RSHA p.88
L 15–19 in
WS 37–42 in

BWHA p.92
L 14–17 in
WS 32–36 in

GRHA p.98
L 14–18 in
WS 32–38 in

STHA p.100
L 15–17 in
WS 33–41 in

HASH p.102
L 18–23 in
WS 40–47 in

COBH p.104
L 20–22 in
WS 40–52 in

ZTHA p.106
L 19–22 in
WS 48–55 in

SNKI p.110
L 14–16 in
WS 42–46 in

HBKI p.114
L 16–20 in
WS 34–38 in

STKI p.116
L 21–24 in
WS 47–54 in

MIKI p.118
L 13–15 in
WS 29–33 in

WTKI p.122
L 14–16 in
WS 39–41 in

AMKE p.128
L 8–11 in
WS 20–24 in

MERL p.132
L 9–12 in
WS 21–27 in

PEFA p.136
L 14–18 in
WS 37–46 in

PRFA p.140
L 15–19 in
WS 35–45 in

GYRF p.144
L 19–24 in
WS 43–51 in

APFA p.146
L 14–18 in
WS 31–40 in

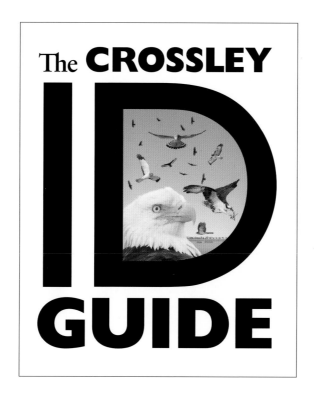

The CROSSLEY ID GUIDE

Raptors

Richard Crossley, Jerry Liguori, and Brian Sullivan

Crossley Books
Princeton University Press

Requests for permission to reproduce material from this work should be sent to Permissions, Princeton University Press

Published by Princeton University Press, 41 William Street, Princeton, New Jersey 08540

In the United Kingdom: Princeton University Press, 6 Oxford Street, Woodstock, Oxfordshire OX20 1TW

nathist.princeton.edu

ISBN 978-0-691-15740-5

Library of Congress Control Number: 2012950890

British Library Cataloging-in-Publication Data is available

This book has been composed in Minio Pro

Printed on acid-free paper ∞

Printed in Thailand

10 9 8 7 6 5 4 3 2 1

CONTENTS

PREFACE

The Crossley ID Guide: Raptors is for beginning birders and everyone else who loves the majesty of raptors and the beauty of the outdoors.

This book is a continuation of the award-winning *Crossley ID Guide: Eastern Birds* with the added bonus of larger plates and lots of question-and-answer pages. The Crossley ID Guide series is intended as a halfway house between reality and old-school traditional guides. It "takes you out to the field," where you can enjoy the beauty of the outdoors and birds from an armchair. At the same time, you can get to know the birds: where they live, what they do, and what they look like. You can try to identify the birds in the book on your own—knowing they are not going to fly away. Then, check the answers to see if you are correct. You have your own personal "tour guide."

The Crossley ID Guides are based on what we now know about the workings of the mind, the way it works most effectively when the goal is to improve knowledge and understanding. With this approach comes the confidence, know-how, and enjoyment to take on the challenge of identifying hawks and other birds at any distance. The key points to bear in mind are these:

1. Facts are empty without being linked to context and concepts—they should be lifelike.
2. The brain learns and remembers more when the experience is interesting and fun.
3. Repetition is how we build the neural pathway; "practice makes perfect."
4. The brain processes parts and wholes simultaneously. The brain puts the parts together to create a more complete and understandable picture.

Whether you want to take this book into the field, bring it on a hawk watch, or just leave it in the car, any of these are fine; however, that is not what it is designed for. A book is no match for reality, a field notebook, looking closely at birds, and asking yourself, "What do I see?"

This book is designed to be the next best thing to reality. You can enjoy the beauty of nature and the outdoors with it. It creates the opportunity for a more complete understanding of what we are watching. It also provides an opportunity to practice that is similar to being outdoors—and you can check the answers to see if you are correct. Practice is the best way to improve and to build confidence and enjoyment. Get a nice comfortable seat, perhaps a glass of wine or a pint of beer, and start looking at it. By studying the plates carefully, you can start to see birds as I do.

HOW TO USE THIS BOOK

The most important thing is to enjoy the book. Perhaps it is by enjoying the visual beauty of birds and nature, working out the answers to questions, enjoying the text, or something else. It does not matter as long as you like looking at it.

If you would like to improve your field skills, I suggest the following. When looking at a plate, do not read the text until you have really studied the plate. Ask yourself, "What do I see?" Training yourself to see and describe a bird in great detail is the key to being a better birder. Initially, it takes time and patience to do this. Think of a bird as a jigsaw puzzle where you fill in all the pieces. The more pieces you can fill in the better. Look away and see how much of the puzzle you can complete. As you spend more time doing this, you will find that not only can you complete the puzzle but you can also do a more complicated one. Jigsaw puzzles are challenging but fun. Bird identification is too.

The photographic accounts of each species cover 2 pages (scarce and localized species) or 4 pages (common or widespread species). These pages start with descriptions of closer and perched birds but progress to more distant views. As you become more familiar with each species, it is only logical they get more distant and harder to identify. Funnily enough, because you can see less detail, the thought process is simplified. Mastering distant shapes and patterns is key: the backbone of ID.

After each group of similar-looking species is described, there are mystery photo pages for you to test your skills. Study the raptors closely and for a long period of time and think very carefully. Many people are surprised at how competent they can become in a relatively short time. Nothing beats structured practice!

Most books show only side-on photos. We show birds from all angles. The mind has no problem understanding in 3-D or seeing images from different angles and combining them. Please look at all the images to create a more complete picture in your mind. In the field, birds are side-on only for a small amount of time. A partial picture will never compete with the full picture. For this reason there are no arrows on the plates pointing to traditional field marks. I feel it is time to move on from highlighting a few plumage marks with arrows as these are just a small part of the whole picture—at best!

It should be noted that there are many raptors that are very difficult to identify—for anyone who is honest or knowledgeable. Over the years I have frequently noticed that many are reluctant to take on the challenge of identifying a bird. Why is this? I often wonder if it is the fear that we might not get the answer right. It is human nature to do something less often when we feel we are not being successful. Please never forget two things: First, the best birders are the best because they have made more mistakes than everyone else—they have also learned from them. Second, it is the voyage of discovery that is most exciting. There is very little thrill in knowing everything, so feel lucky when you are learning—and making mistakes. Always keep in the back of your mind that it is the bird you are trying to learn and not its name. If you learn the bird, you will always be able to work out the name later.

Accompanying the plates are the species accounts. These are assembled in much the same way as *The Crossley ID Guide: Eastern Birds.* The accounts succinctly look at all the important field marks to identify, age, and sex birds. I consider any character that helps to identify a bird a field mark. These are size, shape, distribution, behavior, color pattern, and vocalization. As mentioned, birds have personalities. We try to use language that captures the essence of this if it has not been done in the plate. Before you read the text, please enjoy and look closely at the plates for as long as you can, then cross-reference the text to what you see in the plate. You should be able to create a clear picture of the bird's appearance and personality in your mind.

Most of the text in this book was written by two of North America's best raptor guys, Jerry Liguori and Brian Sullivan. They were asked to think outside the box and "be the bird." The sections they wrote are at the beginning of each species account, starting on page 175. The personalities of the birds are really brought out in these accounts, which will help you understand the relationship between where and how a bird lives. This often goes a long way in explaining its size, shape, and even the probability of it being in a particular area.

The second part of each species account is factual information broken down into sections for easier reading: overview, flight style, size and structure, plumage, geographic variation, molt, similar species, status and distribution, migration, and vocalizations. Jerry's and Brian's lifetimes of watching raptors are self-evident.

The remaining text, starting on page 261, comprises the answers to the many photo quizzes. In many respects, these pages will be the most helpful and "fun" part of the book. Most of us love the challenge of working out answers. This is particularly helpful because it encourages us to look more closely and focus on details that we would otherwise overlook. The answers will explain the key features on which to focus and give you other clues that come from decades of field experience.

There are always difficult decisions to make when writing books. One of the most questionable was the use of the word *morph*. This term has been used in raptor guides forever. A morph is supposed to be a distinctive form with no overlap. Short-tailed Hawk has two distinct forms, one light and the other dark; however, in other species such as Swanson's and Red-tailed Hawks, the distinctions are unclear and often overlap. These ranges of color from light to dark are better thought of as clines rather than morphs.

Raptors are arguably the most studied and majestic group of birds in North America; yet there is still much about them we are not sure of or quite simply don't know. That's part of the fun, the voyage of discovery while enjoying their beauty in the beautiful outdoors.

Richard Crossley

INTRODUCTION

If you've ever witnessed someone's first experience of observing a perched hawk through a spotting scope, seeing an eagle snatch a fish from the water, or catching a glimpse of a hawk in his or her own yard, you know the person is simply mesmerized. What is it that is so exciting about raptors? Is it that they are skillful predators? Is it that they are big and powerful? Is it that they look menacing? Whatever it is, one thing is certain: they are attention-grabbing even to nonbirders, and they are a favored group among birders! This favored status is evident in the throngs of hawk watchers who visit raptor migration sites each spring and fall with an obsession and fervor unmatched in the realm of birding. During the migration seasons, it is common practice for hawk watchers to spend weekends or days off at their local watch sites, spending countless hours staring into the sky in search of raptors. They might even plan an entire vacation to coincide with the peak time for hawk migration. Being present for a "big day" is the highlight of their year, but missing the "big day" is heartbreaking. The biggest hawk flights are the stuff of legend, and to be part of one of these migration events can be the birding experience of a lifetime.

One aspect of hawk watching that is forever a hot topic is identification. There is a mystique about hawk identification, especially in regard to high-flying or distant raptors that are barely visible to the average person. Birders are fascinated when hawk watchers can identify these "specks" in the sky and eager to listen to experienced watchers discuss the finer points of raptor ID. At first, it seems impossible to identify birds at the limit of vision or to tell similar species apart, even up close. But with practice all aspects of hawk identification become clearer and easier to understand. Successful hawk identification relies on becoming familiar with raptors in the field and on understanding which field marks to focus on when observing a raptor in a particular situation. Each species gives a different impression or "feel," but expressing these subjective differences in words and pictures can be difficult. *The Crossley ID Guide: Raptors* presents birds in lifelike scenes so that the images (large and small) become imprinted on the reader, similar to the way one learns a new language by subconsciously absorbing it.

Raptors can be seen flying and perched at a range of distances, at varying perspectives, and in a number of settings. Because of these varying views, many nuances are involved in raptor identification, such as structure, flight style, plumage, habitat, and behavior, and each is equally important to learn. It is also important to know that specific aspects of ID are more reliable than others in certain instances. For example, the shape of a bird may be easier to tell than its plumage on a cloudy day or at a distance, or vice versa. It is helpful to visit migration or winter sites with concentrations of raptors in order to see a number of birds in one day, and often multiple species side by side. Seeing birds again and again is good ID practice and accelerates the learning process. Remember, it is impossible to identify every bird you see, but it's fun to try!

MIGRATION

Raptor migration is dynamic, and the phenomenon itself is still part mystery. We understand that most birds migrate to warmer climates for the winter, but how do they know where to go, and how do they know how to get back to their summer territories? Do they have an internal GPS system? This would make them more advanced than humans in several ways! Regardless, there is nothing more exhilarating than watching hawks pass by one after another on migration. A big movement of anything is exciting to watch—a million robins or dragonflies in a day, a "fallout" of warblers or sparrows—but a steady stream of hawks is absolutely spellbinding. Another dynamic of hawk watching is the social aspect. Many known hawk migration sites are a favorite hangout of birders, just like a coffee shop or bar. In spring and fall, birders meet at these sites on a regular basis just to chat or have lunch together, whether birds are flying or not.

Most hawk migration counts are conducted at locations where birds tend to congregate, and these sites vary, depending on their geographic location and make-up. Since raptors are reluctant to cross over large bodies of water, certain sites along the shorelines of the Great Lakes, the Atlantic and Pacific oceans, and the Gulf of Mexico, such as Cape May Point, NJ, and Hawk Ridge, MN, are great places to see gatherings of birds. Hawks also concentrate along the Rocky and Appalachian mountains at sites such as Hawk Mountain, PA, and the Goshute Mountains, NV, where they can take advantage of the uplift that occurs when winds strike the ridges. At each site, a specific wind condition is most favorable for large flights of birds. The Hawk Migration Association of North America (HMANA) lists more than 1000 hawk migration sites in North America, and there are Web sites for many of them that offer information on count data, weather conditions, site history, and driving directions. Hawks also congregate in winter in large fields, marshes, or agricultural areas with an abundance of prey.

MOLT

Molt is an important process in the lives of birds. Feathers wear out over time, becoming abraded and tattered, and often bleached by the sun. In order for birds to maintain the ability to fly, stay insulated, and yield all the other natural history benefits of feathers, it is important that feathers be replaced when they no longer perform their function adequately. Most birds molt annually, but the extent and timing of molt vary both between and within species.

Why care about molt in raptors? A basic understanding of molt in raptors can help you identify and age many species. Raptors are large birds that spend a lot of time in the air, and it's relatively easy to see molt in the wings and tail. Understanding the molt sequences of raptors can help age birds, and in some cases an accurate assessment of molt is the only way to accurately determine a bird's age (e.g., subadult Golden Eagles). Understanding molt and wear can help you avoid identification pitfalls, too, as raptors in active molt can look atypical. At times, they may look pointy or blunter at the wingtips depending on which primaries are molting or missing, or they may look abnormally short- or long-tailed. A molting bird may appear paler-headed than usual or appear to have an unusual plumage pattern caused by missing or bleached feathers. Recognizing these situations in the field will lead you to become a more careful observer.

Most raptors have the same basic pattern of molt in the flight feathers, beginning with P1 (innermost primary) and continuing out toward the wingtip (P10). Usually these feathers are molted sequentially. Tail molt usually begins with the central and outer

tail feathers, with the interior tail feathers replaced later. Falcons differ in starting their annual molt in the middle of the primaries at P5, then progressing in both directions sequentially. In smaller raptor species, molts are generally complete, meaning that they molt all the flight, tail, and body feathers each year (usually from late spring through early fall). But in larger species that have very long primaries, molts are typically incomplete, and it can take one year or several years for all the primaries to be replaced. In the latter case, raptors often show stepwise molt patterns, a process that allows them to replace more feathers simultaneously without compromising their ability to fly. In some older buteos and eagles, as many as 3–4 "waves" of molt can be progressing through the wings at the same time, causing them to look very tattered in midsummer! Northern breeding raptors tend to have less extensive annual molts, and they usually molt later in the year than southern breeding raptors.

GROUPINGS OF RAPTORS

There are several families of raptors, and each is unique. Their shapes and behavior are adapted to their environment, habitat, and food preference or hunting needs. Many groups or individual species specialize in catching and feeding on a specific type of prey. For most raptors, the sexes are similar, and females are usually larger than males.

Vultures (3 species) are ugly, skittish birds but are beautiful in flight. They are large, mostly dark soaring birds with long, broad wings and bare heads. The largest is California Condor, the smallest is Black Vulture, and the most common and widespread is Turkey Vulture. Vultures often hang out in groups, finding food and feeding together. Their food source is dead animals, which they find by sight or smell. Black and Turkey Vultures attain adult appearance in 1–2 years; Condors take at least 5 years.

Eagles (2 species) are impressive in size and strength, with powerful talons, large bills, and long wings (up to 7 feet wingspan). They soar with ease and can travel long distances using minimal energy. Eagles can hunt a variety of prey; Bald Eagle is known to pluck large fish from the water, snatch songbirds from a marsh, and chase down ducks in flight. It also scavenges or steals prey from other raptors throughout the year. Golden Eagle hunts primarily mammals and large birds but is adept at catching snakes and just about anything it can tackle. It is able to stoop at speeds that rival those of the Peregrine Falcon! Eagles are mostly dark, attaining adult appearance in 4–5 years.

Osprey (1 species) is a large, fish-eating raptor of coasts and inland lakes and rivers. Ospreys are active and fun to watch as they hover, dive, and slam into the water repeatedly (sometimes for hours) until they successfully catch a fish. They are adapted to holding onto fish with their sharply curved talons and the spiny pads on their feet. Ospreys are distinctive, with long, slim, bowed, gull-like wings, and boldly patterned blackish-and-white undersides. Ospreys commonly nest on manmade structures, especially platforms. They attain adult appearance during their second year.

Buteos (12 species) are a diverse group of robust hawks characterized by broad wings and short tails fit for soaring. Sometimes buteos are seen soaring in large flocks or "kettles," especially Broad-winged and Swainson's Hawks. Although robust, some buteos are longer-winged and slimmer overall than others, and there is a significant range in size from the largest buteos to the smallest. Red-tailed Hawk is probably the most frequently encountered and widespread North American buteo, whereas some species are range-restricted. Many species have highly variable plumages, ranging from light to dark below, and some show moderate sexual dimorphism. Buteos usually attain adult appearance in their second year, but a few acquire adult plumage in their third or fourth year. Most buteos prey primarily on small mammals, but almost all will take small birds, reptiles, and even insects. Taxonomically, Common Black-Hawk, Harris's Hawk, and White-tailed Hawk differ from true buteos, though their habits are similar enough that we lump them in with the buteos when making general reference to this group.

Accipiters (3 species) are woodland hawks recognized in flight by their long tails and short, rounded wings. They are bird-eating specialists, and the most likely to be seen at backyard birdfeeders, especially Sharp-shinned and Cooper's Hawks, which wait in hiding to burst toward birdfeeders in a surprise attack, chasing birds into dense cover if need be. Accipiters breed in forested areas, often away from homes, but Cooper's has adapted to suburban areas. Northern Goshawk is rare across North America and the least likely to be encountered. Distinguishing the accipiters from each other in flight requires considerable practice using a combination of shape, flight style, and plumage. Accipiters often fly directly, flapping and gliding intermittently more often than do other raptors, but with sufficient lift they are proficient at soaring. Accipiters attain adult appearance in their second year.

Harriers (1 species) are a large, worldwide family, but only the Northern Harrier occurs in North America. A Harrier's buoyant, languid flight is mesmerizing to watch as it teeters low over marshes and fields in search of mice and voles. It is easy to identify, and often easy to observe, but unique in many ways. Harriers have long, narrow wings, a long tail, and a brilliant white rump that often clinches their ID. They also have a unique facial pattern made up of stiff feathers that form an owl-like facial disk that helps them to hunt by sound as much as by sight, sometimes in near darkness. Harriers perch on the ground or on low posts, but rarely in trees or on high perches. Adult males and females are markedly different in plumage. Harriers attain adult appearance in their second year.

Kites (5 species) are a diverse, lesser-known group of raptors that reside in warmer regions. Three North American species (White-tailed, Mississippi, Swallow-tailed) are characterized by long, pointed wings and are graceful masters of flight. Their aerial maneuverability, especially when taking small prey such as insects on the wing, is unmatched. The other 2 North American kites (Snail, Hook-billed) have paddle-shaped wings and eat mostly snails. Kites attain adult appearance in 1–2 years.

Falcons (7 species) are exciting birds to watch. They fly at high speeds when chasing prey over open country and can perform vertical stoops at speeds so fast they are hard to follow, even with the naked eye! "Typical" falcons (genus *Falco*, 6 species) have narrow, pointed wings and frequently take prey in mid-air. All North American falcons have dark brownish black eyes, and a tomial tooth (notch near the base of the upper mandible). Crested Caracara is considered a type of falcon, but it is very different from the others in appearance and behavior. Caracara has blunt wings, a long tail, and bright facial skin, and it inhabits a restricted southern range. It feeds on carrion and is often seen with vultures. The North American falcons range from nearly songbird size (American Kestrel) to Red-tailed size (Gyrfalcon).

RAPTOR TOPOGRAPHY

Learning all the tracts of feathers and the anatomy of birds will help you understand their appearance and behavior. Practice on the many images in this book and take what you learn into the field.

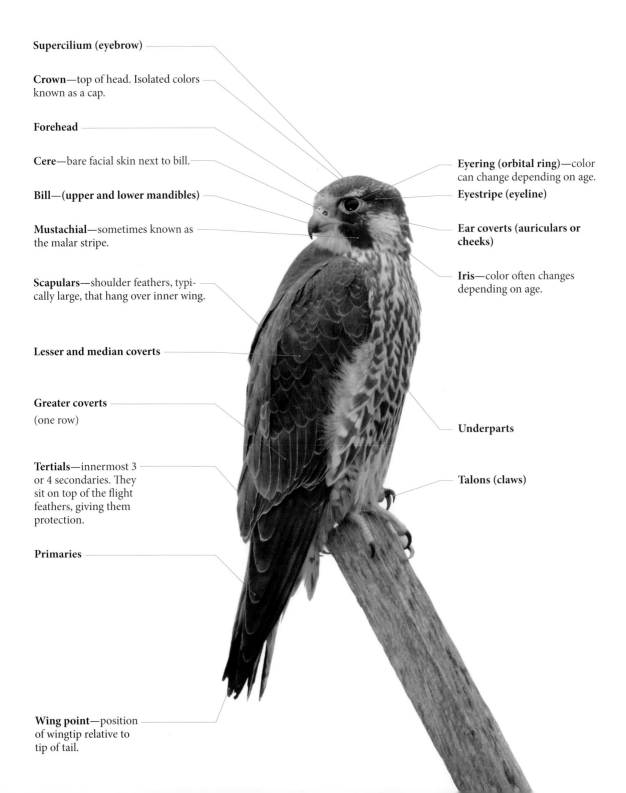

Supercilium (eyebrow)

Crown—top of head. Isolated colors known as a cap.

Forehead

Cere—bare facial skin next to bill.

Bill—**(upper and lower mandibles)**

Mustachial—sometimes known as the malar stripe.

Scapulars—shoulder feathers, typically large, that hang over inner wing.

Lesser and median coverts

Greater coverts
(one row)

Tertials—innermost 3 or 4 secondaries. They sit on top of the flight feathers, giving them protection.

Primaries

Wing point—position of wingtip relative to tip of tail.

Eyering (orbital ring)—color can change depending on age.

Eyestripe (eyeline)

Ear coverts (auriculars or cheeks)

Iris—color often changes depending on age.

Underparts

Talons (claws)

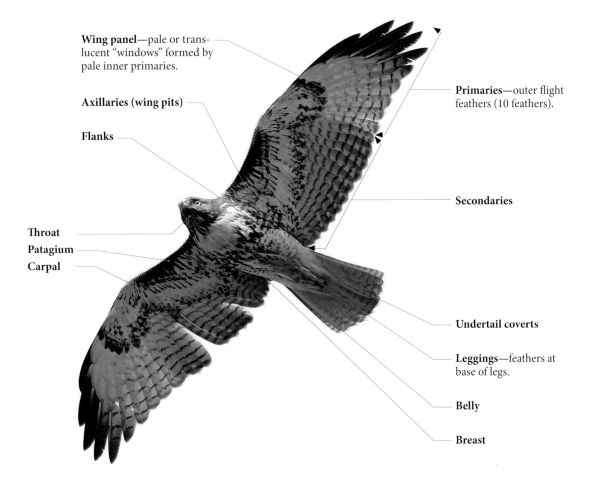

Wing panel—pale or trans-lucent "windows" formed by pale inner primaries.

Axillaries (wing pits)

Flanks

Throat
Patagium
Carpal

Primaries—outer flight feathers (10 feathers).

Secondaries

Undertail coverts

Leggings—feathers at base of legs.

Belly

Breast

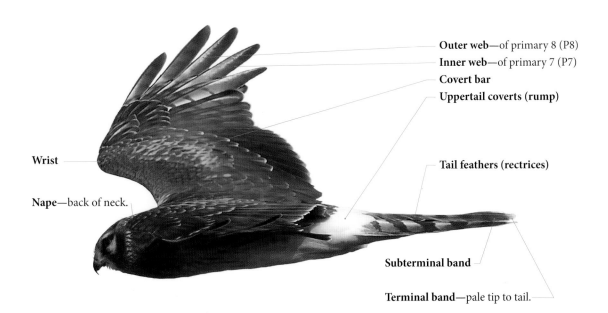

Outer web—of primary 8 (P8)
Inner web—of primary 7 (P7)
Covert bar
Uppertail coverts (rump)

Wrist

Nape—back of neck.

Tail feathers (rectrices)

Subterminal band

Terminal band—pale tip to tail.

juv.

ad.

imm.

juv.

ad.

Turkey Vulture (East) *Cathartes aura* **TUVU** L 24–28 in, WS 63–71 in, WT 3.5–5.3 lb, page 175

On the ground, easily identified by its large size, dark plumage, featherless head, and clumsy movements. But in flight becomes graceful and elegant, and at a distance can be confused with other large, dark soaring birds (especially Zone-tailed Hawk). Unsteady in flight, wobbling from side to side. Always holds wings in a strong dihedral. Appears comparatively smaller-headed than other raptors, and shows plain silvery flight feathers that contrast with otherwise blackish plumage. Long tail usually rounded at tip. Sexes similar in plumage and size. Adult has featherless red head and ivory bill. Ageing 1st-years is straight-forward in fall, but harder in spring. 1st-year has neat, same-age flight feathers with no signs of molt, and broad buffy tips on the upperwing coverts; head and bill grayish changing to pinkish with a dusky-tipped bill as early as 3–4 months old (timing varies). Over the course of the first year, head becomes darker red, completely featherless, and the bill more wholly whitish, as on adult. Some 2nd-years retain faint dusky bill tip in the second fall, usually hard to see in the field. Occurs in any habitat, but

Turkey Vulture (West)

favors woodland and cliffs for nesting. Highly aerial and social, soars in large "kettles," rising and spinning tornado-like on the horizon, and gathers in numbers at kills, during migration, and at roosts. Eats primarily carrion detected mainly by smell. Frequently scavenges along roadsides, attending roadkills with Black Vulture and Crested Caracara. Tears prey with powerful bill, but has relatively weak feet, unlike stronger talons of raptors. The "Turkey Buzzard" leaves its prey reluctantly and rarely retreats far. Often perches on dead snags, radio towers, and utility poles, and frequently holds wings outstretched to help condition flight feathers and increase body temperature (lowering it at night to conserve energy). Partly migratory, mostly retracts from the northern parts of range in winter, especially the Great Basin and northern Great Plains, but has been found in recent years with increasing regularity farther north than usual. Eastern birds average slightly larger and usually have more prominent "tubercules" (colorful, wartlike protuberances near the eyes) on the face than western birds, but some birds appear intermediate.

Turkey Vulture—the effect of light

When identifying raptors in flight, it's important to understand how lighting affects plumage. We know that strong backlighting produces silhouettes, and these can be very challenging to identify, since plumage features seem to disappear. Raptor watchers are frequently faced with variable lighting conditions, changing by the day, throughout the day, or even as they watch birds pass from blue sky to clouds. Using the two vultures as an example, look at how strong sun or shadow affects the overall appearance of these birds. Here, the early morning light gives every-

thing in the sunlight rich red tones. In flat light, like the birds still in the shade, the Turkey Vulture usually shows a moderate contrast between the paler, silvery flight feathers and the darker underwing coverts, as seen on the bird gliding to the right. Depending on whether the underparts are well lit or shadowed, Turkey Vulture can appear highly contrasting or uniformly dark. In flat light, Black Vulture is dark with contrasting whitish outer primaries that appear as white patches on the outer wings in flight. These white patches can all but disappear in dull

light, and in strong sun, they can be washed out when the rest of the bird is brightly lit. In dull light or when backlit, the patterns of all species become muted, and even species with strong plumage contrasts can appear monochromatic. But strong sun amplifies contrasts, and species that usually appear dark can suddenly appear highly patterned. By understanding the effects of lighting on plumage patterns, you can be prepared to more accurately identify birds under a variety of lighting conditions. As always, when lighting is tricky, use shape and flight style to help identify raptors. Despite what the lighting might tell, these vultures can always be distinguished by their shape and flight style differences. The bird on the upper right appears to have whitish outer primaries, indicating a Black Vulture, due to dark shadow on the inner wing caused by the bird's body; however, in the field, its slow, floppy wingbeats and wobbling flight style would readily identify it as a Turkey Vulture. Try to identify and age as many birds as you can; take your time doing this. The distant flock formation is typical of only one of these species.

Double-crested Cormorants

juv.

ad.

ad.

juv.

Black Vulture *Coragyps atratus* **BLVU** L 23–28 in, WS 55–63 in, WT 3.8–5.1 lb, page 177

Shy and wary when breeding, but pugnacious and fearless at roadside carrion and around human settlements and land-fills. Highly gregarious year-round. Most often seen in flight or perched along highways at roadkills, especially in the Southeast, where it is abundant. Frequently roosts with Turkey Vulture on transmission towers. Has weakly developed sense of smell compared with Turkey Vulture, on which it partly relies to find decomposing animals, especially in areas with dense canopy cover. Often flies high, visually searching for gathering Turkey Vultures, which it then follows to kills. Gray or blackish feather-less head helps distinguish it from all but juvenile Turkey Vulture. Sexes similar. Adult has an unfeathered, wrinkled, grayish head with an ivory bill. 1st-year has sparsely feathered black head and black bill, changing quickly to a paler bill with dusky tip by late fall. 2nd-year essentially adult-like, but some may still be in transition, retaining a slightly dusky bill tip through the second fall. Generally sedentary, but range is expanding to the north. Proficient at soaring and often seen flying in large groups with

ad.

Black Vulture

Turkey Vulture, but not as buoyant or graceful on the wing, and needs to work harder to stay aloft. Slightly smaller and stockier than Turkey Vulture, with broader squared-off wings and whitish outer primaries forming pale patches most visible in flight. Short, narrow-based, square-tipped tail imparts tailless appearance in flight. Differs from Turkey Vulture and both eagles by its snappier wingbeats, often delivered in short bursts interspersed with glides. These quick, shallow, "anxious" wingbeats seem odd

for such a large bird and best set it apart from other large raptors. Soaring flight more stable than that of Turkey Vulture, but occasionally wobbles slightly in stronger winds. Somewhat eagle-like and has fooled more than a few top birders. Soars in broad circles with wings arched forward and held in a shallow dihedral or sometimes flat. Glides with a modified dihedral, as opposed to Turkey Vulture, which typically flies in a pronounced dihedral, showing a modified dihedral only on occasion.

Vultures at the dinner table. Squabbling groups of Turkey or Black Vultures feeding on carrion is not an uncommon sight in the Southeast. When seen together on the ground at a carcass, note Black Vulture's more aggressive demeanor, smaller size, shorter tail, and blackish or grayish head. Turkey Vultures usually have reddish or pinkish heads, but some fresh juveniles can be pale gray-headed.

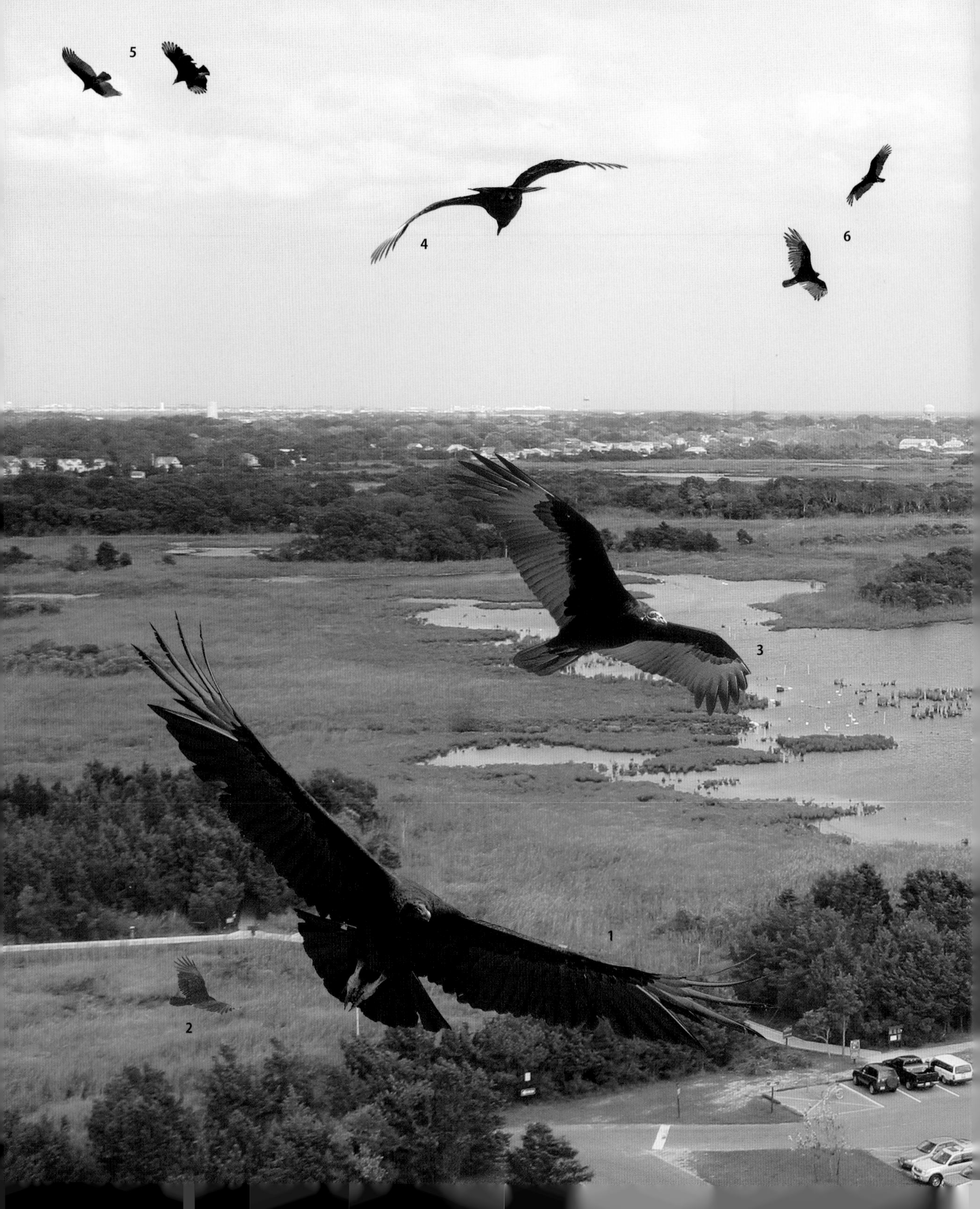
5
4
6
3
1
2

"wobbly" flight and holds its wings in a steeper dihedral than Black Vulture, but the most significant flight style difference is the hurried, snappy wingbeats of Black Vulture compared with the lazy, floppy wingbeats of Turkey Vulture. Try to distinguish these Turkey Vultures and Black Vultures flying over Cape May Point, NJ. Answers p.261.

Crested Caracara *Caracara cheriway* **CRCA** L 21–24 in, WS 47–52 in, WT 1.8–2.8 lb, page 179

Crested Caracara is one of the most distinctive raptors in North America and unlikely to be confused with anything if seen well. At a distance in flight, it can recall a raven when flapping, or even an immature Bald Eagle when soaring, but note Caracara's distinctive patterned plumage, with white primaries and a bold white tail with black tip. When perched, Caracara appears large-headed, and its eponymous "crest" helps create a distinctly square-headed profile. Crested Caracaras are raptors of open country, especially cattle country and mesquite grassland. They often feed on carrion with vultures but also hunt a variety of live prey, including insects, small mammals, reptiles, and birds. Caracaras are comfortable around semideveloped areas and sometimes seen in surprisingly suburban areas. They are gregarious birds, often roosting in small groups with vultures. They frequently perch on manmade structures, including power poles and fence posts, usually in an upright pose. When on the ground or in windy weather, they often stand in a more horizontal manner than other raptors. Crested Caracara is a common resident in south Texas but generally uncommon and local in Arizona (occurring mainly in Pima Co.) and in south-central Florida.

ad.

juv.

Crested Caracara

Crested Caracaras are large and distinctive in flight, with long, narrow, squared-off wings, long tails, and a long-necked appearance, recalling an adult Bald Eagle. Crested Caracaras are rarely seen at high altitudes, instead flying at low to medium height and flapping in a steady, rowing, raven-like manner. Caracaras soar on flat or somewhat bowed wings. Caracaras have 3 age classes differentiated by plumage and head/bill pattern, and they attain their adult appearance in about 2 years. Adults are boldly patterned with a clean white throat, upper breast, and cheeks, a whitish barred lower chest and hind-neck, and black cap and upperparts. The facial skin is vibrant orange-red, and the legs are yellow. The tail is white and finely barred, with a wide, black tip. 1st-year birds have buffy, dark-streaked breasts and dark brown instead of black plumage. The facial skin is pale pinkish. The tail is white but more coarsely barred than adults, with a dark tip. The legs are pale bluish. 2nd-year birds are similar to adults but are browner dorsally and often with orange-yellow facial skin. The tail is adult-like. Males and females are similar and indistinguishable in the field.

ad.

Turkey Vulture

4th/5th-yr.

ad.

California Condor *Gymnogyps californianus* **CACO** L 43–50 in, WS 98–118 in, WT 18–31 lb, page 180

California Condors are rare reintroduced carrion-eaters of mountain canyons and coastal cliffs throughout their range. Nearly unmistakable, their impressive size dwarfs even vultures and eagles. Condors are dark overall but distinctive in having long, broad wings, a slight dihedral, a very short tail, and a massive appearance both when perched and in flight, rendering it unlike both eagles and vultures. Condors of all ages show pale underwing coverts, which are strikingly white in adults. Immature Bald Eagle, to which it is most similar in terms of plumage, can have white along the underwing co-verts, but this is rarely as distinctly contrasting as on Condors (a few 1st-years may approach Condor in underwing pattern); however, all Bald Eagles are smaller with slimmer wings, larger heads (feathered!), and longer tails. Immature Bald Eagles often have a paler brown belly or white on the belly, whereas Condors are uniformly dark-bodied in all ages. Because of their size, California Condors rarely take flight unless lift is optimal (usually midday); often seen perched on rocky hillsides or out-crops for hours at a time, and sometimes even for days when weather is inclement. Big Sur, CA, is a good place to see them.

ad.

2nd/3rd-yr.

2nd-yr.

1st-yr.

California Condor—immature

Condors are extremely slow moving and steady in flight, soaring in wider circles than other raptors. They soar with a slight dihedral but sometimes appear flat-winged in light winds, with the wingtips always showing an obviously splayed, "fingered" appearance. Condors are frequently seen in pairs or small groups, often in the company of Turkey Vultures. Condors' wingbeats are exceedingly slow and heavy, but once airborne they rarely flap. Condors take 5–7 years to attain adult appearance, with progressive change in wing pattern and head color from juvenile to adulthood. All ages are largely dark with contrasting paler underwing coverts. The featherless head changes from grayish to orange-red, and the underwing coverts get whiter, more vibrant, and more extensive with each passing year until adulthood is reached. The secondaries and the greater upperwing coverts become whiter throughout the first 6 years as well. Eye color is dark grayish turning to dark red with age. Males and females are identical in plumage and size. Almost all Condors have numbered patagial markers that identify them as individuals. The last wild birds were captured in 1987 not far from this well-known Condor site at Bitter Creek NWR in Kern County, CA.

Osprey

4th-yr.

ad.

Bald Eagle (sitting) *Haliaeetus leucocephalus* **BAEA** L 27–35 in, WS 71–96 in, WT 4.4–14.5 lb, page 183

Bald Eagles are often found near water, especially lakes, rivers, and bays. They eat mainly fish, and their talons are perfect for grasping slippery prey, and their powerful bills are needed to break through a fish's tough skin. Bald Eagles are exceptional predators catching their own fish throughout the year but they also steal fish from Ospreys and eat carrion. Bald Eagles congregate in large numbers, sometimes hundreds, in areas where food is plentiful. They sit peacefully together on ice packs one minute, then aggressively tail-chase each other the next, usually in squabbles over food. When perched, Bald Eagles are massive, bulky overall with large heads and bills. It takes roughly 5 years for birds

to attain their familiar adult plumage. Immatures are trickier to identify. 1st-years are mainly dark with brown heads and tails, dark brown eyes, and a blackish bill. Subadults (2nd–4th year) become progressively more adult-like, with the head, tail, bill, and eye color changing most notably. Younger immatures have white bellies and upper backs, and older birds generally get darker in these areas. Some 4–5 year-olds looks essentially adult-like, but retain small signs of immaturity, such as dark flecks on the head or tail. Bald Eagles build massive stick nests in large trees, adding on to the nest each year. Some nests become so large and heavy that the braches supporting them collapse from the weight.

4th/5th-yr.

ad.

Bald Eagle (flying)—adult/subadult

In flight, Bald Eagles appear large, slow moving, and mostly dark, and they typically fly on flat wings. Telling adult Bald Eagles in flight is straightforward; they are blackish with starkly contrasting, distinctly separate white heads and tails. Immature Bald Eagles lack the white head and tail and are much less obvious! 1st-year birds are dark brown with white wing pits and white underwing coverts; they show a blackish topside with faded browner upperwing coverts, appearing two-toned on top like Swainson's Hawk, except when recently fledged. 2nd-year birds are still mostly dark overall but are variable with white bellies and white upper backs. Unlike 1st-year birds that have a uniform trailing edge to wing, 2nd-years have a more ragged

juv./1st-yr.

2nd-yr.

3rd-yr.

2nd-yr.

juv./1st-yr.

Bald Eagle (flying)—immature

trailing edge formed by the longer, more pointed retained juvenile feathers and shorter, flatter-tipped, newly grown ones. 3rd-year birds typically have a mix of white and dark on the belly and upper back and show more white on the head, and a yellower bill. They have a cleaner trailing edge to the wing than 2nd-years with typically only 1–3 juvenile secondaries remaining. 4th-year birds are mostly dark on the belly and back with a whitish head and dark eyeline, and a whitish tail with a dark tip and faint dark streaks. The head and tail become whiter and the eyes and bill become yellow as Bald Eagles reach adulthood, but 5th- and sometimes 6th-year birds often still have specks of dark around the eye or on the tail tip, or white on the axillaries or underwings.

ad.

ad.

ad.

ad.

Golden Eagle *Aquila chrysaetos* **GOEA** L 28–35 in, WS 72–89 in, WT 6.6–14 lb, page 186

Golden Eagles are birds of the mountainous West and Northeast, using cliffs almost exclusively as a substrate for their massive stick nests. Adults are nondescript, lacking any striking characters. They are dark brown with a golden hindneck and pale mottling along the upperwings. Adults lack white in the tail or wings shown by immature birds. The wings and tail have faint grayish banding that is difficult to see without exceptional views. Immature (1st- to 4th-year) Golden Eagles have either considerable white in the wings or none at all, but 1st-, 2nd-, and 3rd-year birds always have a

juv.

juv.

subad.

subad.

subad.

Golden Eagle—immature

white-based tail. 4th-year birds and some 5th-year birds have remnants of white in the tail, but it is usually toward the base of the outer tail feathers only. 1st-years differ from other ages in their lack of pale motttling along the upperwings, clean, same-age flight feathers in fall showing no signs of molt and a crisp white-based tail with well-defined blackish terminal band. 2nd- to 4th-year birds can be impossible to tell apart in the field, and many should be dubbed as "unknown age."

juv.

juv.

2nd-yr.

subad.

Golden Eagle

Golden Eagles spend the winter in lower-elevation open areas or hillsides. They are territorial and stake out specific areas as their own, rarely congregating in large numbers like Bald Eagles but can be seen in small groups in parts of Wyoming and California during winter. Golden Eagles catch live prey year-round but will steal prey from smaller raptors or feed on deer carcasses in winter when the opportunity exists. Golden Eagles hunt mostly from high-speed stoops in order to gain the speed

juv.

subad.

subad.

ad.

needed to overtake prey but will cruise hillsides attempting to surprise prey and ambush them before they have the chance to escape. Golden Eagles often perch on utility poles to rest or to scan for prey. When hunting from utility poles, they are typi- cally unable to gain the speed necessary to overtake birds such as grouse and pheasants but often surprise jackrabbits and ground squirrels before they have a chance to escape. Golden Eagles are quite skittish, flushing easily from a perch when approached.

Eagle Comparisons. Bald and Golden Eagles are essentially the same size, and are similar in shape. The overall shapes differ between the two species, with Bald Eagle showing a larger head and broader wings that are held flatter at most times. Golden Eagle has a distinct dihedral that can be seen at distances other field marks can't. Both Bald and Golden Eagles have labored wingbeats, but those of Golden Eagles are shallower and end abruptly on an upstroke. Adult Bald Eagles are easily told from

Golden Eagles by their gleaming white head and tail, but younger Bald Eagles are more similar to Golden Eagles. Telltale clues to immature Bald Eagles are the white axillaries, underwing coverts, and sometimes secondaries, and a dark tail that lacks a clean white base. Golden Eagles never show white bellies or white upperbacks. Adult Bald Eagles have quite slim wings compared with 1st- and 2nd-years. Can you identify all these birds? Ageing them is trickier, but give it a go. Answers p.262

ad. ♀

ad. ♂

juv.

Osprey *Pandion haliaetus* **OSPR** L 21–26 in, WS 59–67 in, WT 2.2–4.2 lb, page 190

Ospreys are almost always found near water, except during migration, when they can be seen over deserts or forests. They build large stick nests on manmade platforms, power poles, signs, buoys, light posts, or large dead trees along lakes, rivers, and marshes. The nest is typically decorated with human material such as fishing line, ribbon, and other plastics. They are quite vocal around the nest and aggressive toward intruders. Ospreys prey almost exclusively on fish and are seen catching other sea life or mammalian prey only on rare occasions. All Ospreys are blackish on top with a white head with dark eyeline, and white underneath with darker flight feathers and wrists. Adult males typically show a clean white breast; adult females and 1st-years usually show a dark, streaked necklace. 1st-years are told from adults by the orange (instead of yellow) eyes and white-tipped

ad.

juv.

Osprey

upperwing coverts. Female Ospreys are slightly larger than males. All Ospreys have large, powerful bills for tearing fish. Ospreys can be seen in small groups along waterways where there are lots of structures to nest on and an abundance of fish. Ospreys have long, narrow wings that they hold drooped at all times, appearing gull-like, and they are often confused for them when flying together along shorelines or contending with them over fish. When soaring, they sometimes look like Bald Eagles, but their wings are slimmer, and the head always appears smaller and less protruding. When gliding overhead, Ospreys display extremely long wings that form a distinct M-shaped silhouette.

Osprey behavior. Ospreys hover and soar over lakes and waterways in search of fish below the water's surface. Although they expend significant energy while hunting, they are well adapted with great stamina and may be airborne for hours at a time. Unlike Bald Eagles, they rarely pluck fish off the surface of the water and are not known to scavenge. They are efficient hunters but must adjust their aim to their underwater target, coming up "empty-handed" much more often than Bald Eagles. When they spot a fish close to the surface, they dive feet-first into the water, partially submerging

to grab the fish with their sharply curved talons. After catching their prey, Ospreys use a great deal of force to propel themselves from the water. As soon as they take flight, they "shake off" any water so they are able to fly more easily with their weighty prey, which they hold aerodynamically head-first. Ospreys are uniquely adapted with acutely curved talons and rough spines, called spicules, on the bottom of their feet that help them to easily hang on to their slippery prey

40

2nd-yr./ad ♂

ad. ♂

ad. ♀

ad. ♂

ad. ♂   ad. ♀

Northern Harrier *Circus cyaneus* **NOHA** L 16–20 in, WS 38–48 in, WT 10–21 oz, page 192

Slimly built with long, narrow wings and a long tail, Harriers are highly aerial and hunt by quartering low over marshes, teetering side to side and showing a bold white rump patch, an obvious field mark of all ages and sexes. Adult males are strikingly white below and gray above, but females and 1st-years are brownish overall and more difficult to distinguish from each other. Adult females are streaked dark below on a buffy body, whereas 1st-years are generally rufous below with little notable streaking. 1st-year sexes are similar, but females have brown eyes

and males have yellowish eyes. By spring, 1st-years have faded to buffy below and can easily be confused with adult females. Adult males are somewhat variable, ranging from clean white below to more heavily washed rufous, and the upperparts range from clean pearl gray to gray washed with brownish. It's tempting to age these brownish adult males as 2nd-year birds, but this is not always the case. 2nd-year males can be safely aged only in the rare cases when juvenile flight or body feathers are retained. Harriers are found in open country, including grassland, marshes,

ad. ♀

juv.

juv.

Northern Harrier—juvenile

fallow fields, and agricultural areas. Active throughout the day, Harriers also frequently hunt well into the evening, unlike many other raptors. They are often the last birds seen coursing over the marsh in the evening, regularly in the company of Short-eared Owls. The "Marsh Hawk" flies steadily but will stop on a dime, hover briefly, then drop on its unsuspecting prey with long legs outstretched. When seen low over a marsh, Harriers are distinctive but during migration they can be confused with other long-winged raptors, especially when soaring or gliding high overhead. The wingtips vary from appearing rounded in slow hunting flight, to quite pointy when gliding. Harriers can always be identified by their proportionately long tail and lanky structure when gliding overhead; also look for the contrastingly dark secondaries shown by females and 1st-years. Unlike many raptors, Harriers rarely perch conspicuously in trees. Instead they favor lower perches such as fence posts or bare ground.

Harrier ageing and sexing. Harriers are found over open country, hunting by quartering low on teetering wings in search of prey, mainly small mammals. All ages and sexes have a bold white rump, but which of the birds here is a male, female, or immature? Male Harriers are always stark whitish below and grayish above, and these are fairly straightforward to ID in the field. Adult females can be more difficult and more like juveniles since they are brownish overall. But note the strongly streaked

underparts of adult females and the tawny upper wing bar. Adult females also tend to have grayish barred primary coverts on the upperwings. Juveniles are similar, though females are generally brown-eyed and males greenish yellow (tough to see in the field). Both sexes show strongly rufous-tinged underparts in fall and fade to an even buff in spring. Many times, however, you won't be able to tell the age/sex of a Harrier and should be satisfied to leave the identification at the species level. Answers p.262

Sharp-shinned Hawk *Accipiter striatus* **SSHA** L 9–13 in, WS 20–26 in, WT 3–8 oz, page 195

Breeding mainly in remote mid- to high-elevation coniferous forests, Sharp-shinned Hawks are not often encountered by birders during the breeding season, but they become more familiar to us during migration and winter, when they occur in large numbers at hawk watches and stake out backyard feeders to prey upon small birds. They are the commonest accipiter, but they are declining in many areas, and now can be outnumbered on some days by Cooper's Hawks at certain hawk watches. Sharp-shinneds are generally less urbanized than Cooper's

Hawks, are more wary, and don't occur in cities or suburban areas during summer. Adults of both sexes are blue-gray above and barred rusty below, with fluffy white undertail coverts and orange eyes that turn deeper red with age, and become darkest on older males. Males average bluer above and brighter rufous below. The tail is banded and usually has a narrow white tip. Adults' heads lack the blackish cap and the pale nape shown by adult Cooper's Hawks. Adults from the Pacific Northwest are darker and more saturated overall, with some birds appearing

juv.

Sharp-shinned Hawk—juvenile

nearly solid rufous on the underparts. 1st-year birds are brown above with tawny or rufous-fringed coverts, and whitish below with dense brownish-red streaking on the underbody. They are typically the most heavily marked of the 1st-year accipiters, and they tend to have more rufous tones to the underparts streaking than Cooper's and Goshawk. When perched, Sharp-shinned Hawk appears diminutive with a stout chest and small rounded head. They often appear "big-eyed". The tail is narrow, and varies from being slightly notched to slightly rounded,

but usually appears somewhat square-cut with a faint whitish tip. Sharp-shinned Hawk has fast, fluttery wingbeats that lack the power of its larger cousins. The wingbeats are punctuated by short glides, and it is easily buffeted by the wind due to its buoyancy. It is more compact than Cooper's Hawk, with a thinner, less rounded tail tip that usually lacks bold white. Sharp-shinned has little head projection beyond the wrists in flight, another good distinction from the bigger-headed Cooper's.

Sharp-shinned Hawk Ageing. At migration sites such as Cape May Point, NJ, thousands of Sharp-shinned Hawks can be seen in a single day. They often fly at low altitude in high winds, but way up high during light wind conditions. Sharpies are small, stocky birds with long, narrow tails and small heads. The tail is short for an accipiter and typically square-tipped when closed, but sometimes

rounded. Shape and flight style are often more easily seen in the field than plumage, so using these characters to tell it from the similar Cooper's Hawk is more reliable. Sharp-shinned Hawks are unsteady and buoyant in flight, and they have rapid, snappy wingbeats that lack power. They rise quickly in a soar and flap more frequently than other raptors. Age all the Sharp-shinned Hawks. Answers p.263

ad.

juv.

2nd-yr.

ad.

Cooper's Hawk *Accipiter cooperii* **COHA** L 14–19 in, WS 28–34 in, WT 10–24 oz, page 197

Cooper's Hawks are a fairly common and increasing inhabitant of low- and mid-elevation forest. They have adapted to humans and are now frequent in urban areas, where they sneak in low and fast to snatch unsuspecting feeder birds. They feed mostly on doves and starlings, but birds their own size are also fair game. In the West, their habitat preference is streamside forest or patches of woodland within open city areas, such as canyon washes, parks, and golf courses, but they also hang out in places such as downtown Los Angeles. Adults are bluish on top and rusty-barred below with fluffy, white undertail feathers, and orange eyes that turn dark red at a few years old. The tail is indistinctly banded with a bold white tip, and the head is dark with a paler nape. The white tail tip is usually more prominent than on Sharp-shinned Hawk. Adult males are bluer on top, with a grayer cheek and more vibrant in color underneath than females, especially birds more than 2 years old. 1st-year Cooper's Hawks are brown on the upperparts and lightly to moderately streaked on the underparts with large, tear-dropped

juv.

Cooper's Hawk—juvenile

streaks. The underparts typically appear paler than on other 1st-year accipiters with streaking usually most concentrated on the breast fading to cleaner white on the belly and under-tail coverts Western birds average more heavily streaked below, and can be confusing. 1st-year Cooper's Hawks are similar in appearance to Sharp-shinned and Northern Goshawks. It is intermediate in size and this is sometimes, but not always, distinctive. Size differences between the sexes are significant: males are close to female Sharp-shins and male Goshawks.

Compared with that of female Sharp-shinned Hawk, the tail tip is more rounded with a broader white terminal band. In flight the longer, broader and more rounded tail are usually distinctive. Wings are narrower-based and longer with a straighter leading edge. The head projects farther beyond the wings and looks contrastingly tawny in juveniles. Cooper's Hawk flies with stiff, shallow wingbeats that come from the shoulder. Adults have broader and rounder-looking wings than juveniles, making them appear more similar to Sharp-shinned Hawk.

Cooper's Hawk ageing. In flight, Cooper's Hawks have stocky bodies with long, narrow tails, and relatively narrow wings for an accipiter. The tail is long for an accipiter and typically round-tipped when closed, but sometimes squared. The head is large and projects beyond the wings more than that of the smaller Sharp-shinned Hawk, and the wings appear lengthy compared

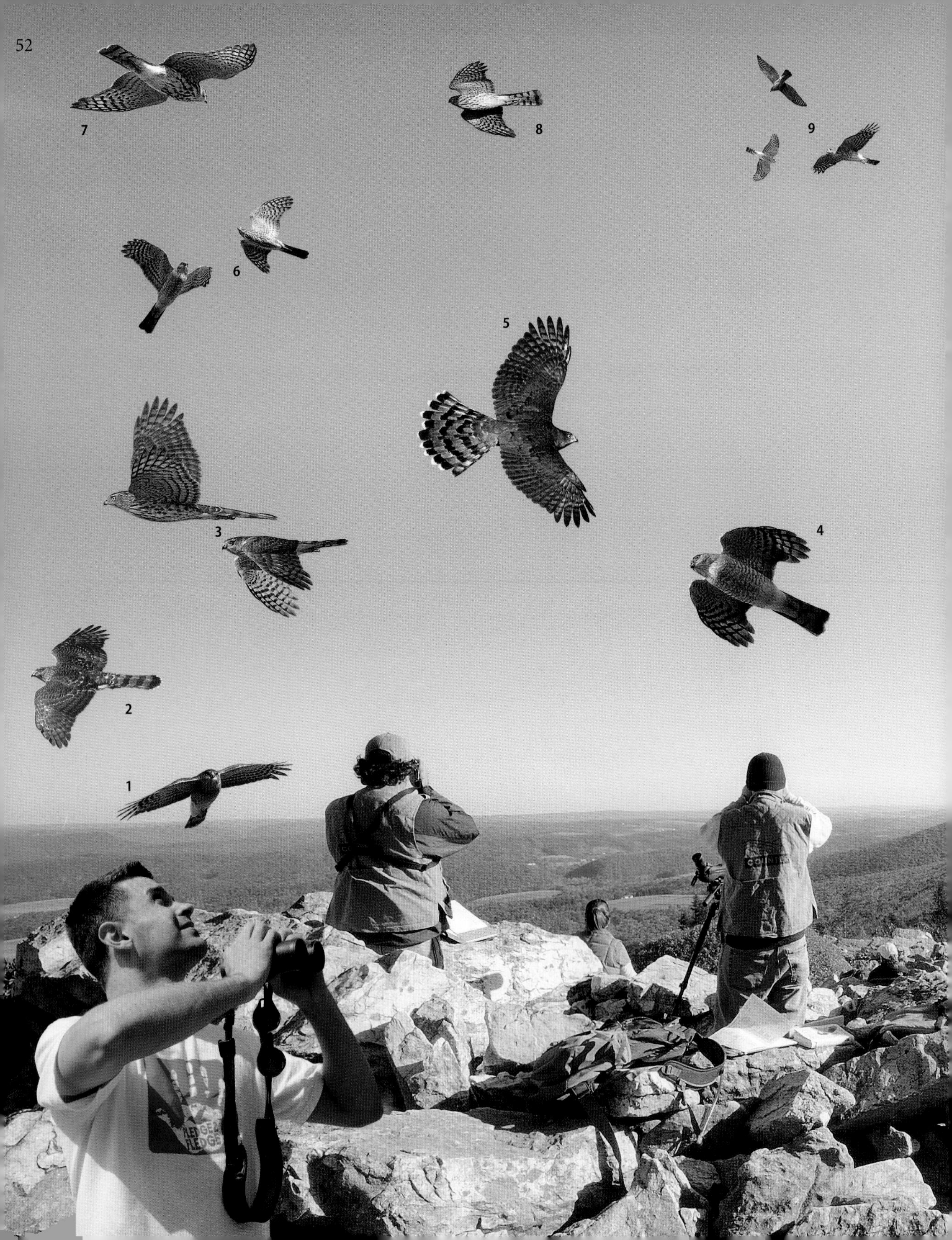
7
8
9
6
5
3
4
2
1

53

Hawks soar on flat wings, but Cooper's Hawks soar with their wings typically held in a slight dihedral, but also flattish at times. On Cooper's Hawk, note the large head, long wings, and long tail that is often rounded at the tip when closed compared with the stockier overall shape and typically square-tipped tail of Sharp-shinned. Identify and age as many of the Sharpies and Coops as you can! Answers p.264

Northern Goshawk *Accipiter gentilis* **NOGO** L 18–24 in, WS 38–45 in, WT 24–43 oz, page 200

Goshawks are the scarcest of the accipiters. They inhabit dense evergreen forest during the nesting season and are usually not found far from forest at any season. They usually stay well hidden, sitting quietly, and will often hunt from perches. They use healthy coniferous trees to support their nest and are quite vocal and aggressive defending their territories. They may even swoop on and strike people who happen upon their nest—they are not to be messed with! Adults are blue on top and whitish gray below with fine, faint, black barring. Adult males are bluer on top and more finely barred underneath than females. Adult Goshawks have orange eyes that eventually turn dark red as they get older. The tail is indistinctly banded with a narrow, white tip, and the head is blackish with a bold white eyeline. 2nd-year birds are adult-like, but some retain a few old tattered and worn brown

juv.

Northern Goshawk—juvenile

juvenile feathers. Goshawks are the scarcest of the accipiters. 1st-year Goshawks are heavily streaked underneath and brown on top. Compared with the similar Cooper's Hawk, they show more pale mottling along the upperwing coverts, a tawny nape, slightly wavy tail bands often mixed with gray, and a bolder eyeline. Underparts are heavily streaked, extending down to the undertail coverts. All Goshawks have broad wings and long tails, with adults being a bit slimmer-winged and shorter-tailed than 1st-years. Goshawks look pointed-winged in flight more often than the other accipiters, especially when flapping or gliding. They have broader, bulging secondaries that enhance the wings' pointed look. Large and heavy-chested, females can look massive, approaching Red-tailed Hawk in size. Males are smaller and more similar in size to the largest female Cooper's Hawk.

Perched Accipiters can be very difficult to tell apart. Sharp-shinned Hawks appear small and Goshawks appear large, but size may be misleading. In general, Goshawks appear broad at the shoulders. Cooper's and Sharp-shinned appear less stout. Cooper's

appears large-headed, and Sharp-shinned appears small-headed. Goshawk is the most likely to show a prominent eyeline, especially adults, though all 3 species can show a paler eyebrow at times. Identify and age as many as you can! Answers p.264

Accipiters in Flight. These 3 widespread accipiters are very similar in shape and plumage, and telling them apart can be difficult. Goshawks are much larger than Sharp-shinned Hawks, but male Goshawks are nearly the same size as female Cooper's Hawks, and male Cooper's are nearly equal in size to female Sharp-shinneds. This makes judging size a difficult task in many cases; however, their heavy wingbeats and steady flight make Goshawks appear large in flight, and the buoyancy and snappy wingbeats of Sharp-shinneds make them appear dainty in flight. Plumage traits such as the bold eyeline and mottled

upperwings of 1st-year Goshawks or the bold tail tip of 1st-year Cooper's can be helpful for topside views, but shape and flight style are often the keys to telling the accipiters apart in flight. Goshawks are stocky with broad chests, and they have the broadest wings of the accipiters that taper toward the tips. Cooper's have the longest tail, slimmest wings, and most protruding head. Sharp-shinned Hawk has the smallest head, slimmest, shortest tail, and shortest wings. Note the Red-tailed Hawk for compari-

Red-tailed Hawk (East) *Buteo jamaicensis* **RTHA** L 17–22 in, WS 43–56 in, WT 1.5–3.8 lb, page 203

The quintessential roadside raptor, Red-tailed Hawk is familiar and common throughout much of North America, frequently seen sitting motionless in roadside trees and on power poles, white breast gleaming in the sun. Heavily built with broad wings and a relatively short, broad tail; appears particularly large and stocky when perched. Though highly variable in plumage, across the majority of its range light morphs predominate, so becoming familiar with the field marks of light Red-taileds will enable you to id most Red-taileds encountered range-wide. East of the Great Plains, Red-tailed Hawks show little variation, occurring mainly as light morphs, with dark and rufous birds occurring very rarely during migration and winter. Light Red-tailed Hawks can be identified by their distinctly dark patagium (leading edge of the wing), dark bellyband contrasting with unmarked white breast, and red tail (adults). Adult Eastern Red-taileds have whitish-buff underparts with dark-spotted bellybands, and generally lack the strong rufous wash underneath of western birds. Eastern adults breeding in the Lower 48 usually lack distinct dark tail bands, but some Florida breeders and boreal forest breeders can show this. Eastern Red-taileds occasionally have dark throats.

juv.

juv.

Hunt efficiently from the air, often hovering and kiting from mid- to high elevation, as well as from a perch, typically a roadside power pole or tree, and can stoop at high speeds to surprise, flush, or overtake prey. Large and powerful with even-paced, moderately heavy wingbeats; its wingbeats and flight style differ from all other buteos. The broad wings usually held in a shallow dihedral when soaring, but sometimes flat. 1st-years lack the adult's red tail, instead having a brownish-banded tail throughout the first year, becoming adult-like in the second fall. 1st-years also pale-eyed; eastern birds tend to be pale-throated with white to buffy underparts and blobby dark bellybands. 1st-years rangier than adults, with narrower wings and longer tails, lack the adult's bold dark trailing edge to the wings in flight and show distinct pale wing panels on the outerwings. 2nd-years sometimes identifiable by retained juvenile outer primaries and secondaries. Found in a variety of open habitats; generally avoids dense tracts of continuous forest. A true generalist, feeding on everything from mice to rabbits, as well as birds and snakes. The typical call is the Hollywood raptor scream, very familiar even to nonbirders, but often passed off as an eagle on the big screen.

62

ad. light

juv. light

ad. light

ad. light

Red-tailed Hawk (West)

Common throughout open country of the West and often seen sitting on power poles, western Red-taileds are generally richer-colored and more boldly patterned than eastern birds, with most light birds washed with rufous below. From the Great Plains westward, body plumage is highly variable, though the vast majority are light morphs; rufous morphs are uncommon, and dark morphs are rare. Light-morph adults usually show brown-ish throats and a mix of barring and spotting on the belly, and often have more heavily marked underwing coverts than eastern birds. The tail is variably barred dark, usually with heavier, wider bands than eastern birds. Rufous and dark birds both appear darkish overall below at a distance, but up close most rufous birds have an orange chest and a darker belly, whereas true dark morphs are completely brown or black below. Flight style

ad. dark

juv. dark

ad. intermediate

juv. light

juv. dark

nearly identical to eastern birds, though western Red-taileds average slightly longer-winged and generally look a bit lankier in the field. Western 1st-years are more heavily marked below than their eastern counterparts, usually with barring on the leggings and more heavily marked underwing coverts. 1st-year rufous morphs are dark below with variable tawny streaking, and the underwing coverts are completely mottled, disguising the dark patagial bars shown by light morphs, but occasionally showing a ghost of that pattern. True dark morphs are very rare and solidly brownish black below, showing no hint of a belly-band or darker patagials. Juvenile flight feathers of all morphs are similar but average a bit more heavily banded than eastern birds. The outer primaries of western 1st-years are typically solidly dark, whereas easterns can be banded or solidly dark.

ad.

ad.

juv.

Red-tailed Hawk (Krider's)

Generally scarce as a breeder on the northern Great Plains, Krider's is a pale variant of Red-tailed Hawk that was formerly considered a subspecies, but is now being swamped out by interbreeding with Eastern, Western, and Harlan's Red-taileds. Adult Krider's are variable, but extreme examples are white-headed with darker malar marks, and white-tailed, usually with a pinkish tip. The underparts can be completely unmarked, lacking a bellyband and patagial marks altogether, but more often the bellyband is reduced to a few spots and the patagial marks are faint. Females are darker overall, and perhaps indistinguishable from some Easterns, and the high proportion of intergrades makes it difficult to ever be certain of a Krider's that isn't on the extreme end of the spectrum. 1st-years are similar to paler Easterns but usually have distinctly whiter heads, more extensive white mottling on the upperwing coverts, and whitish tails with narrow black banding throughout. The wing panels are usually more distinct than on Eastern. Krider's winters on the southern Great Plains south to the Gulf Coast and east into the Mississippi River Valley; it rarely reaches the Southeast and Peninsular Florida. Breeding in Alaska and northwestern Canada, Harlan's is

Red-tailed Hawk (Harlan's)

usually seen by birders during migration and winter, especially on the Great Plains. It is local in the West and rare east of the Mississippi. Harlan's differs from all other Red-taileds in its highly variable tail pattern on adults. Tail pattern ranges from nearly wholly blackish to completely white, but most have some mix of white, gray, and red. Most are washed with smudgy grayish mottling. Body plumage ranges from completely black to stark white with a blobby blackish bellyband, but most birds are darkish with a white speckled breast. Light morphs are generally starker black and white than other subspecies, but some are browner

and more like Eastern Red-taileds. Adult flight feathers usually show some mottling but occasionally none. 1st-years are also highly variable, but generally have darker brownish black ground color, a white-speckled breast, and bolder, thicker barring in the wing and tail feathers than other subspecies. The outer primaries are usually boldly banded. Light morphs are very similar to Krider's, but light Harlan's usually has a bolder dark bellyband and patagials, and a darker brownish ground color to the tail. Both can be very white-headed. To identify Harlan's, a good assessment of tail pattern and flight-feather pattern is critical.

Red-tailed Hawks on the Prairies. Many races of Red-tailed Hawk occur on the prairies. Determining the age of Red-tailed Hawks of any subspecies is usually relatively straightforward. Only adults have red tails, and adults of all subspecies show a broad dark trailing edge to the wings. 1st-years of all subspecies and morphs have brownish tails with variable black banding above, and all lack the bold dark trailing edge to the wings shown by adults. Red-tailed Hawks have pale eyes in their first year, and older adults have brownish eyes, but sometimes 2nd- and even 3rd-year birds can show very pale eyes, so be careful when using this as a field mark for ageing Red-taileds. 2nd-years often have the outer primaries retained from juvenile plumage, and this can be a good thing to look for to accurately age 2nd-year birds. Be careful when trying to put Red-tailed Hawks into subspecie

categories, especially 1st-years. A good view of the underside, the upperparts, and the tail pattern is often required to make a subspecies determination, and without these you're usually left guessing. No single field mark is unique to any subspecies. Plumage characters overlap between all the subspecies, and there are many intermediate birds out there that are not safely assigned to any subspecies. Harlan's is the most distinctive race, yet Harlan's are also highly variable, and many adults show intermediate characters, sometimes looking more like Easterns or Westerns. Look for the distinctive dusky mottling on the upperside of nearly all adult Harlan's tails. 1st-year Harlan's are generally blacker than other Red-tailed races, and usually have more heavily banded flight feathers, often with outer primaries banded out to the tips. What race and age are all of these? Answers p.266.

68

Red-tailed Hawks on the Southern Great Plains. The highest diversity of Red-tailed Hawk subspecies can be found on the southern Great Plains in winter. Here the mix of plumages can be bewildering, and many birds cannot be safely assigned to a particular subspecies, especially 1st-years. The variety of light morphs here ranges from heavily marked western and northern-breeding eastern birds, which can be nearly identical, to the palest

light variations of Krider's and Harlan's. The status of the subspecies Fuertes is in question, but generally birds breeding on the southern Great Plains west to New Mexico and Arizona can be Eastern or Western-like, but have virtually unmarked bellies and are recognized as Fuertes by some authors. Identify race and age if you can!

Swainson's Hawk *Buteo swainsoni* **SWHA** L 17–22 in, WS 47–54 in, WT 1.3–2.7 lb, page 209

Elegant raptor of western open country, best distinguished by its long, tapered, dark flight feathers that contrast with paler underwing coverts in all but the darkest of plumages. Swainson's are highly aerial buteos, hunting mainly small mammals from medium to high elevations, using spectacular stoops to pounce on prey. They regularly hover and kite, and soar unsteadily on smoothly raised wings, occasionally held flatter. Equally comfortable on the ground, often occurring in large flocks in a field with abundant insect prey, which they eat during migration and winter. Found in a variety of open country, ranging from treeless expanses of grassland to disturbed agricultural areas. Extremely variable ventral plumage, though the majority of birds can be characterized as light, intermediate, or dark. Light adults vary from being unmarked white below with a distinct brown or rufous bib, to having barred bellies and variously mottled underwing coverts, but always paler than the flight feathers. Intermediate birds are generally rufous below with paler underwings, and true dark morphs range from wholly brown to

Swainson's Hawk

blackish, but almost always with pale undertail coverts. The upperparts, wing, and tail feathers are similar on all Swainson's Hawks. The sexes are similar, but males are generally more lightly marked with brighter rufous bibs and gray heads in light morphs, and they are generally blacker overall in dark morphs. Dark and intermediate birds usually look dark at a distance, whereas light morphs show the strikingly patterned underparts and dark-light underwing contrast. The upperparts are generally darkish with a pale U-shaped band at the base of the tail. At a distance, the upperparts show a vague two-toned appearance, with darker flight feathers and paler brownish back and upperwing coverts. The darkest birds lack contrast underneath, with completely dark underwings. On these dark extremes, look for paler undertail coverts, which are barred but paler on even the darkest birds. Adults have a grayish brown tail with darker narrow internal bands and a bolder, dark subterminal band.

1st-s.

juv.

2nd-s. light

2nd-s. light

Swainson's Hawk—immatures

1st-years are slightly narrower-winged than adults, and they lack the bold dark trailing edge to the wings shown by adults; beware, some darker 1st-years can have a fairly prominent dark trailing edge. 1st-years range from being essentially whitish buff below with spotted darker upper breast sides to being essentially blackish brown below with faint tawny streaks. Even the darkest 1st-years have some tawny streaking on the underparts. 1st-years of all morphs have buff-fringed upperwing coverts, though these are fainter on darker birds. In spring, returning migrants are often very pale-headed, even the darkest birds. These can be confusing for birders, so be aware that for a species such as Swainson's, which winters on South American

juv.

juv.

juv.

juv. dark/intermediate

juv. light

grassland, the sun can drastically bleach and fade the upperparts. Unlike many big buteos, Swainson's take 3 years to reach adult plumage; they have a distinctive 2nd-year plumage where birds look intermediate between 1st-year and adult. 2nd-years have molted in adult-like flight feathers and tail feathers, but in some cases retain several outer primaries, which appear very pale and worn. A good rule of thumb for identifying 2nd-years is to look for juvenile-like birds underneath (streaky), but with a bold, dark trailing edge to the wings and a wide, dark subterminal tail band. In general, 2nd-years are streaked below, whereas adults are barred or smoothly patterned. 2nd-years appear "blotchy" below when molting from second-summer plumage into adult plumage.

Swainson's Hawk on Migration. Swainson's Hawks have one of the most spectacular migrations of any raptor, with some birds migrating from the northern Great Plains to the grasslands of Argentina. En route, they form large flocks, passing over the Great Plains in big groups and over hawk watches such as Corpus Christi and sites in the Lower Rio Grande Valley of Texas. The biggest flights pass through Veracruz, MX, and Panama, where birds are funneled into a narrow bottleneck before continuing south into South America. Swainson's Hawks have the most variable plumage of any buteo, with perhaps the exception o

Red-tailed Hawk, but the good thing about Swainson's is that all birds can be identified by the same suite of few characters: long tapered wings, dark flight feathers, usually paler underwing coverts, and almost always pale undertail coverts. The upperparts, wing, and tail feathers of all variants are similar in appearance, so focus on the body and underwing coverts to get a sense of the variation of Swainson's. Many of these birds can be aged, but if you are lucky enough to come across a large movement of

ad.

3rd-yr.

White-tailed Hawk *Geranoaetus albicaudatus* **WTHA** L 18–23 in, WS 50–53 in, WT 1.9–2.7 lb, page 212

A big, strikingly patterned hawk of south Texas prairies and agricultural areas. Often congregates in fall and winter around burning sugarcane fields and actively tilled agricultural lands, frequently in association with Crested Caracara. Adults are nearly unmistakable, with beautiful grayish upperparts, rufous shoulders, clean white underparts, dark flight feathers, and a clean white tail with a broad black band at the tip. Somewhat intermediate in shape between Red-tailed Hawk and Swainson's Hawk, White-tailed is broad-winged but has tapered hands, and it has darkish finely banded flight feathers that contrast with the clean white or lightly barred underwings. Importantly, on perched birds of all ages, the wingtips extend well past the tail tip, but especially so on adults and older immatures. White-tailed Hawks are steady in flight and soar in wide, lazy circles the way other large buteos do. They hold their wings in a modified dihedral. Their direct flight is with stiff, deep

juvs.

juv.

2nd-yr.

White-tailed Hawk

wingbeats, similar to Red-tailed or Swainson's Hawk. While North American White-tailed Hawks are not polymorphic like Swainson's and Red-tailed Hawk, the longest age progression of any North American buteo, taking 4 years to achieve full adult plumage. Add to this a highly variable 1st-year plumage that ranges from blackish below with a large white breast splotch (typical), to variably paler with dark patagial marks and a bellyband, recalling juvenile Red-tailed Hawk. 1st-years often have a bold head pattern, with pale patches above and behind the eye. 2nd-years are similar overall to 1st-years but have darker heads and adult-like wing feathers, usually with 2–4 outer primaries retained from juvenile plumage. 3rd-years are similar to adults but usually darker slaty-gray above, and have barred bellies and flanks and rufous-tinged underwing coverts.

ad. dark

ad. light

dark

Ferruginous Hawk *Buteo regalis* **FEHA** L 20–26 in, WS 53–60 in, WT 2–4.5 lb, page 214

Western grassland, sagebrush desert, and shrub-steppe environments are the preferred breeding habitats of the Ferruginous Hawk, but in winter it can be found in more altered landscapes such as agricultural land, especially when ground squirrels are present. Light adults are strikingly beautiful birds! They are pure white underneath with bold rufous leggings and spectacular rufous upperwings. Plumage of adults is variable, with many showing faint to heavy rufous mottling on the underwing co-

verts and rufous streaking on the underbody with whitish flight feathers. Light adults have whitish primaries that "flash" white on top, and whitish, grayish, or even reddish mottled tails. Dark adults are solid dark rufous-brown below with a grayish brown "bib" and head, or dark brown underneath with a rufous bib, but still show the strikingly contrasting whitish flight feathers. Dark adults typically have grayish tails and have reduced pale primary panels above. 1st-year Ferruginous Hawks are

juv. dark

juv. light

juv. light

Ferruginous Hawk—juvenile

similar to adults in plumage and shape. 1st-year light birds are noticeably white underneath, appearing plain and unmarked at a distance, but brown spotting on the flanks and dark commas at the wrists can be seen on close birds. Topside is "warm" brown with obvious white primary "panels" and a white-based tail. 1st-years lack the brilliant rufous upperwings of adults. 1st-year dark birds are nearly identical to adult dark birds. Differences are minimal, with 1st-years dark brown underneath

with a slightly more rufous chest and a brown head. The tail of 1st-year dark birds is often dark grayish brown with slightly darker narrow banding but appears dark overall in the field. Some dark 1st-years show a white-based tail. Dark birds that are "black" underneath are very rare. The outer primaries of all Ferruginous Hawks show dark tips, which are limited compared with most other buteos. All 1st-year birds have pale eyes that take up to several years to become dark brown as adults.

Ferruginous Hawks over the Canyons. In flight, Ferruginous Hawks are long-winged, large-headed, and fairly long-tailed compared with other buteos. The wings are fairly slim overall and pointed at the tips, but the body is stout and "chesty" and appears powerful. Ferruginous Hawks fly with a dihedral or modified dihedral in all postures, especially when gliding. They are buoyant for such a bulky bird, soaring and rising with ease, and even "wobbling" from side to side on ridge updrafts. The

7

8

9

10

wingbeats are stiff but easy and slightly quicker on the upbeats. Light birds appear brightly plumaged in most situations, but in poor light, even they can appear dark underneath. Ferruginous Hawks are found in open, unobstructed country habitats such as the badlands shown here, but also in surprisingly agricultural and even suburban settings during migration and winter." They are active, territorial, and vocal on the breeding grounds. Answers to their age are on p.269.

Rough-legged Hawk *Buteo lagopus* **RLHA** 18–23 in, WS 48–56 in, WT 1.6–4 lb, page 217

Light adults are pale underneath with a dark belly and wrist patches, with paler underwings, chest, and head. The underwing coverts can be lightly or heavily marked. On males, the underwing coverts are sometimes mottled throughout, and the dark wrist patches become lost within the dark mottling. On females, the underwing coverts are typically buffy with brownish mottling. All light adults have a white-based tail with a dark tip, and a dark trailing edge to the wings (more bold and defined compared with 1st-years). Males usually have multiple dark tail bands; females show a nearly solid dark band toward the tip. Males and females can have a dark "bib" on the chest, but this is more typical of males, which often have a mottled belly and barred flanks compared with the solidly dark belly and flanks of most females. Some adult males have a white belly! Adult males are grayish brown above, especially the back (note bird on power pole), compared with the even brown upperside of females.

juv. light

Rough-legged Hawk—juvenile light

Adult males and females differ in plumage, but overlap occurs between the sexes, making some birds impossible to sex. The feathered legs of Rough-legged Hawks are sometimes noticeable on perched birds. 1st-year light Rough-legged Hawks have a solid dark belly and wrist patches with paler underwings, chest, and head (sometimes the "bib" is dark like light adults), and dusky tail tip and trailing edge to the wings, which is less bold and defined than those of adults. 1st-year males and females are identical in plumage. Like some other buteos, 1st-year Rough-legged Hawks have pale primary panels that are most noticeable on the topside and visible from below only at certain times. The upperside is "plain" brown with a pale head, and a white-based tail. Be aware that 1st-year birds can appear very similar in plumage to adult females, but they always show a dusky, ill-defined trailing edge to the wings. All 1st-year birds have pale eyes that take a year or two to become dark brown as adults.

84

ad. dark

Rough-legged Hawk — dark

Dark Rough-legged Hawks are dark brown below with slightly paler underwing coverts, and dark above. The upperside of adults is mottled compared with the unmarked uppersides of 1st-years. Some adult males are a beautiful, uniform black underneath with a slaty blue sheen on the back. Adults show a

dark trailing edge to the wings and a defined dark tail tip from below. The tail pattern on adult dark birds is all-dark above or dark with multiple white tail bands. Both sexes can have tail bands, but the white bands on males are typically neat and well-defined. 1st-years have an indistinct dark tail with faint grayish

juv. dark

juv. dark

ad. intermediate/dark

broken bands that appears whitish with a smudgy dark tip from below. 1st-year dark birds also have a paler face than dark adults. Rough-legged Hawks are high-Arctic breeders. Rough-legs winter on marshes, farmland, and other open countryside, often in the harshest environments. They can often be seen soaring with wings in a modified dihedral or hovering to spot unsuspecting rodents. Any raptor sitting on the very highest snag surveying the surrounding countryside is likely to be this species.

Rough-legged Hawks in the Cold. Rough-legged Hawks occupy open fields, agricultural areas, grassy hillsides, and marshes in winter. They hover and soar relentlessly with amazing stamina in search of mice and voles hidden in the grass, plunging to the ground after spotting prey. They also perch-hunt from power poles, fence posts, and watering pivots. In flight, the wings are lanky

overall but still buteo-like, and usually held in a dihedral or modified dihedral. They are buoyant but steady, teetering from side to side only in high winds. The wingbeats are easy and reminiscent of a Northern Harrier, but somewhat stiffer and with more power. Plumage differences between the ages and sexes can be difficult to observe in the field, but try on the birds here. Answers p.269.

juv.

ad.

juv.

ad.

ad.

juv.

Red-shouldered Hawk (East) *Buteo lineatus* **RSHA** L 15–19 in, WS 37–42 in, WT 1.1–1.9 lb, page 220

Eastern Red-shoulders are found in swampy woodlands in summer, but they occur in more open habitats during migration and winter, especially along field edges. They take flight less frequently than most raptors, remaining perched for long periods waiting for prey. 1st-years are brown on top and pale below with dark streaks on the underbody. The tail is banded brown and blackish, but fairly indistinct, and usually the brown bands are narrower than the blackish ones, showing a hint of the adult tail pattern. All ages and races have unique, pale, comma-shaped, translucent "windows" on the outer primaries that show up from below and above. The primary commas are white on adults and buffy on 1st-years. Adults are gorgeous, with strik-

Red-shouldered Hawk—Florida

ing black-and-white banded flight and tail feathers, rufous underparts, and rufous upperwing coverts or "shoulders"! Florida Red-shouldered Hawks are found in semiopen swamps or dense, swampy woodland. They fly in only short spurts, sitting most of the day, and they are tamer than the other races, often allowing close approach. They may hunt and display right in front of people, while other raptors are much more aware of their personal space. Adults are similar in plumage to eastern adults but are considerably paler overall, and especially pale gray on the head. 1st-years are similar in plumage to 1st-year Eastern as well; oddly, they are often more heavily marked underneath than eastern birds. Birds of southern peninsular Florida average palest.

Red-shouldered Hawk (West)

California Red-shouldered Hawks live in a variety of woodland habitats, including small patches of trees within suburban areas. They can be seen hunting grassy fields and roadside edges as well in winter. Adult California Red-shouldered Hawks are the darkest, most vibrant rufous underneath of the races, often showing a solid rufous breast. 1st-years are brown on top and pale below, with dark streaks on the underbody, but they are typically heav-ily marked with rufous brown streaks and sometimes barred on the chest, appearing adult-like below. The flight and tail feathers are also adult-like on many 1st-years, with neat black-and-white bands and whitish primary commas. Red-shouldered Hawks are somewhat stocky with square-tipped wings compared with other buteos; however, they can show tapered wings at times, especially when gliding. They are similar in shape to

Broad-winged Hawk

Broad-winged Hawk

Red-tailed Hawk

Red-shouldered Hawk

Red-tailed and Broad-winged Hawks, and very similar in plumage to Broad-winged Hawks. Both species are barred rufous underneath, but adult Broad-winged lacks the boldly banded flight feathers of adult Red-shouldered, and the tail has broad white bands compared with the narrower white tail bands of Red-shouldered. 1st-year Red-shouldered Hawks are told from 1st-year Broad-winged by their broader tail, less tapered wings,

and comma-shaped primary windows. One of the most distinctive traits of Red-shouldered Hawk is its accipter-like wingbeats, which easily separate it from Red-tailed Hawk. Red-shoulders also lack a bellyband and have shorter, less bulging wings and a longer tail. Red-shouldered Hawks soar on flattish wings that are arched slightly forward and glide on bowed wings.

1st-s.

ad.

1st-s.

ad.

Broad-winged Hawk *Buteo platypterus* **BWHA** L 14–17 in, WS 32–36 in, WT 11–17 oz, page 223

Broad-winged Hawks are found in swampy deciduous and mixed woodland in summer throughout their North American range. Most migrate to Central and South America for winter, where they can be seen along field edges and within forests. They hunt mostly from a perch, remaining still until their prey reveals itself; they rarely hunt from the sky. 1st-years are brown on top and pale below with dark streaks on the underbody, though they are highly variable, with some heavily streaked underneath and others almost unmarked. They have squarish, translucent "windows" on the outer primaries that show up from below. The tail is indistinctly banded with a broad, dark tail tip. Adult Broad-winged Hawks are barred rufous on the underbody with buffy

dark

juv.

Broad-winged Hawk—juvenile

underwings. The upperside is dark solid brown, and the tail is boldly and evenly banded black and white. Adults have a defined dark trailing edge to the wings compared with the faint dusky terminal band of 1st-years. Broad-winged Hawks are small, stocky buteos with pointed wings in all postures. The tail appears broad when fanned but narrow when closed, sometimes appearing somewhat long and accipiter-like. Dark birds are uniformly dark on the underbody with pale flight feathers. Dark adults solidly blackish below with flight feathers similar to light adult. Dark juveniles are brownish-black below with variable tawny streaking, sometimes entirely blackish, and have darker upperwings than light juveniles. Wing and tail feathers are similar to light morphs.

A Broad-winged Hawk Kettle. On migration, Broad-winged Hawks often gather in large flocks or "kettles," sometimes with other birds, such as Swainson's Hawks and Turkey Vultures. These kettles can be overwhelming to comprehend or count, and a thrill to observe. Broad-winged Hawks show stocky, pointed wings in a soar, and spiral in tight circles compared with larger hawks. When they glide from a kettle, the wings are short but sharply pointed, and the tail is narrow. They may fly from sunup

to find the Red-taileds. If the bird has a plainer underwing pattern, it's a Broad-winged or a Red-shouldered. Red-shouldereds usually show streaked breasts and a more square-handed look to the wingtips than Broad-wingeds, which are quite variable below but always have more tapered wingtips. Identify and age these widespread buteos in upstate New York on fall migration. Answers p.270

ad.

1st-s.

Gray Hawk *Buteo plagiatus* **GRHA** L 14–18 in, WS 32–38 in, WT 13–23 oz, page 226

Gray Hawks are medium-sized, striking buteos restricted to a few areas in the South and Southwest, usually found along rivers and dry creek beds in Arizona, New Mexico, and south Texas. Scarce but numbers increasing. Gray Hawks perch-hunt, and while they soar readily and often quite high on midmorning thermals, they typically do not stoop on prey from a height. Instead they sit quietly in the shady areas of large cottonwoods waiting to pounce on lizards, small mammals, birds, and insects. Adults are simply remarkable and unlikely to be confused with any other North American raptor, but 1st-years are more variable and frequently confused with 1st-year Broad-winged and Red-shouldered Hawks. From below, Gray Hawks often appear very pale when soaring, with few notable field marks (but see tail pattern). Unlike those of many buteos, the underwings are very plain and unmarked. Gray Hawks soar on flat wings in steady circles. Their direct flight uses snappy, accipiter-like wingbeats that are gener-

Gray Hawk—juvenile

ally faster than those of other buteos. 1st-years are overall brown above, and variably marked dark brown on buff below, with a notably striking head pattern combining a white cheek, dark malar, dark eyeline, and white supercilium; most have a dark central throat stripe. The tail pattern is unique, with many broad, brown bands that become narrower near the base. The flight feathers are finely barred, even the outer primaries, and are largely translucent in flight on both 1st-years and adults. 1st-years are told from

1st-year Broad-winged Hawk by their more distinct head pattern, with bold pale cheeks, shorter wings (compare when perched), a longer tail with progressively narrow bands toward the base, and lack of a dusky trailing edge to evenly translucent flight feathers (vs. pale panels on juvenile Broad-winged). 1st-year Gray Hawk is told from 1st-year Red-shouldered Hawk by its bolder head pattern and the lack of pale crescents on the outer primaries.

juv. light

ad. light

Short-tailed Hawk *Buteo brachyurus* **STHA** L 15–17 in, WS 33–41 in, WT 12–20 oz, page 228

Medium-sized highly aerial raptor of mainly tropical distribution, with a small population in south Florida and a few nesting pairs in southern Arizona mountains. In all plumages, note broad wings with relatively tapered tips, and dark flight feathers that contrast with paler outer primaries. Wings appear somewhat pinched-in at the base, accentuated by bulging secondaries. When gliding, carpal protrudes. On light morphs, note pale underwing coverts contrasting strongly with dark flight feathers. Ages differ; sexes similar. Adult light morph is clean white below with dark brown head and pale throat, often with rufous tones on the neck sides. Tail pattern variable, ranging from lightly to heavily banded, but always with a wider dark subterminal band. The topside is dark brown, lacking any mottling, appearing similar to adult Swainson's Hawk. 1st-year light morph is brown above and buffy below, with variable brown streaking (sometimes absent) on the sides of the upper breast, a more diffuse dark trailing edge to flight feathers than on adult, and translucent primaries. Tail pattern similar to adult, but usually lacks the well-defined, broad, dark subterminal band. Short-tailed Hawks are aerial hunters, and kite but do not hover. Often

juv. dark

ad. dark

Short-tailed Hawk—dark

hang motionless at high elevation, turning abruptly on one wing and falling into a stoop, pouncing on birds, rodents, and reptiles. Rarely seen perched, and typically do not sit on roadside wires or poles like other small buteos. Occurs in light and dark morphs, but no known intermediate plumages. All Short-tailed Hawks share similar flight feathers that are mostly dusky grayish with the outer 3–4 primaries notably paler. Adult dark morph is dark brown above with wholly blackish underparts. 1st-year dark morph is variably dark below, but typically shows extensive tawny streaking on the body and underwing coverts; rare ex-

amples are completely dark. Most birds show light speckling on the belly and underwings. The flight and tail feathers are similar to 1st-year light morphs. Short-taileds soar steadily on flattish wings with the tips characteristically upturned, sometimes also with a smooth dihedral. In most flight positions, the bird does not appear particularly short-tailed, but when seen head-on, its tail can appear quite short in relation to the broad wings. Short-tailed Hawks fly with even-paced, smooth wingbeats, somewhat between the manner of a Broad-winged and a Red-tailed Hawk.

ad.

Harris's Hawk *Parabuteo unicinctus* **HASH** L 18–23 in, WS 40–47 in, WT 1.3–2.6 lb, page 230

Large, distinctive raptor of the arid Southwest, shaped somewhat like an oversized accipiter with long, broad wings, long legs, and a very long tail that is always white-based. Harris's are found in open to semiopen habitats with well-spaced perches, usually tall cacti (standing atop the thorns), power poles, or trees, and are frequently found in surprisingly suburban areas such as around Tucson. They are generally social during both nesting and winter, and the hunting tactics of Harris's Hawk are among the most complex and unique of any bird. Hunting groups usually consist of a pair of dominant adults assisted by several immature or adult birds, often offspring of the adults or even birds from other nesting pairs. These groups cooperatively hunt prey year-round, sharing the catch, but Harris's Hawks are also capable of hunting alone. Harris's Hawks are known to practice "back-standing," where one hawk perches atop another to gain a better view of the territory. Although most North American Harris's Hawks breed in spring, in some cases they can breed year-round when food is plentiful.

Harris's Hawk—juvenile

Generally confiding, they often allow close approach. Formerly called the "Bay-winged Hawk" because of its striking rufous upperwing coverts, Harris's Hawk has 2 distinct plumages: 1st-year (juvenile) and adult. Adults are solidly blackish brown overall with rufous underwing coverts and rufous uppertail coverts. 1st-years are variably streaked below, sometimes with a more solid breast and finely banded flight feathers. Both ages have a blackish tail with a conspicuous white base, but adults have a bolder white tip than 1st-years. First-summers are in transition from juvenile to adult plumage and have a mix of juvenile and adult feathers; they are adult-like by second fall. Sexes similar. Harris's Hawks soar steadily on flattish or bowed wings, and glide on bowed wings with the tips curled upward. When flapping, the wingbeats are even and heavy, somewhat recalling a Red-tailed Hawk. They are impressive sprinters as well, accelerating quickly at the first sign of prey.

Common Black-Hawk *Buteogallus anthracinus* **COBH** L 20–22 in, WS 40–52 in, WT 1.4–2.9 lb, page 232

Common Black-Hawks are generally shy and retiring during the breeding season, nesting along perennial streams lined with sycamores or cottonwoods in the desert Southwest. There are relatively few places where birders can access their nesting areas, most of which are in Arizona. In flight, adults are nearly unmistakable, with very broad wings and a short black-and-white banded tail. But perched adults can be challenging, as their general coloration closely matches another Southwest specialty, the Zone-tailed Hawk. 1st-years are very different from adults, having a plumage pattern similar to several streaky-plumaged juvenile buteos,

with which they are often confused. Black-Hawks soar briefly in midmorning (the best chance to see one), but then return to the gallery forest canopy, where they quietly perch-hunt amphibians, reptiles, and fish. Occasionally they hunt on the ground, even wading in shallow water with their long legs. When soaring, Black-Hawks do so on flat wings, lacking the shallow dihedral shown by Black Vulture. They soar in wide, steady circles, and their direct flight is with stiff, labored wingbeats. On perched Black-Hawks, the wingtips nearly reach the tail tip, especially on adults, and the bill is less sharply curved than on most other raptors.

Common Black-Hawk

Common Black-Hawks are large raptors, roughly the size of a Red-tailed Hawk, but more similar in shape to Black Vulture than to any buteo. Ages differ; sexes similar. Adult completely black below with dark, finely banded flight feathers, an extremely broad, dark trailing edge to the wings, and a single bold white tail band that creates a white-rumped look from above. The upperside is otherwise blackish with a bluish sheen, but the cere and flesh in front of the eye are pale. Note pale bases to the outer primaries. 1st-year streaked dark below, with finely banded flight feathers, a bold face pattern, and multiple wavy white tail bands

with a black tip that are striking from above and sometimes from below. The upperwings are dark brownish black, with pale panels on the inner primaries. By the first summer, 1-year-old birds look intermediate between 1st-year and adult, as they are molting from the streaky juvenile plumage to the solidly dark plumage of adults. 1st-years are much lankier than adults, with narrower wings and longer tails, and much more likely to be misidentified or passed off as a buteo. The shape difference between 1st-year and adult Common Black-Hawk is the most dramatic age-related difference of any North American raptor species.

Zone-tailed Hawk *Buteo albonotatus* **ZTHA** L 19–22 in, WS 48–55 in, WT 1.3–2.4 lb, page 234

Zone-tailed Hawk is a large raptor of riparian woods, mountains, canyons, and arid hills of the South and Southwest. Highly aerial, spending most of the day hunting on the wing, usually in association with kettles of Turkey Vultures, but also singly. Hunts birds, mammals, and reptiles, usually capturing through spectacular aerial stoops, but sometimes perch-hunts in the early morning. Thought to mimic Turkey Vulture in order to prey on animals that have become conditioned to the vulture's harmless presence; one of few cases of evolutionary mimicry in birds. As a result,

Zone-tailed Hawk is often confused with and passed off as Turkey Vulture, which it closely resembles in flight. It shares Turkey Vulture's teetering flight and strong dihedral, but Zone-tailed's wingbeats are quicker and stiffer, and it is able to make quicker, more agile turns and stoops than vultures. Zone-tailed Hawks also differ in that they are smaller, larger-headed, square-tailed, and have slightly narrower wings. Plumage differences from Turkey Vulture include banded flight feathers with a bold dark trailing edge (adults), a yellow cere and feet, and different tail patterns.

with Turkey Vultures

juv.

ad.

Zone-tailed Hawk

There are 2 age classes: adult and 1st-year (juvenile). The sexes of 1st-years are identical, but adult males and females differ slightly in tail pattern. It is possible that 2nd-year birds have mostly adult female-like tail characteristics, but more study is needed. Zone-tailed Hawks take 1 year to attain adult plumage. Adults are black below with contrasting grayish, heavily banded flight feathers with a bold dark trailing edge. The long tail has 1 prominent white band when closed and seen from below. When the tail is spread, adults show 2–5 inner bands, but the number varies between individuals, and tail pattern overlaps between the sexes. Males average fewer inner tail bands than females. 1st-years are similar to adults, but have fine white spotting on the breast, finely banded flight feathers out to the tips, and a finely banded tail with a wider black subterminal band. The flight feathers lack the bold dark trailing edge of adults, making 1st-years more similar to Turkey Vulture than to adults. The pale inner primary panels are visible from above and below, but are not so striking or obvious as on many other juvenile buteos.

Dark Raptors of the Southwest. At any point in the day when one is birding in the southwestern United States, the majority of soaring birds in the sky are Turkey Vultures; however, other species frequently join them. It is quite easy to overlook some

of these, particularly if you are basing identification on color. Check this group out. The more you look, the more you see! It's always good to scan a flock this size at least 3 times! How many different species are there? Answers p.271

Snail Kite *Rostrhamus sociabilis* **SNKI** L 14–16 in, WS 42–46 in, WT 12–21 oz, page 236

Distinctive raptor of freshwater marshes, drainage ditches, and flood channels in Florida. Feeds on the large freshwater apple snail, using its slim, specially adapted bill to sever the muscle that holds the snail to its shell. Unlike the Osprey, Snail Kites do not plunge-dive for prey. Instead, they forage over very shallow water, delicately plucking a snail from the water by extending just their legs and talons beneath the surface. Snails are then carried to a favored perch for consumption. Gregarious, often nesting in loose colonies, and roosting communally with herons, egrets, and vultures. In fall and winter, large roosts can form near good forag-

ing areas, sometimes with more than 100 birds, but usually fewer than a dozen are seen in any given marsh. Medium-sized and distinctively shaped, Snail Kites couple broad, rounded wings with slim bodies and long tails. They fly slowly, deliberately, and quite low over marshes, with heavy wingbeats, accentuated by glides on deeply bowed wings. They make agile, quick changes in direction when prey is detected. Snail Kites rarely soar high, but when they do, confusion is possible with other raptors, especially the lankier 1st-years. Perched, they are slim overall, with long wings that reach the tail tip, and a long, narrow, sharply curved bill.

♀

ad. ♂

Snail Kite

Snail Kites differ by age and sex, usually taking 2–3 years to attain full adult plumage. General plumage progression is from a streaky 1st-year plumage where both sexes are similar, to an intermediate plumage in the second year where sexual characters begin to develop, to adult plumage in the third year. All ages show a distinctly white-based tail. Adults are stockier overall with wider wings than 1st-years. Adult males are dark overall, with bright red eyes, facial skin, and legs; facial skin less vibrant during nonbreeding. The flight feathers are mostly blackish, but some have minimal white mottling. 2nd-year males similar, but typically have pale throat, mottled flight feathers, and paler eyes. Some have faint streaking below. Adult females are brownish overall with a slaty blue-gray cast to the upperparts. Underparts much like 1st-year, but generally darker and variably marked with tawny streaks. The head is usually dark with red eyes, but some marked whitish. Flight feathers have a broad, dark trailing edge (bolder than on 1st-year), typically with whitish-based outer primaries. 2nd-year females similar to adult, but usually have brownish eyes. 1st-year Snail Kites have a bold head pattern and dark underparts with variable tawny streaks, fading to buff by winter/spring.

Snail Kites are scarce and local in central Florida wherever there is a plentiful supply of apple snails. They can be seen gracefully quartering reed beds, somewhat harrier-like. With talons and a bill designed to do maximum damage, they pluck the

snails from the surface and usually disappear to a favorite post or branch to eat.

ad. ♀

ad. ♂

Hook-billed Kite *Chondrohierax uncinatus* **HBKI** L 16–20 in, WS 34–38 in, WT 8–12 oz, page 238

Hook-billed Kites are distinctive raptors of mainly tropical distribution, restricted in the U.S. to the riparian corridor along the lower Rio Grande in south Texas. Even along the Rio Grande it is quite rare, and a concerted effort must be made to see it. Because of its habit of hunting quietly from perches in the canopy, it is typically encountered only in midmorning, when it soars briefly before disappearing into the forest at a favored feeding site. Hook-billed Kites feed almost exclusively on land snails, which they extract with their oversized, odd-looking bills. Hook-billed Kites are rarely seen perched but can occasionally be seen sitting on open snags above the forest in early morning. Hook-billed Kites usually fly relatively low over the treetops, with somewhat floppy wingbeats, yet at the same time they can recall an accipiter or small buteo. At times, they join kettles of soaring vultures and hawks, and they can be especially confusing when seen high overhead. The long, boldly banded tail is distinctive when seen at close range, but at a distance, Hook-billed Kite can be confused with soaring Cooper's Hawk, Red-shouldered Hawk, and Harris's Hawk. Hook-billed Kites are medium-sized. In flight, note long, banded tail and broad, rounded wings that pinch in near the

ad. ♂

Gray Hawk

juv.

Harris Hawk

ad. ♂ dark

ad. ♀

Hook-billed Kite

body, creating unique, odd, paddle-shaped wings, held bowed or flattish when soaring. When perched, whopping hooked bill accentuated by a smallish head, and unique face pattern with bold yellow-orange lores. Ages and sexes differ; usually attain adult appearance in about 1 year. Adults have whitish eyes; 1st-years have dusky eyes. Adult male dark slate blue-gray above and below, with coarse white barring underneath. The primaries are boldly banded, and the secondaries are largely dark. The tail is black with 2 whitish bands below, but from above it looks mostly gray. Rare dark-morph adults are mostly blackish with white spotting on the outer primaries. The tail usually shows only 1 broad white band. Adult female slate-gray above, with rufous underparts coarsely barred with white. Note bold rufous face, throat, and collar, all set off by a distinct blackish cap. The flight feathers are overall heavily banded, and the tail has 2 whitish bands. 1st-year light morph similar to adult female but lacks rufous tones and has pale-edged upperparts; 1st-year dark morph similar to adult dark morphs, but the upperparts are edged paler, and the flight feathers are evenly banded throughout. 1st-year, sexes similar.

ad.

ad.

Swallow-tailed Kite *Elanoides forficatus* **STKI** L 21–24 in, WS 47–54 in, WT 11–18 oz, page 240

The Swallow-tailed Kite is perhaps the most striking and grace-ful bird on the planet! In flight it is simply mesmerizing, moving through the air with unparalleled elegance, buoyantly floating above the treetops in search of prey. Its shape and plumage pat-tern are likewise a study of simple elegance: long pointed wings, a slim body, and an amazingly long, forked tail that twists be-hind it through artful mid-air arcs, dives, and turns. Patterned in contrasting black and white below, and glossy iridescence

above, it is indeed a remarkable bird, and one that is unlikely to be confused with any other species in North America given reasonable views. Adults and juveniles are very similar, but fresh juveniles have a buffy wash on the breast that quickly disappears in late summer, and juveniles have more shallowly forked tails on average, though this can be really difficult to judge on some birds, and beware broken outer tail feathers on worn adults. Swallow-tailed Kites feed on a variety of prey items, especially

Swallow-tailed Kite

insects, lizards, and even nestlings that they snatch from the upper canopy of tall trees. Because of this low altitude foraging, they often provide great views for birders, but they also have a sneaky habit of disappearing way too quickly! Unlike their other kite cousin the Mississippi Kite, Swallow-taileds do less aerial foraging, preferring to take larger prey, though they are equally adept at capturing dragonflies and other aerial insects on the wing. In late afternoon, groups of Swallow-taileds can get stratospheric, reaching the limits of vision. They are early spring migrants, arriving back in Florida in late February, after a nonstop flight across the Gulf of Mexico. They depart early in fall, with the bulk of the population leaving in August, and the species completely vacates North America in winter to pass the colder months in South America. Swallow-tailed Kite is an uncommon wanderer north of its mapped range, especially in April and May, sometimes reaching the Great Lakes and the Northeast.

ad.

juv.

ad.

juv.

Mississippi Kite *Ictinia mississippiensis* **MIKI** L 13–15 in, WS 29–33 in, WT 8–13 oz, page 242

Mississippi Kites are medium-sized, elegant raptors found mostly across the South and on the southern Great Plains, but they are expanding their range farther north and west in recent years. They are often colonial, nesting in large trees, often near water. In the western parts of their range they frequently nest in small towns with big trees, zipping over the treetops in search of food, mainly aerial insects but also lizards, birds, and small mammals. They are often noisy, betraying the presence of their nests

by aggressively chasing intruders, including humans! Juveniles are on the wing as soon as their feathers are fully grown, and they depart the nesting areas earlier than the adults. 1st-summer birds are regular wanderers north of the breeding range, mainly in May and June. Adults are grayish overall with a whitish head and dark flight and tail feathers (tail can be faintly banded). The primaries are washed rusty above, though this can be hard to see in the field, and the secondaries are whitish. Juveniles are brown

1st-s.

ad.

Mississippi Kite

above and pale below with dark streaking, and a dark tail with faint pale bands. The flight feathers are usually somewhat banded, but can be plain gray. 1st-year birds molt throughout winter, and in their first spring and summer have a mix of adult grayish body feathers with retained juvenile flight feathers. Mississippi Kites are exceptional fliers, and they are highly maneuverable and buoyant on the wing, whirling around quickly at the sight of a dragonfly, which they snatch from mid-air with agile talons. They are slimly built, with small heads; long, narrow, pointed wings; and a slim, slightly notched tail that flares at the outer tip. They are sometimes mistaken for a Peregrine Falcon at first glance, but kites lack the heavy, chesty build of Peregrine, and its powerful rolling wingbeats. Mississippi Kites fly on flat wings, gaining lift easily, and flap with smooth, deep, fluid wingbeats.

Mississippi Kites migrate in fall, traveling south around the coastal bend of Texas through Central America to winter mainly in South America. They migrate in large flocks, sometimes numbering hundreds or thousands through east Texas and Central America. On migration, note the falcon-like shape with strongly pointed wings when gliding and soaring. Groups of kites rise up on strong

thermals spinning into big "kettles" before streaming out at high elevation in search of the next source of lift. In the morning kites stay lower, hunting for insects, such as dragonflies, which they capture through graceful aerial stoops and then rip apart on the wing. Look for their dark, angular silhouettes streaking high across the bright blue Texas sky, mainly in April and again in September.

White-tailed Kite *Elanus leucurus* **WTKI** L 14–16 in, WS 39–41 in, WT 10–13 oz, page 243

White-tailed Kites are slim, delicate raptors with long, pointed wings. Roughly the size of a Northern Harrier, they are generally slimmer and more angular by all comparisons. Across their restricted range, White-tailed Kites prefer open country. They hunt grassland, savanna, roadsides, and agricultural areas, and are surprisingly more regular in disturbed areas than most raptors, sometimes even in suburban settings. Often form large winter roosts (dozens of birds) near optimal foraging areas. White-tailed Kites are distinctly white overall in all plumages, with strongly contrasting black shoulders and dark carpal spots on the underwings that vary slightly in extent. Ages differ. Adults are clean white below, with plain grayish upperparts and black shoulders; males average paler above than females, with a whiter head, but differences are marginal. 1st-years have boldly scaled brownish white upperwing coverts and backs, and a rusty wash lar to adults but have pale-fringed primary coverts. Also note the dusky, thin subterminal tail band on 1st-year birds. When perched, they appear small, thin, and somewhat small-headed.

juv.

White-tailed Kite

All White-tailed Kites have orange to orange-red eyes. Unlike other kites, White-tailed Kite does not hawk insects in the air; instead, it feeds mainly on small mammals. In general behavior, White-tailed Kite recalls a large, white Kestrel, regularly perching on roadside wires, hovering frequently, and pouncing on prey from low to moderate heights. Like Harriers, White-tailed Kites fly with a dihedral, usually strong but smooth when soaring, and modified with flatter hands when gliding. Their direct flight is with languid, Harrier-like wingbeats, but faintly stiffer and deeper. White-tailed Kites frequently hover with wings raised above the shoulders and the body angled at 45 degrees, usually with dangling legs. They stoop with wings in a distinctive strong V-shape, instead of completely folded up like most stooping raptors. Unlike American Kestrels, White-tailed Kites do not kite. While hovering for extended periods, they often break off with a few languid flaps, a long glide, and then go straight back to hovering over a new location.

White-tailed Kites nest in a variety of coastal prairie and open habitats throughout their range, and in late summer through winter can be seen in rather large concentrations near communal roost sites, and in places where foraging is good. They are

...ften seen in association with Northern Harriers, as the two feed on the same prey and occupy the same habitats. Can you find the Northern Harrier in this plate?

Mystery Kites in the Southeast. Kites are an odd group of birds. Some species are highly aerial, with long pointed wings, and others are specialized for feeding on snails, with broad rounded wings. Swallow-tailed and Mississippi Kites are the most likely to be seen soaring high on thermals overhead, often at the limit of vision, but even at a great distance. Swallow-tailed Kite

5

6

7

8

American Kestrel *Falco sparverius* **AMKE** L 8–11 in, WS 20–24 in, WT 3.4–5.3 oz, page 245

American Kestrels can be found in fields and pastures in remote areas or within suburban areas, nesting in cavities made by woodpeckers and sometimes in nest boxes. They are often seen perched on wires, fence posts, or billboards near grassy fields or roadsides scanning the surrounding environment for mice or small prey hidden in the grass. Kestrels frequently hover low over the ground while hunting. Females are pale underneath with rufous streaks on the body and black-and-white checkered underwings. They are orange on top with blackish barring, blackish primaries, and multiple black tail bands. Adult males are pale underneath with black spots on the belly and a rufous wash to the chest. The upperside is gorgeous, with dazzling blue upperwing

American Kestrel

coverts, an orange back with black barring, blackish primaries, and an orange tail with a black tip. All Kestrels have two black "sideburns," unlike other North American falcons that have a single black sideburn. 1st-year male Kestrels are nearly identical to adult males, but show dark streaks on the chest; however, they hold this plumage only for a short time, molting body feathers throughout their first fall and becoming indistinguishable from adults by early winter. Note that all male Kestrels can show multiple black tail bands when the tail is spread, but always show a broad black tip (subterminal band). 1st-year females are usually not distinguishable from adult females in the field, though on average they lack the broad dark subterminal band shown by adults.

1st-yr. ♂

American Kestrel is a beautiful raptor. Sadly, it is declining rapidly in many areas as a result of habitat loss. Is it worth protecting?

132

Merlin *Falco columbarius* **MERL** L 9–12 in, WS 21–27 in, WT 4.5–8.3 oz, page 248

Boreal forest is the home of the Taiga Merlin. The taiga race is the most widespread and common of the three races. It does not nest within earshot of Bald Eagles (on nest), but does occupy the same habitat. Recently, like a number of other raptors, it has adapted to humans and is increasingly moving to urban areas to feed and nest. Adult males have slate-blue upperparts with bold tail band-ing. They are paler below with rufous-brown streaking and a yel-low-orange wash, especially the leg feathers and wrists on many males. Adult females are dark slate-brown above with multiple whitish tail bands, and heavily streaked below with "checkered" underwings. They often appear dark. A prominent broad white tail tip on barred tail is distinctive. All Merlins are similar in size

Merlin

to Kestrels, but are more compact, with slightly stockier wings and chests, and exhibit much stiffer wingbeats and direct, dashing flight. Their speed in a full sprint humiliates the Kestrel. They are partial to sitting on the top of snags where they can scope out the surrounding countryside. 1st-year Taiga Merlins of both sexes are extremely similar in plumage to adult females, and it is often impossible to tell them apart in the field. They often lack the slaty tone to the upperside and head of adult females, but some 1st-year birds appear slaty on top. The streaks on the underbody are often less blobby or teardrop-shaped, and the undertail coverts are less heavily marked; however, because of plumage variability, it may be difficult to see clear differences between the two ages.

134

ad. ♂ Prairie

♀/imm. Prairie

Prairie Merlin

Merlins come in a variety of colors, from the palest version, known as "Prairie" Merlin, to the darkest race, known as "Black" Merlin. Prairie Merlins breed mainly on the northern Great Plains and winter throughout the western United States. Black Merlins breed in the Pacific Northwest but can be seen throughout the West in win-

ter when all 3 subspecies can be seen side by side in rare cases. 1st-year and adult female Prairie Merlins are pale below with rufous streaks, and pale brown above with obvious tail banding. Adult male is powder blue on top with bold tail bands, and pale below with rufous body streaking and leg feathers. Both sexes have pale heads compared

Black

ad. ♂ Black

Black Merlin

with the other races. As the name suggests, they are typically found in the prairies, dashing across open ground and sitting on posts and snags. They usually go to roost in the tallest evergreens in villages and small towns. Black Merlins are extremely heavily marked below and very dark on top with somewhat obvious to absolutely no tail bands or spots in the flight feathers. The "sideburns" on the face are often indistinct. Darker variant Taiga Merlins can approach the plumage of Black Merlin, especially 1st-years and adult females. It is sometimes better not to try to give subspecific status to some of these birds. Adult male Black Merlin has dark slate-blue upperwings and head.

2nd-yr.

juv. Tundra

ad. Tundra

ad. tundra

ad. tundra

juv. tundra

Peregrine Falcon *Falco peregrinus* **PEFA** L 14–18 in, WS 37–46 in, WT 1–2.1 lb, page 251

Peregrine Falcons are found in a variety of habitats. They nest on steep cliff faces in the Arctic, and on bridges and buildings in the middle of big cities where they are conspicuous and easy to see. In wild, remote places, they feed on all types of birds, from shorebirds to waterfowl, but hunt mainly pigeons in urban areas. Regardless of their environment, they rely on their amazing hunting abilities and lightning speed to pursue and overtake prey. The Peregrine's legendary missile-like stoop has been clocked at speeds faster than any other land or sea animal in the world. Reintroduced birds have a great array of appearances, making subspecific identification of many birds impossible. Tundra Peregrines are the palest, least marked of the races. They average slightly smaller and slimmer than other races. Adults are blue-gray on top with a black head and "sideburns". They are pale below with barred bellies and "checkered" underwings. 1st-years are brown above (typically with a distinctive pale golden forehead extending on to the crown) and pale below but heavily streaked on the body. The mustachial is typically narrower at all ages than

juv. *anatum*

ad. *anatum*

ad. Peale's

juv. Peale's/dark

ad. *anatum*

Peregrine Falcon—Peale's and Anatum

other races. 2nd-year birds may have leftover juvenile body and flight feathers that are brown and faded and sometimes visible in the field. *Anatum* Peregrines inhabit western mountainous regions in summer and are found in mostly coastal areas in winter. They are similar in appearance to Tundra birds, and plumage overlap between the races occurs, but adult *anatum* is typically more heavily marked underneath and slightly darker on top. 1st-year *anatum* is heavily streaked on the underbody, which has an orangey wash, and usually lacks the pale forehead of Tundra. Peale's Peregrine originates from the Pacific Northwest and is the darkest and largest of the races. Both adult and 1st-year birds are heavily marked below and dark on top compared with Tundra and *anatum*. The head is nearly solid blackish. Peale's is uncommon and usually found along the West Coast in winter, but it is rare throughout the Interior West outside the breeding season. Reintroduced birds are widespread, particularly in the East. They show characteristics of several races and make subspecific identification of many birds impossible.

2nd-yr.

Peregrine Falcon

On migration, Peregrines can be seen in numbers, especially along the East Coast and to a much lesser extent along the Rocky Mountains. They are extremely steady fliers, able to fly long distances using powered flight instead of thermals and ridge updrafts like other birds. They readily cross over large bodies of water without hesitation and are sometimes seen

juv.

migrating miles out over the ocean. Peregrines flap with fluid, deep, forceful wingbeats with which they are able to reach blinding speeds in seconds! They soar and glide on slightly drooped or flat, long, pointed wings. The tail is broad and long with a slight taper toward the tip (Kestrels and Merlins show narrower, straighter tails). The head and body are broad.

juv.

ad.

ad.

Prairie Falcon *Falco mexicanus* **PRFA** L 15–19 in, WS 35–45 in, WT 0.9–2.1 lb, page 254

Solitary raptor of western open country, nesting in cavities on cliffs along rim-rock canyons, on buttes, and on rocky outcrops. During winter found more widely across the West, even in surprisingly suburban areas with some open space. Unlike the similar Peregrine, Prairie hunts mainly ground squirrels, captured through low, surprise-attack flight, as well as by perch-hunting. Prairie Falcons also eat medium-sized open country birds such as meadowlarks, Horned Larks, and pipits. Prairie Falcons are overall sandy brown above and whitish below, with contrasting blackish underwing linings that vary slightly in extent and dark axillaries (wing pits). Note whitish eyebrow and a pale cheek that offset a narrow black malar. Prairie is large with long, tapered wings, and a medium-length, tapered tail. Slimmer overall than Peregrine (males can be Kestrel-like), but the wings, tail, chest, and head are still broad like those of Peregrine. Distinguishing Prairie from Peregrine at a distance can be one of the toughest identifications in birding. When perched, Prairie appears large and broad-shouldered like Peregrine but often bobs its

Prairie Falcon

head up and down like a Kestrel, atypical of Peregrine. Adults are lightly spotted below with faintly barred upperwing coverts. Males average more lightly marked below, but it is often difficult to sex Prairie Falcons in the field. Adults' tails are often paler than the upperwings, showing a slight overall contrast above. 1st-years (juveniles) are darker brown above than adults, with pale-fringed upperwing coverts. Creamy buff below with variable dark streaks when very fresh, but the buff fades to whitish by the first fall. 1st-years have a bluish cere, eyering, and feet/ legs, changing to yellow during the first winter or spring. Prairie Falcons are steady, strong, and fast in flight with Peregrine-like wingbeats, but with a slightly stiffer, shallower quality. Like Peregrine, Prairie soars and glides mainly on flat or slightly bowed wings. Often, the flight feathers appear pale or translucent against the sky, making the wings look slimmer than normal, and making the tail appear pinkish red. On occasion, they hover or stall in flight while hunting, but only for a few seconds at a time, and not for extended periods like American Kestrel.

Peregrine or Prairie? Peregrine and Prairie Falcon are nearly identical in size, shape, and manner of flight, so telling the two

part is difficult without plumage clues. See if you can identify and age these falcons based on plumage traits. Answers p.271

ad. gray

juv. gray

ad. gray

Gyrfalcon *Falco rusticolus* **GYRF** L 19–24 in, WS 43–51 in, WT 2.2–4.6 lb, page 256

Gyrfalcon is the largest, most heavily built, scarcest, and most sought after of the North American falcons. It is a predator of the Arctic, rarely occurring in winter in the Lower 48. Gyrfalcon is usually found in open areas that have ample food and whose habitat roughly mimics the open Arctic tundra they prefer (e.g., flat agricultural areas, grassland, dunes, beaches). Most Lower 48 birds are 1st-years and often confused with 1st-year Peregrines. Gyrfalcons nest mainly on cliffs above vast, treeless expanses where they hunt large birds (e.g., ptarmigan, waterfowl), and sometimes medium-sized mammals (e.g., arctic hare). Gyrfalcon hunts primarily using

"surprise-and-flush" tactics, cruising low over bumpy or flat terrain, hoping to flush avian quarry. When prey is flushed, Gyrfalcon chases it down with heavy, forceful wingbeats that enable it to gain speed in a matter of seconds. After a fantastic tail-chase, prey is typically struck in the air and then captured on the ground. Gyrfalcon occasionally stoops from high altitudes as well. It prominently perches on rock outcrops, hilltops, and manmade structures, especially utility poles during winter. Gyrfalcon is often fearless, allowing close approach by humans. Gyrfalcon is a real powerhouse, with a hulking chest, back, and shoulders, tapering toward the belly and

juv. white

ad. white

juv. dark

Gyrfalcon

tail, all combining to impart a small-headed and bulky-bodied appearance. Females can be similar to Red-tailed Hawk in size and bulk, but males are smaller and slimmer-winged, and appear equal in size to female Peregrine and Prairie Falcons. In flight, the wings are slightly broader than those of Peregrine and the wingtips more bluntly pointed, most apparent when Gyrfalcon is soaring or in a shallow glide. In direct flight, Gyrfalcon's wingbeats are shallower and less "whiplike" or rolling than those of Peregrine. Gyrfalcon soars on flattish wings, but sometimes also with a slight dihedral in lazy, wide circles. Gyrfalcons have long and broad tails, and the wing-tips fall well short of the tail tip on perched birds. Gyrfalcon is highly variable in general coloration, ranging from nearly wholly white to completely dark, with a complete continuum between. For convenience, most birds are lumped into 1 of 3 categories: white, gray (intermediate), or dark. Gray morphs are most frequently encountered in North America, while white and dark morphs are rare. 1st-years and adults differ in plumage; sexes similar. Adults have barred upperwing coverts, generally spotted underparts, and yellow cere and eyering. 1st-years have pale-fringed upperwing coverts, streaked underparts, and blue-gray ceres and eyerings well into the first spring.

ad. ♀

ad. ♂

juv.

Aplomado Falcon *Falco femoralis* **APFA** L 14–18 in, WS 31–40 in, WT 8.4–16 oz, page 259

Elegant, long-winged, and long-tailed falcon favoring grassy savanna dotted with yucca in its tiny U.S. range in south Texas and New Mexico. Sleek and speedy, bursting from a perch to tail-chase prey, primarily small birds, but also small mammals and insects. Frequently perches conspicuously on roadside wires, power poles, and bush tops, but sometimes conceals itself in the inner branches of a shrub. Distinctive in both structure and plumage, Aplomado Falcon is unlikely to be confused if seen well. Flight is fast and direct with fluid wingbeats, especially when chasing small landbirds. Occasionally soars to high altitudes, but typically does not hunt from

high elevation. Soars steadily with wings held flat. When perched, Aplomado Falcons appear particularly lengthy, and the long tail extends well past the wingtips. In all plumages, note the bold head pattern (black cap and thin sideburn with bold, white eyeline and cheek), dark vest, grayish brown topside, and white trailing edge on the secondaries. Adult sexes differ slightly: males are cleanly patterned with unmarked white breasts, females are lightly streaked. 1st-years are tawny below with heavily streaked buffy breasts, tawny leggings, and brownish upperparts. The cere and orbital ring are bluish for the first few months. 1st-year sexes are similar.

South Texas Falcons. Focus on size, shape, and broad patterns of plumage. Kestrels are slim and rufous overall, whereas Merlins are compact and dark. Aplomado is elegant, long-winged, and dark-backed, with a striking head pattern. Peregrine is grayish and heavily built, looking much bigger and sturdier than any of the other falcons on this plate. Try to identify, age, and sex all of them if you can! Answers p.272

Perched Buteos. Identifying perched buteos can be a challenging task since most look similarly sized and shaped. The wingtip of the longer-winged buteos (such as Swainson's Hawk) may reach the tail tip when perched, while those of others may fall well short. Some buteos appear particularly broad-chested when perched (Ferruginous Hawk), some stocky overall (Broad-winged

Hawk). Regardless, there are often plumage traits that stand out on perched buteos, even when viewed while driving past at 70 mph. See if you can note them on these perched birds. Answers p.273

Buteos on the Midwest Prairie. The prairie grassland is a place where a variety of buteos can be seen soaring and hunting in the wind on any given day. In flight, each species has its own distinct mannerisms, wingbeats, and way in which they hold their

wings. The shape of each buteo species also differs. See if you can recognize these buteos using plumage…but don't hesitate to confirm your IDs with shape characteristics. Answers p.273

The Widespread Common Raptors. In many areas, raptors of all sorts can be seen. Several species are common or widesprea[d] throughout North America, so your understanding of which species to expect in a certain area or habitat may narrow you[r] choices. Then try to decide what type of raptor (falcon, accipiter, buteo…) you are watching; this helps to narrow your choice[s]

153

...even further. Mastering the identification of these species will create a great platform for wherever you travel. See if you can identify, age, and sex all these common raptors that are frequently encountered. Answers p.274

Hovering Birds. There are many species of raptor capable of hovering for short periods, but some with the stamina to do so employ this tactic frequently while hunting. Remaining close to the ground and stationary in the air with the use of powered flight can be an advantage to a bird of prey. It allows it to search an area from a chosen vantage point, with only a short gap to

close when prey is spotted. Knowledge of behavior is very important in bird identification. Watching the characteristics of a hovering raptor will significantly reduce the number of species it could be. See if you can tell these hovering birds apart. Answers p.275

156

Hazel-Bazemore Hawk Watch. The Hazel-Bazemore hawk watch is a unique site for raptor watching. Many birds of various species pass over Texas each spring and fall on their way to and from warmer climates south. Located in southern Texas along

9

10

12

13

11

16

15

14

he Gulf of Mexico shoreline, Hazel-Bazemore sees huge numbers of migrants that follow the shoreline as they head south in fall. It is also a promising site to see the "Southwest specialties." Try to identify and age all the birds seen here. Answers p.276

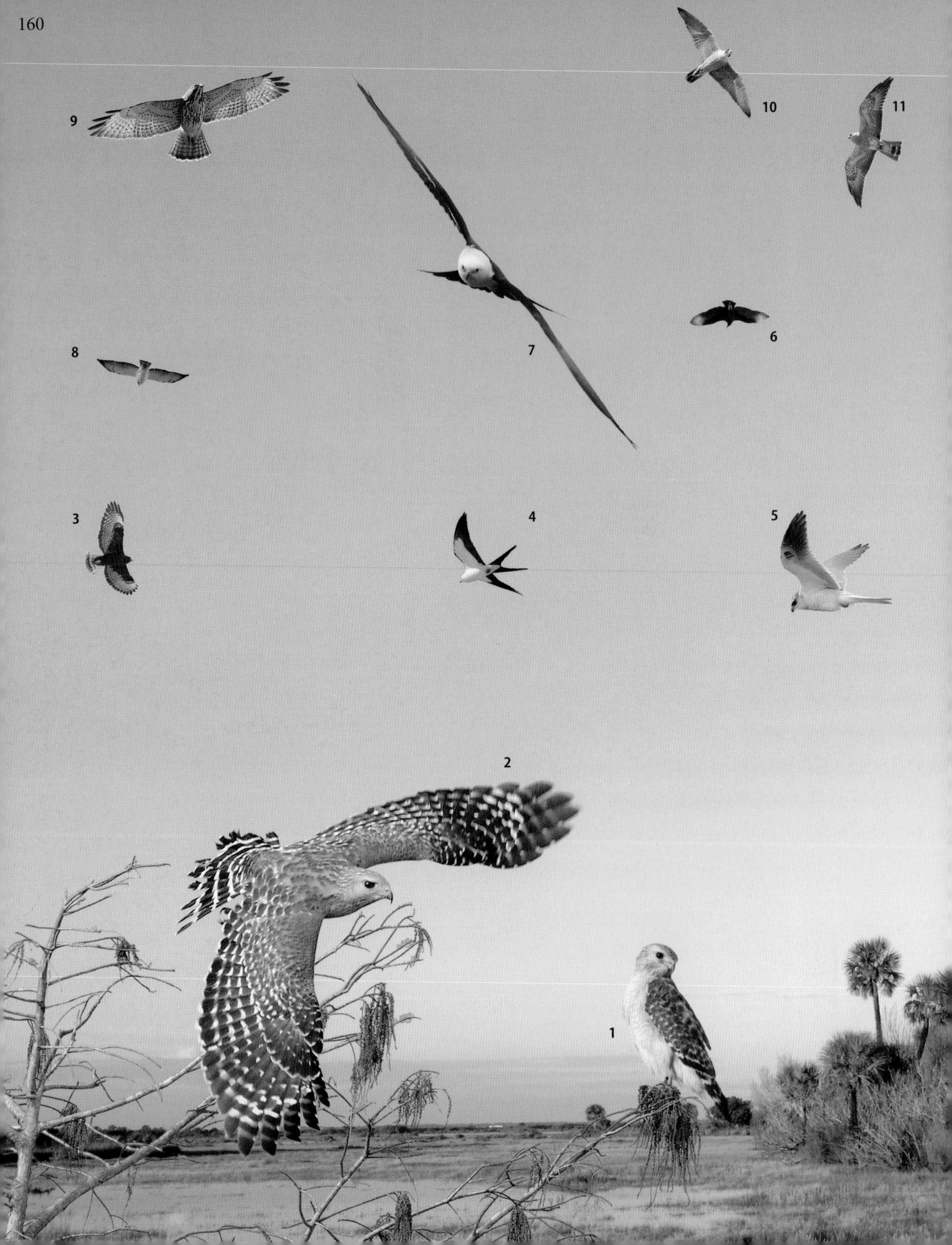
9
10
11
7
6
8
3
4
5
2
1

there are also plumage traits that are very helpful when separating dark raptors from each other, and these traits are a must-know in many situations. On birds up close, sometimes the plumage is much easier to note than the shape, so give these close-up and distant birds a try. Answers p.279

Going Away! Birders tend to give up on identifying birds once they have passed by, with the thought that it must be a hopeless endeavor; however, birds flying away still reveal plenty of clues to their identification. All birds look shorter-tailed and longer-winged when headed away, but the relative lengths between each component are still comparable, and plumage and flight styl

accurate IDs. The ability to see patterns as "shades of gray" helps. And of course, structure and manner of flight are always keys to raptor ID. Challenge yourself to distinguish these early morning raptors. Answers p.282

Into the Sun! How many times have you followed a flying raptor until it has reached the sun, but still haven't made the ID? Most silhouettes, even of the most boldly marked birds, appear blackish. Some species with pale areas in the flight and tail feathers will show bold

patterns where the sun shines through. When birds are near the sun, their shape and plumage may appear altered, but there are still ~~traits that will tell them from the others. Be aware of this altering effect, but try to identify these hawks with confidence. Answers p.283~~

172

I look off into the distance. Rays of sunshine cast their beams onto the hillside, and I can see forever. Right at this moment, I see a speck. Even from this distance it looks majestic. It soars in circles and owns the sky. With its long, broad soaring wings, it has to be an eagle, or does it? I strain my eyes for more clues, but from this distance, there's no way to be sure. But I'm not really bothered. After all, I'm just happy to be here, sharing the beauty of it.

Whose world is this? Thinking more carefully, I realize it's both of ours. We have more influence on birds than birds do on us. Yet somehow, as I watch, I know that I'm living in a world that truly belongs to the birds and to nature. It's too big and too beautiful to belong only to us. We need to take better care of it, because it's more fragile and more precious than we realize. Right now, we both see how gorgeous it is—the colors, the patterns, the tricks of light. But how I would love to be up there floating around together—free as a bird!

Turkey Vulture *(Cathartes aura)* **TUVU** page 12

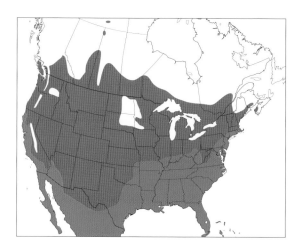

As you speed down the road on a hot, humid day, the radio blasts, and the sea and sand are in your sights. You turn a narrow bend, and the rank smell of decay smacks you in the face. On the roadside, a dead animal is being ravenously torn to pieces by a group of large, black birds. The birds spook and jump into the air as you pass, taking flight easily despite their large size. Their bald, red heads and flashing silvery flight feathers help identify them as Turkey Vultures, known carrion eaters. Just seconds ago these birds were repulsive as they fed on the bloated carcass, but in the air they become quite graceful, almost beautiful. Their buoyant, wobbly flight is captivating as they float in wide circles, keeping watch on the carcass below. As you move farther away, the vultures fall out of the sky with legs dangling and run tentatively, unsteadily back to the carcass. A glance skyward reveals dozens more circling overhead, and several are perched in a dead tree nearby with wings outstretched, as if summoning evil spirits. You can't help but feel the ominous boding of these birds and their obvious association with death.

Overview: Turkey Vultures are easy to identify, even at considerable distances. They are large birds with long, broad wings and long tails. Their heads appear small compared with those of other raptors. Turkey Vultures are social and can often be seen in large "kettles" on migration, and in large gatherings at communal roosting sites. They often perch in the open on dead snags, radio towers, utility poles, and other manmade structures, and they frequently hold their wings outstretched to help condition the flight feathers in the morning, evening, and sometimes midday.

Flight Style: Turkey Vultures are buoyant for such a large bird, and they fly in a wobbly manner, constantly swaying from side to side, making them distinctive among the larger raptors, which are typically steady in flight. Turkey Vultures appear slow-moving in the air and soar in wide, lazy circles. They hold their wings in a strong dihedral at most times but often glide with a modified dihedral, and they can be surprisingly flat-winged in light winds. Turkey Vultures have lofty, easy wingbeats that end abruptly on an upstroke.

Size and Shape: L 62–72 cm (24–28 in), WS 160–181 cm (63–71 in), WT 1.6–2.4 kg (3.5–5.3 lb)
Turkey Vultures are large birds, only slightly smaller than eagles. They have long, broad wings, and long tails that are typically wedge-shaped at the tip. Their heads are small in comparison with those of other raptors, and exaggeratedly so because they lack feathers; when perched, they appear bulky with particularly small heads. Their legs and feet are weak and underdeveloped compared with those of other large raptors, and their talons are much less sharply curved.

Plumage: Turkey Vultures have blackish underparts with silvery flight feathers, imparting a two-toned appearance. In poor light, the flight feathers of Turkey Vultures look black; thus, they can appear uniformly dark. Over snow or other highly reflective surfaces, the flight feathers can appear whitish, creating strong contrast with the blackish underparts. They are mostly blackish above with paler-fringed upperwing coverts; some birds show minor fading along the upperwings (unlike the obvious fading that eagles can exhibit) but still appear overall dark at a distance. The head and bill are grayish on juveniles, changing to a pinkish head and dusky-tipped white bill at about 3–4 months old. Timing varies, but most lose the grayish head and bill by late fall, and some can transition much faster, being pinkish-headed shortly after fledging. Over the course of the first year, the head becomes darker red and the bill more wholly whitish as on adults. By the second fall, most are indistinguishable from adults, though some may retain a faint dusky bill tip. Head color is difficult to see at a distance, but the white bill of adults frequently shines noticeably when it is seen overhead. Males and females are identical in plumage and size. All Turkey Vultures have black eyes.

Geographic Variation: Three subspecies of the Turkey Vulture occur in North America: *C. a. septentrionalis* of the East; *C. a. meridionalis* of the West; and *C. a. aura* of the Southwest border region. We treat *C. a. meridionalis* and *C. a. aura* together as "Western" Turkey Vulture, as they are essentially identical under field conditions. Eastern and western birds are identical in plumage, but eastern birds are slightly larger, and the tubercules (colorful, wart-like protuberances) on their faces are usually more prominent than on Western birds. These tubercules usually appear as whitish or bluish bumps running in front of and below the eyes.

Molt: Turkey Vultures have an unusual molt pattern for such a large bird; they can replace all their flight feathers each year instead of having a stepwise molt pattern in the wings that slowly replaces the flight feathers over several years like many large raptors (e.g., eagles, some buteos). To achieve this, spring adults molt their flight feathers starting at about P5 and progress outward. When the molt reaches P8 or P9 in early summer, it initiates also at P1. As the outermost primaries are molted, so are the innermost, continuing through P4 or P5 in most birds. This progression results in fall adults having a fresh block of inner primaries, and an obviously older, more faded block of outer primaries, with the outermost being fresher and darker.

Juveniles employ a similar strategy in their first year to "catch up" to the molt timing and pattern of adults. Juveniles molt their flight feathers beginning in mid- to late first-winter, starting with the innermost primary. The wing molt then continues out sequentially through about P8, at which time (early summer) a new wave of primary molt begins again at the innermost primary! Since first-year birds replace the inner 4–5 primaries twice in the same cycle, 1-year-olds in fall have essentially the same molt pattern as adults.

Similar Species: When seen up close, Turkey Vultures are quite obvious, but at a distance they are similar to several species in flight. All the large, dark soaring birds can be confused with Turkey Vulture (e.g., California Condor, Black Vulture,

immature Bald Eagle, Golden Eagle, and dark buteos); however, Turkey Vultures always teeter in flight, hold their wings in a strong dihedral, and appear comparatively smaller-headed. The species that appears most like a Turkey Vulture is Zone-tailed Hawk. At a distance in flight, the two are exceedingly similar, and Zone-tailed frequently soars with kettles of Turkey Vultures. In direct comparison, Zone-tailed is slightly smaller, larger-headed (because it is feathered instead of bare), and has a different wing pattern. Adult Zone-taileds are fairly distinctive, with a dark trailing edge to the wings and a boldly banded black and white tail. But juveniles are more similar to Turkey Vulture. Note the usually white-speckled breast of juvenile Zone-tailed, and the finely barred flight and tail feathers. Chances are if you are close enough to see these details, you can easily distinguish between the two.

Status and Distribution: Turkey Vultures are common breeders from southern Canada throughout the United States (March–August), and are especially abundant throughout the Southeast. Populations are generally expanding northward, with increasing annual counts at more northerly hawk watches, and increased frequency of overwintering reports at the northern limits of their range. Many southern breeders are resident, but most northern populations are migratory. The Eastern subspecies presumably winters mainly throughout the Southeast, but birds from the Great Plains and west winter as far south as northern South America.

Migration: Turkey Vultures are seen during migration at all eastern hawk-watch sites in spring, mainly from early March through April, and in fall from September through November. The Great Lakes hawk watches such as Hawk Cliff, ON, Lake Erie Metropark, MI, Brockway Mountain, MI, Braddock Bay, NY, and Derby Hill, NY, have peak daily high counts of several thousand. East Coast migration sites, such as Cape May Point, NJ, Kiptopeke State Park, VA, and Curry Hammock, FL, see significant numbers of Turkey Vultures in November. Western coastal hawk watches, such as Marin Headlands, see fair numbers of vultures each fall, but West Coast movements are perhaps more of a dispersal than true migration. The intermountain West migration sites, such as the Goshute Mountains in Nevada and the Wasatch Mountains in Utah, see good numbers every fall from September through October, and in spring (Wasatch) from March to early May. Corpus Christie in Texas is also a great site to witness Turkey Vulture migration. Of course, the largest migration of Turkey Vultures in the world occurs at Veracruz, Mexico, where more than a million can be seen in a day in November! Massive numbers also move through Panama.

Vocalizations: Mostly nonvocal, but Turkey Vultures occasionally grunt when aggressive or scared. Call is a raspy, gargling hiss.

Black Vulture *(Coragyps atratus)* BLVU page 16

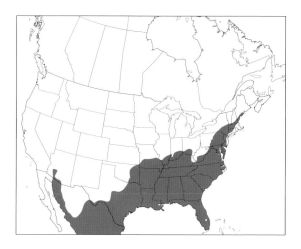

It's late morning, and a group of birders have just arrived at the local hawk watch. The air is still and humid, and as thermals build, raptors begin to rise above the treetops. Turkey Vultures soar in small groups, lazily teetering from side to side on long, up-turned wings. As the crowd begins to scan the birds, one observer scrutinizes a distant shape through a spotting scope. It is a "speck" in binoculars, but it is visible through the haze. The bird looks completely dark, is soaring on flatter wings than the nearby Turkey Vultures, and appears more stable in flight. A birder excitedly declares, "Bald Eagle!" But as the bird flaps its wings in a snappy, accipiter-like manner, it is immediately recognized as something different—a Black Vulture. As the bird nears and soars overhead, its stocky silhouette and pale outer primaries become more visible, helping everyone confirm the identification. Despite these obvious distinguishing characteristics, Black Vultures can be "chameleons" when seen at a distance, and even experienced hawk watchers can be fooled by their eagle-like appearance.

Overview: Black Vultures are shy and wary birds while breeding, but are pugnacious and fearless at roadside carrion, chasing away larger Turkey Vultures that may be present to dominate a carcass. Highly gregarious year-round, Black Vulture is often seen eating roadkill, and at landfills eating refuse. With a weakly developed olfactory system compared with that of Turkey Vulture, Black Vultures rely partly on Turkey Vultures to find decomposing animals, especially in areas with dense canopy cover. They nest in the tops of broken tree trunks, in vacant buildings, or on the ground in places that offer sufficient overhead cover. Black Vultures are proficient at soaring, and are often seen flying in mixed groups with Turkey Vultures. They also associate with Turkey Vultures at roost sites.

Flight Style: Black Vulture's flight is more stable than that of Turkey Vulture, but it sometimes "wobbles" slightly in strong winds. Black Vultures soar in lazy circles with wings arched forward and held in a shallow dihedral or sometimes flat. They glide with a modified dihedral, as opposed to Turkey Vultures, which typically show strong dihedrals in all postures. The most unique trait of the Black Vulture is its quick, shallow, "anxious" wingbeats that seem odd for such a large bird and are very different from those of eagles and Turkey Vultures.

Size and Shape: L 59–74 cm (23–28 in), WS 141–160 cm (55–63 in), WT 1.7–2.3 kg (3.8–5.1 lb)
Black Vultures are large birds, only slightly smaller than Turkey Vultures, but they are stockier overall with broad squared-off wings, small heads, and very short, narrow-based, square-tipped tails. They are the only raptor in North America whose feet typically project beyond the tail. Black Vulture's somewhat flat-winged soaring profile appears similar in shape to Bald Eagle's when seen at eye level, but Black Vultures are always stockier in comparison, with smaller heads and shorter tails. When perched, Black Vultures appear large and stocky, but are small-headed

with an elongated bill, and short wings and tails.

Plumage: Black Vultures are black overall with contrasting pale "silvery" outer primaries. Only on the darkest overcast days do Black Vultures appear uniformly dark. From above, the pale outer primaries are obvious, even in poor light. There are two age classes differentiated by head and bill pattern—adult and juvenile. *Adults* have an unfeathered, wrinkled, grayish head with an ivory bill. *1st-years* (juveniles) have a sparsely feathered black head and all-black bill when first leaving the nest, changing quickly to a paler bill with dusky tip by late fall and early winter. Adult-like head characteristics are obtained by the second fall. *2nd-year* birds are essentially adult-like, but some may still be in transition with a slightly dusky bill tip. Sexes are identical. All Black Vultures have dark eyes.

Geographic Variation: There are 3 subspecies of Black Vulture, but only 1, *C. a. atratus*, occurs in North America; they are considered monotypic by some authorities. Northern populations average larger with less extensive pale markings on the undersides of the outer primaries than the southern forms, though the latter have not been quantified and differences are difficult to assess.

Molt: Black Vultures undergo their first wing molt during the first winter and spring. It begins with the inner primaries as early as January and continues through the second fall. Before it is complete, however, the wing molt starts again at P1 during the first summer, generally stopping at P3–P4 before suspending for the second winter. Body plumage is also replaced during the first summer. Adults molt their flight feathers beginning in early spring with the inner primaries as well as resume molting where the previous molt was suspended, resulting in 2 waves of active molt. Similar patterns are followed throughout their lifespan, effectively enabling these aerialists to complete a full wing molt each year, unlike many other large soaring raptors.

Similar Species: Black Vulture is told from Turkey Vulture and both eagles by its overall stockier shape, snappy wingbeats, pale outer primaries, and smaller size. Black Vulture is superficially similar to adult Common Black-Hawk but has faster wingbeats, unmarked flight feathers lacking a distinct black trailing edge, a smaller unfeathered head, and a solid black tail.

Status and Distribution: Black Vulture is a common breeder across the Southeast west to central Texas, and ranging north to New Jersey and Pennsylvania, but recently increasing in numbers farther north. It breeds in southern Arizona but is relatively uncommon there, with that area being the northernmost extension of its western range. It is a rare vagrant outside its mapped range.

Migration: Black Vulture migration is poorly understood. Some perhaps join migrant Turkey Vultures that leave the northern extremes of their range in winter, but others are year-round residents. It's difficult to determine whether numbers seen at hawk watches in North America are local groups on foraging flights, dispersing young birds, or true migrants. In the Southeast, distinguishing potential migrants from local residents is impossible. Sites that see concentrations of Black Vultures during fall migration are Kiptopeke State Park, VA, and Cape May Point, NJ.

Vocalizations: Black Vultures are generally silent, but they occasionally make eerie "hissing" sounds when aggressive or alarmed.

Crested Caracara *(Caracara cheriway)* CRCA page 22

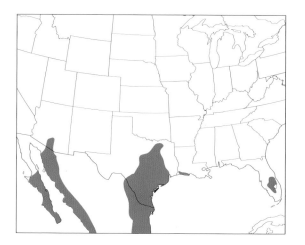

they do so on flat or somewhat bowed wings.

Size and Shape: L 54–60 cm (21–24 in), WS 118–132 cm (47–52 in), WT 800–1300 g (1.8–2.8 lb) Crested Caracaras are large birds, only slightly smaller than the 2 vulture species with which they often associate. They are distinct in shape, having long, narrow, squared-off wings, long tails, and a long-necked appearance, recalling an adult Bald Eagle in flight. When perched, Caracaras appear big-headed, and the crest helps create a distinctly square-headed profile. They have large bills compared with those of most other raptors, which they use to tear carcasses open.

Plumage: Caracaras have 3 age classes differentiated by plumage and head/bill pattern. Males and females are similar and indistinguishable in the field. Caracaras attain their adult appearance in about 2 years. Eye color changes from brownish amber to yellowish after several years.

Adults are boldly patterned with a clean white throat, upper breast, and cheeks, a whitish barred lower chest and hindneck, and black cap and upperparts. Their facial skin from the bill to the eyes is a vibrant orange-red, but changes to yellowish when they are excited or agitated. The legs are yellow. The tail is white and finely barred, with a wide, black tip. The outer primaries are nearly whitish, but similar in all ages.

1st-years (juveniles) have buffy, dark-streaked breasts and dark brown instead of black plumage. The facial skin is pale pinkish. The tail is white, but more coarsely barred than adults, with a dark tip. The legs are pale bluish.

2nd-years (subadults) are similar to adults, but have browner upperparts and yellowish facial skin (beware worn adults that appear browner above). The tail is adult-like.

Geographic Variation: Caracaras are monotypic but formerly considered a subspecies of a much larger-ranging taxon that stretches through southern South America and the Falkland Islands. North American breeders are now considered conspecific with those of Central and northern South America, while several former subspecies have been elevated to species status (e.g., Southern Caracara, *C. plancus*).

This land is flat and open, mainly cattle country and grassland, with a few mesquite shrubs scattered throughout. A group of vultures has gathered to feed on a road-killed calf that wandered outside the fence. Among the familiar vultures is something vastly different. Unlike the all-black, bald-headed vultures, this bird is boldly patterned, with a big, square head. It is smaller than the vultures, but more aggressive and unafraid, staring them down and getting its fill. Its bright orange face, long legs, and upright carriage are odd looking, and when taken together create a very striking bird. It bumps off the roadside and lands on a fence post, in the process revealing bold white patches in the outer wings, and a white tail with a crisp black band. What is this distinctive bird that feeds with the vultures, but looks like a hawk?

Overview: Crested Caracaras are distinctive, strikingly plumaged raptors of open country, especially cattle country and mesquite grassland. While they readily feed on carrion with vultures, they are not necessarily a carrion specialist, also hunting a variety of live prey including insects, small mammals, reptiles, and birds. Caracaras are comfortable around semi-developed areas and are sometimes seen in surprisingly suburban areas. They are gregarious birds, often roosting in small groups with vultures. They frequently perch on manmade structures including power poles and fence posts.

Flight Style: Crested Caracaras are rarely seen at high altitudes, often flying at eye level and flapping in a steady, rowing, raven-like manner. When they soar,

Molt: Juveniles may have a very limited molt of body feathers during the first fall/winter, but generally begin their first complete molt in late winter continuing through summer. Second-year plumage is attained by the second fall. Adult appearance is acquired during the second summer/fall. Molts thereafter are generally complete, mainly from March to September. Caracaras are considered falcons taxonomically and share a falcon's flight-feather molt sequence, beginning in the middle of the primaries and then spreading inward and outward simultaneously.

Similar Species: Crested Caracaras are one of the most distinctive raptors in North America, and they are unlikely to be confused with anything else if seen well. At a distance in flight they can recall a Chihuahuan or Common Raven when flapping, or even an immature Bald Eagle when soaring. But note Caracara's distinctive patterned plumage with white primaries and a bold white tail with black tip.

Status and Distribution: Crested Caracara is a common resident in south Texas but generally uncommon and local in Arizona (occurring mainly Pima Co.) and in south-central Florida. The overall population is stable and even expanding in some areas of Texas. In Florida, it is considered threatened because of habitat loss, with numbers exceedingly low, but is generally thought to be stable.

Migration: Crested Caracaras are nonmigratory, but some birds disperse postbreeding, occasionally wandering north of their normal range. Sightings outside the normal region of occurrence are on the rise, especially along the West Coast, but possible escapees confuse the true status of Crested Caracaras as a vagrant.

Vocalizations: Generally silent, Crested Caracaras occasionally vocalize during aggressive encounters. Their call is a low-pitched mechanical rattle and raven-like modulated croaking *klak, klak, klak; gree-aaaaaa.*

California Condor *(Gymnogyps californianus)* **CACO** page 24

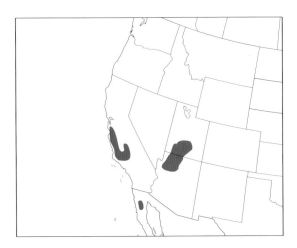

The setting is undeniably astounding…anyone who has been here would concur. Standing on the rim of the Grand Canyon, I try with all my senses to take it in, but the canyon is just too massive, too deep and infinite to assimilate. This vista is worthy of the countless movie scenes and poems dedicated to it. I look over the horizon in awe of the vivid reds, yellows, and blues, listening to the roar of the raging Colorado River that carves out the canyon below. It is argued that this canyon was here when the dinosaurs walked the earth, and it is easy to picture a pterosaur soaring over these vast expanses. My imagination wanders in this prehistoric place until I remember what I came here for—to see the prehistoric-looking California Condor! These birds are old souls in their own right, taking longer than almost any other bird to reach maturity, and still teetering on the verge of extinction.

I scan the horizon for my target species… nothing yet. It's noon now, and warm enough that these birds should be up in the air. I scan the horizon again and notice two birds turning wide, slow circles in the distance. Even with the naked eye, they appear *massive*—as big as dinosaurs. "These have to be condors," I say to myself, verbalizing my impressions. Just then, the two huge birds set their wings and glide toward me. As they come head-on I note their exaggerated, splayed primaries, spread out like fingers catching the wind. Now they're quite close, and I can see the gaudy orange head of the adult and the grayish head of a younger bird. As they glide by below eye level, they dwarf a Turkey Vulture that has joined them. The three catch the stiff, uplifting wind and rise overhead, circling in wide, lumbering spirals. Their wing linings are brilliant white, and the numbers on their wing tags are visible: 83 and 16, a sign that these modern-day dinosaurs now exist in the world of man.

Overview: The California Condor is a bird of mountain canyons and coastal cliffs found in parts of central and southern California, northern Arizona, and southern Utah. It is nearly unmistakable; its impressive size dwarfs even vultures and eagles. California Condors are indeed massive, with heavy bodies and extremely long wings that can reach nearly 10 feet across. Because of their size, California Condors rarely take flight unless lift is optimal (usually midday), and they are often seen perched on rocky hillsides or outcrops for hours at a time, sometimes even for days when weather is inclement.

California Condors eat carrion of all sorts. They are notoriously curious and ingest things such as plastic and garbage that sometimes tragically kill them. They once ranged widely across the West, but the wild population diminished to only a few birds that were brought into a captive-breeding conservation program in 1987. Through the successes of this program and the hard work of many conservation organizations, free-flying Condors are now back in the wild in a few places, but the population is not yet self-sustainable without ongoing help from conservationists.

Flight Style: Condors appear extremely slow moving and steady in flight, soaring in wider circles than all other raptors. They soar with a slight dihedral but sometimes appear flat-winged in light winds. Condors are frequently seen in pairs or small groups, often in the company of Turkey Vultures. Like Turkey Vultures, they occasionally incorporate deep wing flexes when gliding. The wingbeats of California Condors are exceedingly slow and heavy, but once airborne, Condors rarely flap.

Size and Shape: L 109–127 cm (43–50 in), WS 249–300 cm (98–118 in), WT 8.2–14.1 kg (18–31 lb) California Condor is a massive bird, dwarfing Redtailed Hawk and Turkey Vulture, and even notably bigger than both Golden and Bald Eagles. Condors have long, broad wings, a short narrow-based tail, and a small head. In a soar, the wings are rounded at the tips, with the outer 8 primaries obviously splayed, giving a distinct "fingered" appearance to the wingtips. While Condors usually appear to have rounded or even squared wingtips, the wingtips can appear surprisingly tapered when gliding, especially when primaries are missing due to molt. When perched, they often stand slightly hunched and not perfectly upright like some other large raptors, sometimes even spending extended periods lying on their bellies. They show hulking shoulders, a small head, and a short tail, and a ruff of elongated feathers is usually obvious around the base of the neck.

Plumage: Like eagles, California Condors take several years (usually 5–7) to attain adult appearance, with progressive changes in wing pattern and head color from juvenile to adulthood. All ages are largely dark with contrasting paler underwing coverts. The featherless head changes from grayish to orange-red, and the underwing coverts get whiter, more vibrant, and more extensive with each passing year until adulthood is reached. The secondaries and the greater upperwing coverts become whiter throughout the first 6 years as well. Eye color is dark grayish turning to dark red with age. Males and females are identical in plumage (and size). Almost all condors have numbered patagial markers that identify them as certain individuals. These numbers can be input at the Web site www.condorspotter.com to find the date each bird was hatched, giving an exact age.

Adults (*5th-year* and older) are more distinctly marked overall than immature birds, with colorful orange-red heads, pale bluish bills, and clean white wing linings that form a distinct, elongated triangle on the underwings. The upperwings have a distinct, pale panel on the greater coverts, appearing as a narrow white line along the base of the inner secondaries; some have silvery inner secondaries that are obvious when fresh. Fifth-years usually have more dusky bills and less colorful heads than older ages.

1st-year (juvenile) Condors are overall black, with grayish heads scattered with black down, dusky bills, and grayish white mottled wing pits and underwing coverts. The upperwings are plain blackish, and the trailing edge of the wings lacks any unevenness that would be shown by older birds as a result of molt.

2nd- and *3rd-year* birds are difficult to distinguish from one another and are best aged by molt patterns in the wings. Second-year birds usually retain an all-dark head and bill, and typically have

4–6 outer primaries retained from juvenile plumage. Usually only 1 or 2 secondaries have been replaced. Third-years show a dusky bill turning paler at the base, and a mostly dark head with a few yellow-orange patches, especially on the throat. The underwing coverts remain mottled gray but are a bit more prominent. The upperwings are still dark, lacking the narrow white wing bar on the greater coverts shown by older birds. Most third-years have two waves of molt in the primaries and secondaries, and they generally look "messier" along the trailing edge of the wings than second-year birds.

4th-years are more adult-like, with the head still showing dark patches, but changing to orange. The bill is mostly dark but with a pale base. The underwing coverts are clean white. The upperwings now have a narrow white wing bar on the secondary coverts.

Geographic Variation: None.

Molt: Because of their exceptionally long primaries and secondaries, Condors do not replace all the flight feathers in 1 year like some smaller birds. Instead, they have a stepwise replacement of flight feathers throughout their immature plumages similar to both eagles, where older immature birds can have three or more molt "waves" simultaneously. Adults usually molt very slowly, growing 1 or 2 primaries at a time from spring through early fall, mostly suspending molt during the winter. Juveniles molt inner primaries during their first spring/summer, and retain the juvenile outer primaries through the second year. Second-year birds usually have 2 active waves of molt in the primaries and secondaries, and subsequent ages can have 3 or more.

Similar Species: California Condors are dark overall but distinctive in having long, broad wings, a slight dihedral, a very short tail, and a massive appearance when both perched and in flight, rendering them unlike both eagles and vultures. Condors of all ages show pale underwing coverts, which are strikingly white in adults. Immature *Bald Eagle*, with which it is most similar in terms of plumage, can have white along the underwing coverts, but this is rarely as distinctly contrasting as on Condors (a few juveniles may approach Condor in underwing pattern); however, all Bald Eagles are smaller with slimmer wings, larger heads (feathered!), and longer tails. Immature Bald Eagles often have a paler brown belly or white on the belly, whereas Condors are uniformly dark-bodied in all ages.

Status and Distribution: Condors are generally rare, but rather easy to find within their limited range. They are year-round residents at Big Sur, CA, San Jacinto Mountains, CA, Vermilion Cliffs, UT, and Grand Canyon, AZ (and northern Baja Mexico). They are exceptional outside their normal range, but some birds occasionally wander between core occurrence areas. The California Condor reintroduction program is generally considered a conservation success story, with a few hundred birds now living in the wild. A few pairs have recently fledged young in the wild in CA and northern Mexico, but the species has not yet been able to sustain its population in any of the reintroduction locations on its own. Its persistence still largely depends on human-provided supplemental food. Condors sometimes die when they ingest poisons such as automotive antifreeze on a roadside, or lead shot while scavenging dead animals, and this indirect poisoning continues to hamper reintroduction efforts.

Migration: California Condors are year-round residents within their limited geographic range. At times, they may wander outside their core range, but these strays usually return quickly to their local haunts. Birds from the Grand Canyon, AZ, have been known to travel to Zion National Park, UT, and back in one day. In California, birds have wandered north to San Francisco and east to the Sierra Nevadas.

Vocalizations: Condors are generally silent, but often hiss and grunt when threatened.

Bald Eagle *(Haliaeetus leucocephalus)* **BAEA** page 26

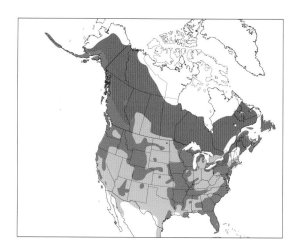

It's overcast, icy, and snowing, making it a challenge just to keep the car on the slick refuge road as you carefully roll along. Most of the freshwater impoundments are now frozen, but a few open pools remain where large groups of waterfowl congregate. Thousands of ducks of various species feed alongside groups of larger, snow-white Tundra Swans. Along the ice are several large, dark shapes that appear faint but visible through the light snow. Most are variably patterned in brown and white, but one is clearly recognizable, a blackish figure with a gleaming white head—an adult Bald Eagle. The onlookers of the same build are immature Bald Eagles of various ages. The adult has a half-eaten duck in its talons and tears off pieces with its large, yellow bill, keeping a watchful eye on the immature birds eager to steal its meal. One after another, the younger birds make their pass at the adult in an attempt to snatch the duck away, and each one is fended off. Out of the snow, another adult barrels in, and the adult with the prey in its talons quickly takes flight. The intruding adult follows its every move, turning and twisting in rhythm with a swiftness thought possible only of smaller hawks. The eagle finally drops its prey, and the thieving intruder swiftly plucks the lifeless duck from midair. As you look off into the distance, the scene repeats itself … waterfowl and eagles … ice and cold.

Overview: Adult Bald Eagles are perhaps the most readily identified and well-known raptor in the world. Even nonbirders are familiar with the Bald Eagle's fierce expression and distinctive white head and tail, as it is the national symbol of the United

States. But immature birds are more difficult to identify and are often confused with other large raptors because of their variable appearance. Bald Eagles generally change from a dark overall appearance to full adult plumage over a period of about 4–5 years.

Bald Eagles are often found near water, where they build massive stick nests in the tops of large trees, and in some cases on manmade structures and platforms. Though they are closely tied to water for nesting, they are frequently seen far away from it during migration and winter. Bald Eagles are often communal during migration and especially in winter, when large concentrations (hundreds and even thousands) can gather at plentiful food sources (e.g., salmon runs, fish die-offs), and they usually roost together at specific sites each night, generally in very large trees. Despite their fierce reputation, Bald Eagles prefer to scavenge dead animals rather than hunt, and they readily steal prey from other raptors when given the chance. They frequently nest near Ospreys and steal fish from them all summer long. Bald Eagles favor fish as their main food, but they also eat birds and mammals when available. When hunting live prey, Bald Eagles are agile and extremely efficient at plucking fish from the water's surface, but they do not submerge to catch fish like the Osprey. They are also quite maneuverable and swift in flight when capturing ducks and other birds.

Flight Style: Bald Eagles are very large and appear slow-moving and steady in flight. They soar in wide circles with virtually flat, planklike wings and typically glide on slightly drooped wings. Occasionally, Bald Eagles fly with a slight dihedral, which is more commonly seen on adults. In direct flight, Bald Eagles display powerful, stiff wingbeats with lofty upstrokes. They usually end their flapping on the downstroke with a slightly hesitant leveling-out of the wings; Golden Eagle usually ends on the upstroke, more directly and abruptly into a dihedral.

Size and Shape: L 70–90 cm (27–35 in), WS 180–243 cm (71–96 in), WT 2.0–6.5 kg (4.4–14.5 lb)
Bald Eagle is very large, notably larger than vultures, and nearly twice the size of a Red-tailed Hawk. Even when perched, a Bald Eagle appears as a hulking figure. Although size is difficult to determine on lone birds in the field, eagles have a way of looking sizable

in flight, regardless of how far away they are. This appearance is due in part to their steady, slow-moving manner of flight.

Bald Eagle has extremely long, somewhat broad wings, and a large, protruding head. The wings of adult Bald Eagle appear to lack any bulge along the trailing edge and taper less toward the body than those of Golden Eagle. Adults appear particularly large-headed, accentuated by the contrasting white head against the blackish body, but the white head and tail can also "disappear" at a distance, especially against white clouds or snowy backdrops, when adults look like a brown, flying board. Juveniles and second-year birds are wider-winged than older birds, appearing a bit stockier overall.

Plumage: Bald Eagles show several plumages before reaching adulthood at about 5 years old; the head and tail turn from dark to white, and the bill and eye color turn from dark to yellow.

Flight feather molt patterns can sometimes be seen in the field, and these are the best way to reliably age birds. Look especially at the secondaries, as the number of longer and faded retained juvenile secondaries helps age second- and third-year birds. Females and males are identical in plumage, but females are notably larger; this is obvious when a pair is seen side by side. Classifying immature birds between 2 and 4 years old can be particularly challenging in the field as plumages overlap somewhat between these ages.

Adults have the famous brilliant white head and tail, blackish brown body, and yellow bill and eyes. Although distinct at most times, adults can look uniformly dark (as with any age) in poor light. Against a white background such as snow or bright clouds, adults can look "headless"; however, most times the white head and tail are visible and obvious at great distances. Some birds in their first adult plumage (4–5 years old) appear almost identical to adults, whereas some birds over five years of age still have minimal dark streaking on the head. Since individual eagles molt at slightly different rates, the plumage of birds more than 3 years old may not always match their actual age.

1st-years (juveniles) are brownish overall with dark eyes and bill, variable amounts of white on the underwing coverts and the undersides of the secondaries, white wing pits, and pale tips to the innermost primaries that appear as translucent 'windows'. The secondaries are long, pointed, and uniform, as opposed to those of older birds that show shorter, square-tipped secondaries. The tail of first-year birds is mostly black with varying degrees of white mottling, usually appearing dark-tipped from below. By spring, many first-years develop a pale or tawny belly, whereas second- and some third-year birds are typically whitish. The upperparts are blackish brown overall. By fall, the back and upperwings fade to brown (and sometimes almost whitish), and contrast with the blackish flight feathers, usually appearing two-toned at a distance; vultures and Golden Eagles do not show this broadly contrasting pattern.

2nd-years are quite variable in plumage. Most develop a white belly (very few are still brown) and back, pale crown, uniform blackish upperwings, and a dusky grayish bill with hints of yellow at the base. The eyes are still mostly dark, but can become paler in some birds. The white bellies of second-years are often obvious even in poor light. Since second-years retain most of their juvenile secondaries (which are longer, worn, faded, and paler), they show an uneven edge to the back of the wings because of the new shorter secondaries mixed in with the old longer ones. Molt limits are more difficult to discern in the primaries, but typically the outer 4–6 primaries are retained juvenile feathers, and are paler brown and more worn than the newly replaced inner primaries.

3rd-years are similar to second-years but the head and tail are typically whiter and the eyes and bill show more yellow. Most third-years have limited white on the axillaries and underwing coverts, and have darker bellies than second-years. The white on the back is less prominent than on second-years, but the white on the head is more prominent. Third-years have largely replaced their juvenile flight feathers, but some birds retain 1 or 2 worn, longer juvenile inner secondaries, and the 2 outer juvenile primaries are typically retained (also worn and paler brown). Also note in third-year birds the slimmer wings with smoother, more even trailing edge, imparting a more adult-like wing shape in flight.

4th-years are variable in appearance and can appear adult-like overall with blackish brown body and a white head and tail, but with a few apparent signs of immaturity, such as some dark flecking in the head and on the tail tip (beware of muddied feather tips on true adults), or limited white mottling on the body or underwings. Some fourth-years still have a fair number of dark feathers on the head (similar to the dark eyeline of an Osprey) or obvious dark-tipped tail feathers, and they may appear similar to immature Golden Eagles. The eyes are yellow and bill is yellow, but some still retain a dusky tip. Beware of confusing fourth-year with first-year birds: both ages may appear nearly all dark in the field. Head, bill, belly, upperwing, and eye color will differ slightly between the two ages; the secondaries are pointed on first-years vs. square-tipped on fourth-years.

Geographic Variation: Bald Eagles are monotypic, but some authorities recognize up to 3 subspecies. Northern breeders average larger, but there is much individual variation, and a general gradation from north to south in decreasing body size suggests that no subspecies are valid.

Molt: Most large birds, such as Bald Eagles, do not replace all their feathers in a single annual molt cycle. Instead they utilize a stepwise molt pattern that replaces the flight feathers in "waves" (see Introduction). Because Bald Eagles breed across a range of latitudes (e.g., from Florida to Alaska), molt timing differs among populations, generally being earlier and perhaps more extensive annually in southern birds. Juveniles retain their plumage throughout the first year, perhaps with a limited molt of body feathers during the late first winter and spring. In the late first spring and summer, juveniles begin flight feather molt, replacing the inner 3–4 primaries and a few secondaries. During this time the body transitions into the first of 2 "white belly" age classes, and most typically have white on the upper back. This plumage is retained until the second late spring/summer, when molt of the flight feathers begins again, but this time in 2 places: where it left off at P4 or P5, and simultaneously again at P1, resulting in 2 active waves of primary molt. Usually the outer 2 primaries are retained but sometimes more.

In the third spring/summer, the flight feather molt process begins again, this time in 3 places simultaneously in the primaries: where the previous molt left off at P8 or P9, and at P4 or P5, and again at P1. In this molt any remaining juvenile outer primaries and secondaries are replaced, resulting in the even, narrower-winged appearance of adults. The body changes to mostly darkish, and the head and tail become mostly adult-like. With the next molt, beginning late in the fourth spring/summer, adult-like appearance is typically attained.

Similar Species: Adults are straightforward; immature, however, can be mistaken for Golden Eagle,

Osprey, and both vultures (at a distance). All Bald Eagles share flat, planklike wings in flight, though first-years can appear a bit wider-winged and longer-tailed, and adult Balds can soar with a shallow dihedral at times. *Golden Eagle* is most similar, but appears smaller-headed, soars with a distinct dihedral, and has dark underwing coverts and axillaries in all plumages (beware molting Goldens, which can show white exposed feather bases along the underwing coverts). Immature Golden Eagles have white restricted to the bases of the flight feathers; Bald Eagles have white underwing coverts and axillaries. *Osprey* flies on distinctly crooked, lanky, gull-like wings and is smaller, slimmer, and more boldly patterned black and white than Bald Eagle.

Black Vulture is often confused with immature Bald Eagle at a distance, but Black Vulture is compact in build with a very short tail and particularly small head, and it shows pale outer primaries (unlike eagles). *Turkey Vulture* is also particularly small-headed compared with Bald Eagle, with adults showing a distinct (featherless) reddish head and white bill. Turkey Vulture almost always flies with wings held in a prominent dihedral, and the 'silvery' flight feathers are often visible. The unstable, teetering, buoyant manner of flight displayed by Turkey Vulture is also very different from the unwavering, stable flight of Bald Eagle.

Hybrids: Bald Eagle may hybridize very rarely with Steller's Sea-Eagle and White-tailed Eagle. But because of these species' extensive plumage variation and long maturation process, hybrid eagles are difficult to confirm. More study is needed.

Status and Distribution: A conservation success story, Bald Eagles were critically endangered across most of their range in the mid- to late 20th century. But the banning of DDT, a toxic pesticide that caused eggshell thinning and subsequent breeding failure, has resulted in a strong rebound in the population. The bird is now fairly common and increasing throughout most of its range. Large populations occur in Alaska, the Pacific Northwest, the Chesapeake Bay region, and in Florida, and the species now can be found fairly easily throughout most of its breeding range. Large numbers leave the north in winter and augment residents nesting in the Lower 48. Some stay in pockets farther north (e.g., Homer, AK) where food resources are abundant through the winter.

Migration: Bald Eagle migration is difficult to delineate in some regions because of overlapping resident breeders and migrants. In general, northern populations are migratory mainly from February through May (spring), and August through December (fall), but they winter as far north as coastal Alaska and Newfoundland. Most migration occurs with interior breeders, whose breeding grounds (e.g., lakes) may completely ice over in winter. Southern populations are largely resident, but northward, postbreeding dispersal occurs. In the Great Lakes and Chesapeake Bay region, large numbers of dispersing Bald Eagles from the Gulf region, especially Florida, are noted during mid-May to mid-June. It is unknown to what extent this northward dispersal occurs in more northern breeding populations. Not all Bald Eagles migrate, especially adults. Tracking data show that some birds move only short distances from the breeding grounds when a reliable food source is found nearby.

Vocalizations: Bald Eagles have relatively weak voices. Instead of the classic "Hollywood" Red-tailed Hawk scream with which it is often associated, it gives a series of weak, high-pitched, descending whistles. It frequently calls during aggressive encounters, when claiming dead fish among other eagles, when chasing other birds (e.g., Osprey), and when nesting.

Golden Eagle *(Aquila chrysaetos)* **GOEA** page 30

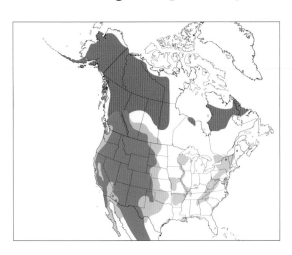

Soaring high above a rim-rock canyon, a Golden Eagle has a commanding view of the surrounding terrain. Below, a roaring river snakes along the canyon bottom. Steep-sided cliffs offer ample substrate to build a nest, safe from any mammalian predator. Off to the north stretches a vast sagebrush desert, and in the distance a few sage grouse shuffle about nervously on a lek. Jackrabbits, the eagle's favored prey, hide below, wary of its presence high overhead. But the eagle is not concerned with food at the moment. This male is 5 years old, and after wandering the surrounding states for a few years, it's now ready to secure a territory and find a mate. It will need to defend this place against many rivals, but it'll be worth it—there is ample food to raise young. In the distance another large, dark figure soars against billowing purple clouds. The young male initiates a spectacu-

lar territorial display, tucking his wings and swooping downward in blinding, roller-coaster-like dives. The intruder seems unimpressed at first but quickly changes direction when pressed by the young male and is tail-chased at high speed. The young male lets this intruder go with a warning this time, an emphatic "Get lost!" The intruder drifts farther away, over the horizon—gone for good. This young male has claimed this place as his domain now—and his territorial displays will dominate this rugged, open landscape for years to come.

Overview: Golden Eagles are magnificent hunters of open country, preying mostly on medium-sized mammals (especially jackrabbits), but capable of catching large mammals and birds (e.g., grouse, ptarmigan). They hunt using a variety of tactics including low-level surprise-and-flush techniques, perch-hunting, and high elevation aerial stoops. Unlike Bald Eagles, Goldens only rarely feed on carrion, instead preferring to hunt live prey. Found throughout the West but scarce in some areas, Golden Eagles prefer grassland, sagebrush, and semiopen clearings in mountainous terrain. In the East, Golden Eagles are much more rare, nesting in the Canadian Arctic from Quebec to northern Newfoundland and Labrador on cliffs and sometimes in trees at forest edges.

Unlike the gregarious Bald Eagle, Golden Eagles are generally more solitary, often found singly or in pairs, but never in large concentrations. Golden Eagles maintain a large home range (several square miles) and are highly territorial; they have even been known to kill smaller raptors that trespass, leaving them dead on the scene without any interest in feeding on them. Golden Eagles often perch prominently on power poles, fence posts, and rocky outcrops during breeding and winter.

Flight Style: In flight, Golden Eagles appear slow-moving because of their large size, soaring in wider circles than most raptors. Golden Eagles are impressively steady, even in the strongest winds. They display slow, heavy wingbeats that end abruptly on an upstroke into a shallow dihedral. The similarly heavy wingbeats of Bald Eagles are stiffer, with deep upstrokes that end with the wings held level. Flying on light winds along a ridge, Golden Eagles can exhibit shallower, "wristy," intermittent flaps. Golden Eagles are highly maneuverable aerialists when chasing prey or defending territories.

Size and Shape: L 70–90 cm (28–35 in), WS 185–225 cm (72–89 in), WT 3.0–6.4 kg (6.6–14 lb) Golden Eagles are very large, roughly the size of a Bald Eagle, and distinctly larger than both vultures. The only larger raptor in North America is the California Condor. Golden Eagles have extremely long, somewhat broad wings, which are held in a dihedral when soaring, and bowed or in a modified dihedral when gliding. Since the wings pinch-in at the body, Golden Eagles are more buteo-like overall than Bald Eagle, especially juveniles and second-year birds that have broader secondaries than adults and older subadults. Females are notably larger than males when the two are side by side. The largest females have more labored wingbeats and more pronounced dihedrals than males (sometimes as steep as those of Turkey Vulture), but it is often difficult to sex lone birds.

Plumage: Golden Eagles are dark overall with prominent golden hackles. Immature birds, from 1 to 4 years old, have varying amounts of white in the wings and tail, but at about 5 years old, most Golden Eagles attain full adult appearance, lacking any white in the plumage. Males and females are essentially alike in plumage. Ageing Golden Eagles in the field is difficult. Many birders assume that birds with no white in the wings are adults, and that birds with lots of white in the wings are juveniles, but these assumptions are often wrong. The amount of white in the wings is sometimes related to age progression in Golden Eagles, but varies greatly within age classes. Some juveniles lack white in the wings altogether,

and some 3- to 4-year-olds can show a surprising amount of white. It's safe to say that if there is notable white in the wings and tail, the bird is not an adult. Accurate ageing is best accomplished by a combination of close study of the tail pattern, which varies little within age classes, and an assessment of molt patterns in the secondaries and primaries. Both these things can be difficult to see in the field, especially on birds gliding overhead, so many migrant Golden Eagles must be left as *unknown* age.

Adults are dark brown overall with variable grayish banding on the flight feathers and generally a well-defined dark trailing edge to the secondaries. The wings of adults (and older subadults) appear two-toned underneath, similar to Turkey Vulture, especially over snow cover. The tail is dark with variable grayish banding, limited to only a few broad bands, or multiple narrow bands. Adults (and nonjuveniles) have paler greater coverts forming a distinct tawny upperwing bar.

1st-years (juveniles) are dark overall with a well-demarcated white base to the tail and variable white patches in the wings. The white in the tail is typically extensive, covering more than half the tail, but can be more restricted on some birds. The white patches in the wings are often solid but in some cases may be split. On white extreme individuals, the upperwings also show small white primary patches. Some juveniles have little or no white in the wings, so birds with prominent white on the wings can be the same age or older than birds with no white in the wings. And birds with all-dark wings can be any age (assessing tail pattern on these is key!). The dark brown secondaries lack the grayish banding and dark trailing edge to the wings of later ages, and these feathers are longer and more pointed than in subsequent age classes. The upperparts are uniform dark brownish; by spring, the upperwing coverts fade to paler brown, but lack the tawny greater coverts of older birds. Juveniles are best aged by their uniform flight feathers that lack signs of molt, their uniformly dark upperwings, and their largely white tail with crisp black tip.

2nd-years retain most of their juvenile feathers and appear nearly identical to juveniles at a distance. With close views, however, they usually have 3–4 new inner primaries and 1–3 new secondaries. The new secondaries are slightly shorter and usually banded grayish. The tail is made up mostly of retained juvenile feathers, with a few subadult feathers in the center and the outer tail. These subadult tail feathers are slightly darker than the retained juvenile tail feathers, but still have a white base with a narrow, smudgy gray band. Some upperwing coverts on second-year Golden Eagles are replaced with the new pale feathers forming a narrow, mottled "tawny bar"; however, this upperwing bar on second-year birds is sometimes very limited compared with that on older birds. Second-year birds finishing their inner primary molt in the fall can show a "gap" along the back edge of the wings as older birds can; otherwise second-year birds not actively molting are difficult to age.

3rd-years are more variable in plumage. The tail comprises mostly subadult feathers, with perhaps a few retained juvenile feathers, especially T5 (second from outermost), appearing fully white-based and juvenile-like in the field. Some third-year birds have new, adult-like dark central feathers, making the tail appear split with white patches on each side. From below, this split-tailed appearance may be visible only when the tail is spread. Primary molt occurs toward the outer end of the wings on birds still in active molt in fall, often resulting in 1–3 retained juvenile outer primaries that are worn and pale, contrasting with the rest of the darker, fresher primaries. The secondaries are now mostly subadult feathers, with 1–3 retained browner, longer, worn, and faded juvenile feathers. Any white in the wings is typically limited to the secondaries. Because of their extensive molt and wear at this age, third-year birds typically appear more ragged along the trailing edge of the wings than other Golden Eagles. The tawny upperwing bar becomes obvious at this age.

4th-years are adult-like overall, with scattered signs of immaturity still visible. The tail has white patches on the base toward the outer edges (often the only way to tell fourth-year birds from adults), and the wings are usually all dark, but some fourth-year birds can still have specks of white at some secondary bases. The white on the tail is apparent from below only when the tail is fully spread, and from above only with good views. The upperwings are identical to those of adults. Careful scrutiny of fourth-years is necessary for ageing in the field, as most are passed off as adults.

Geographic Variation: Worldwide there are 4–6 subspecies of Golden Eagle, but in North America there is only 1: *A. c. canadensis*. This form is medium-sized compared with the larger European and smaller Asian forms.

Molt: Golden Eagles are very large birds, with long flight feathers, and as such they cannot replace all their flight feathers in a single annual molt the way smaller raptors can; instead they use stepwise molt to replace their flight feathers in several waves. Because they breed across a range of latitudes (e.g., from Arizona to Alaska), molt timing and extent differ among populations, being earlier and probably more extensive in southern birds.

Juveniles undergo their first flight feather molt starting as early as late winter and progressing until fall. Molt begins with inner primaries at P1 or P2, generally stopping at P4 before suspending for winter. Body plumage is also replaced during this stage but is generally very limited. Each successive molt begins in early spring simultaneously with the inner primaries and where the previous molt was suspended, resulting in 2 or more waves of active molt. Similar patterns are followed throughout their lifespan, with several waves of molt typical in adults. Tail molt begins at the center (T1), followed by the outer feathers (T6), progressively molting in a stepwise pattern, next with T3 and T4, until eventually attaining a full adult tail that concludes with the replacement of T2 and T5. The complete replacement of juvenile to subadult to adult tail feathers generally takes 4 or 5 years.

Golden Eagles that are actively molting underwing coverts often show variable white patches below. These are not white feathers, but instead are the exposed white bases of underlying feathers that are usually covered by the dark coverts. Birds in heavy molt can show quite a bit of white mottling in the underwing coverts, and they can be confused with immature Bald Eagles.

Similar Species: Golden Eagles are frequently mistaken for Turkey Vultures, Bald Eagles, and even dark buteos. Immature birds with prominent white wing patches and white-based tails are usually distinctive, but darker-plumaged birds are more frequently confused.

Bald Eagle and Golden Eagle are similar in shape and flight style, but Golden Eagle is more buteo-like with a smaller head, slightly longer tail, and wings that pinch-in at the body. Bald Eagle flies with its wings held flat, slightly drooped, or in a very slight dihedral. Golden Eagle flies with a noticeable dihedral or modified dihedral in most situations. The wingbeats of Bald Eagles are slow and stiff, with deep upstrokes that end with the wings held level, whereas Golden Eagle displays easy wingbeats that end abruptly on an upstroke into a dihedral. Immature Bald Eagles are dark in plumage like Golden Eagles, but they lack golden hackles, and most plumages have white on the wing pits where Goldens are always dark. Golden Eagles don't show a white belly, white on the upper back, or striking two-toned upperwings like immature Bald Eagles.

Turkey Vulture is similar in shape and plumage to Golden Eagle. Both are dark overall, but Turkey Vulture does not have golden hackles or white in the wings and tail like immature Golden Eagles. The featherless reddish head and white bill of adult Turkey Vulture are distinctive when seen. Even young vultures with dark heads and bills appear small-headed in comparison. Turkey Vultures and Golden Eagles can both appear to show silvery flight feathers, but this occurs only on older Golden Eagles, which also show a dark trailing edge to the wings that vultures lack. One key to telling Turkey Vultures in general is their buoyant, "wobbly" flight, and their distinct way of holding their wings in an exaggerated or modified dihedral.

At first glance, *dark-morph buteos* are similar in appearance to Golden Eagles; however, all buteos are much smaller than Golden Eagles, with smaller heads and shorter wings. Golden Eagles are also more stable in flight, soar in wider circles, and have heavier wingbeats than buteos. Most buteos have pale flight feathers with narrow, dark bands. Those with dark flight feathers (e.g., Swainson's Hawk) have slimmer, more pointed wings than Golden Eagle.

Status and Distribution: Golden Eagles are uncommon to fairly common in the West. The breeding range extends from Alaska through northern Canada and throughout the western United States. They also occur in northern Mexico. In the East, Golden Eagles are much more rare, nesting in the Canadian Arctic from Quebec to northern Newfoundland and Labrador. Historically, they nested in the Appalachian Mountains, but they are no longer found there. Eastern birds winter mainly in the West Virginia Appalachian Mountains (and sparingly in parts south and north along the range), and a scattered few in coastal salt marshes of the Mid-Atlantic. They are rare in the Southeast in winter.

Migration: Golden Eagle migration takes place mainly from February to May in spring, and from September through December in fall. Northern populations of Golden Eagles are migratory, whereas most Lower-48 breeders are resident. Golden Eagles are seen in numbers along the foothills of the Rocky Mountains in spring and fall, and along the Cascade Mountains on the West Coast. Sandia Mountains, NM, Goshute Mountains, NV, Wasatch Mountains, UT, Rogers Pass, MT, Bridger Mountains, MT, and Gunsight Mountain, AK, are all good sites to see Golden Eagles on migration—but the best sites by far are Mt. Lorrette and South Livingstone in Alberta, where thousands are counted each fall and spring. These birds breed mainly in Alaska. In the East, Hawk Mountain, PA, Hawk Ridge, MN, Derby Hill, NY, Franklin Mountain, NY, and especially Tussey Mountain, PA, are good sites to witness Golden Eagle migration.

Vocalizations: Not especially vocal, and rarely heard away from the nesting grounds. When breeding and during courtship, pairs give an agitated, repeated, scratchy yelp, or *seeachup, seeachup*.

Osprey *(Pandion haliaetus)* OSPR page 36

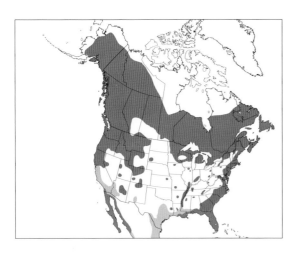

You wouldn't believe the bird we saw today! We were fishing down at the pier, getting "skunked" as usual, kept company by the gulls, pelicans, and cormorants—the birds we're used to seeing, the ones that take handouts when they're too lazy to fish for themselves. But then we saw something different. A fishing hawk! The bird was gigantic, and flew sorta' like a gull with long, droopy wings. It was black and white underneath, and had a white head like an eagle. The most unusual thing about it, though, was how it caught fish. We watched it fly in from over the dock and then hover in midair. Then it plunged feet-first into the water, but couldn't get back out. It was flapping its wings like it was trying to swim to shore. We thought it was drowning, and we got worried. But finally it got up in the air again and flew right over our heads, and it had a big fish in its talons, bigger than anything we'd caught all year. It almost dropped the fish as it shook off water like a wet dog, but then turned it around so it was facing head-first, and it flew off down the shoreline with it. We asked another fisherman what it was, and he told us it was called an Osprey—or what the locals call the "Fish Hawk."

Overview: The Osprey is certainly unique. It is found near water when breeding, building bulky stick nests in dead trees and snags, and on tall light fixtures, power poles, or raised platforms provided especially for it. Unlike the Bald Eagle, which merely prefers to eat fish, Osprey relies on them almost exclusively as its main prey item. Instead of scavenging like the eagle often does, the Osprey actively fishes, plunging feet-first into the water to capture medium-sized to sometimes surprisingly large fish. Ospreys have specialized feet for grasping fish: all 4 talons are long and strongly curved, more so than on other raptors, and the toes have tiny spines or "spicules" on the bottom that help it hang onto its slippery prey. Most raptors have 3 toes in the front and 1 in the back, but the Osprey can rotate the outer toe backward and forward to help grab and carry fish, which it typically carries head-first for better aerodynamics. When intruders come into their territory, Ospreys often swoop down and drag their feet along the water's surface. During migration, Ospreys can be among the highest migrants passing over a given site, and are frequently seen in kettles with other soaring raptors.

Flight Style: Ospreys are extremely steady fliers, soaring in wide circles and gaining lift easily. They readily use powered flight for long stretches, and do not avoid water crossings the way most raptors do. The wingbeats of Osprey are stiff, shallow, and almost mechanical, seeming somewhat incongruous because of the length of the wings. When flapping earnestly, Osprey appears to struggle as its head and chest bob up and down. Unlike the typically flat-winged profile of Bald Eagle, the wings of Osprey are drooped in all postures.

Size and Shape: L 53–66 cm (21–26 in), WS 149–171 cm (59–67 in), WT 1.0–1.9 kg (2.2–4.2 lb)
Osprey is a large bird, only slightly smaller than an eagle, but with a distinctly slimmer body and narrower chest. Ospreys are easy to identify even at long distances, making them a favorite among birders. They have extremely lanky wings that appear gull-like but lack sharply pointed wingtips. In a glide, the wings form a distinct M shape. Males and females are nearly equal in size. When the bird is perched, note the dovelike head of Osprey, caused by the lack of a supraorbital ridge above the eye that gives most raptors a fierce appearance.

Plumage: Osprey superficially resembles whiter examples of immature Bald Eagles. It is overall dark on top with a white head, but the head has a broad, well-defined black eyeline similar to that of subadult Bald Eagles. Osprey is brilliant white underneath with blackish flight feathers and wrists, unlike immature Bald Eagles, which have whitish bellies and darker breasts. All Ospreys have a blackish tail with faint white bands, but from below the white can be prominent when the tail is fanned. When backlit, the tail can look reddish, causing confusion with Red-tailed Hawk for an instant. Males and females are often identical in plumage, but adult males tend to be cleaner white below, lacking the streaked bib on the chest shown by most adult females and juveniles.

Adults have yellow eyes and unmarked brownish black upperparts. *1st-years* (juveniles) differ only slightly from adults, having pale-fringed upperparts through the first fall, but these wear away over the course of winter. Juveniles have orange eyes and a rufous wash to the underwings, especially in early fall, but be cautious as some adults show this faint wash as well. Juveniles are more likely to show streaking on the crown, which makes the head appear less brilliantly white than on adults. Because of feather wear and fading, it is nearly impossible to age Ospreys in spring; however, because many immature birds remain on winter grounds for up to 2 years, Ospreys migrating in the spring are typically adults. In fall, Ospreys with signs of flight-feather molt are adults.

Geographic Variation: Osprey is one of the few raptor species that occurs worldwide. There are 4 subspecies, but throughout North America only 1 subspecies (*P. h. carolinensis*) occurs; the Caribbean form (*P. h. ridgwayi*) could occur as a vagrant to Florida. On average, *P. h. carolinensis* has a darker forehead and eyeline than *ridgwayi*, and the breast is typically more heavily streaked; however, field identification is difficult with perhaps only extreme individuals being identifiable.

Molt: Osprey is a large bird, and as such it does not replace all its flight feathers in a single annual molt; instead it uses a stepwise molt strategy to replace flight feathers. Because it breeds across a range of latitudes (e.g., from Florida to Alaska), molt timing differs among populations, being earlier in southern birds. Osprey is interesting in that it has an accelerated molt of the primaries compared with other large raptors. The first wave of primary molt begins in midwinter, when the bird is roughly 5 months old, beginning with the first primary (P1) and continuing out through outermost primary (P10) over the course of about 1 year. But prior to completion of that first sequential molt, usually when it reaches about the eighth primary (P8), a new wave begins again at P1. So by the second winter, 2 waves of primary molt

are obvious. By the second summer, a third wave has begun, starting again at P1 when the second wave reaches the middle of the wing (about P5–6). In the third fall, yet another new wave begins at P1. After the third winter, Ospreys typically suspend molt for their northward migration, and afterward they molt the primaries in waves during the nonbreeding season. Adults can have up to 5 waves of molt in the primaries alone!

Similar Species: Osprey is among the most distinctive of the North American raptors, not only in behavior and plumage, but also in size and structure. But at a distance, confusion is possible with immature Bald Eagle and large gulls. Osprey is told from immature *Bald Eagle* by its smaller size, slimmer, lankier wings, boldly patterned flight feathers, and cleaner white underparts. Osprey soars and glides on crooked, bowed wings, appearing more gull-like in flight than Bald Eagle. The gull most similar to Osprey, adult *Great Black-backed Gull*, has cleaner white underwings and a pure white head and tail. When gliding head-on or high overhead, *Swainson's Hawks* can appear superficially Osprey-like, but note Swainson's more chesty build and shorter, more pointed, and less bowed wings.

Status and Distribution: Osprey breeds throughout North America near lakes, rivers, and marshes. It is generally common and increasing throughout its range, especially in the Northeast and the Mid-Atlantic. In some areas, populations can be very dense, especially along the East Coast (e.g., Florida, Chesapeake Bay), with Osprey nests on just about every suitable platform. Like the Bald Eagle, the Osprey suffered greatly from the effects of DDT, but it has rebounded strongly in its historic breeding areas. Northern breeders winter in coastal areas from mid-latitudes in the continental United States south to South America, and more rarely inland along major rivers and lakes.

Migration: Osprey has a broad migration window in both spring and fall. It migrates north mainly from March through May, and south from August through November. Osprey is seen at all migration sites in North America, but large numbers can occur in fall along the Atlantic Coast (Cape May, NJ; Kiptopeke, VA). Spring migration is more dispersed. Ospreys can be seen inland far from water during migration. As excellent fliers unreliant on thermals for soaring,

194

Ospreys are often the first and last birds in the sky during migration.

Vocalizations: Vocal year-round, but especially in

their nesting territories, Ospreys are often heard high overhead while soaring or defending the nest. Call is a high-pitched, repeated, well-spaced, rising *sphee-sphee-sphee-sphee* becoming raspy near the end.

Northern Harrier *(Circus cyaneus)* **NOHA** page 40

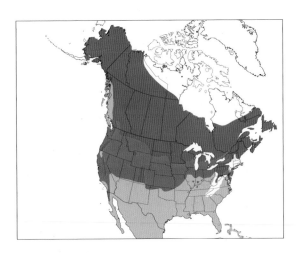

Late afternoon light splashes gold across a western marsh. In the distance 2 silhouettes float inches above the windblown reeds. They are hawks, evident by their long wings and large size, yet they are slim, buoyant, seemingly weightless, and in constant motion. The autumn wind buffets them as they teeter delicately back and forth, unsteady in the breeze. As they course the landscape, holding their wings in a shallow V, they periodically accelerate with deep, fluid wingbeats. As they approach more closely, plumage differences become apparent; one is pearl gray above and snow white below, the other dark brown above and washed cinnamon-rufous below, impossibly orange in the warm autumn light. They hunt intently over the marsh, constantly searching, often pausing to hover with long legs dangling. Occasional flashes of brilliant white across the rump help reveal their identity, as they turn in an instant, pouncing on an unsuspecting rodent below.

Overview: Northern Harrier occurs in open areas throughout most of North America and is the only North American representative of the extensive worldwide genus *Circus*. It is often compared with owls because of its similarly prominent facial disks, acute hearing, and ability to hunt and migrate in low light, and occasionally in complete

darkness. However, Harriers typically migrate and hunt during daylight hours, when they spend much time aloft, coursing over meadows and open fields. Harriers are distinctive in flight, remaining low to the ground when hunting rodents and small birds, often tilting and turning in a "wobbly" demeanor that reveals their characteristic white rump patch, a key field mark. Their long legs are adapted for capturing voles or mice in tall grass, or snatching a passerine out of the air that is startled from the ground. During migration, they are often the highest-flying hawks in the sky, which can fool birders unaccustomed to seeing them at such altitudes. And despite their distinctive shape, they are frequently mistaken for other raptor species.

Flight Style: Northern Harriers are lightweight and able to gain lift more easily than most raptors. They are dynamic and tireless aerialists, perching only briefly on low, single, post-type perches or on the ground, and only rarely perching in trees. Unlike many raptors, they readily utilize powered flight to cross large bodies of water or expanses of desert, especially during migration. In direct flight, their wingbeats are deep, slow, and relaxed. Harriers soar freely, occasionally to very high altitudes. Harriers almost always hold their wings in a pronounced dihedral or modified dihedral, except when gliding on strong updrafts, typically along ridges, when they display slightly bowed wings. A Harrier's buoyancy is much like that of a Turkey Vulture, teetering from side to side in rather unstable fashion, seemingly buffeted by even the slightest breeze, but Harriers differ in their ability to maneuver quickly and often display split-second bursts of speed and radical direction changes when in pursuit of prey.

Size and Shape: L 41–50 cm (16–20 in), WS 97–122 cm (38–48 in), WT 290–600 g (10–21 oz) Northern Harriers are lightweight birds that have a lengthy appearance in flight. When soaring, their silhouette is distinctive among raptors. They have long, narrow wings and long, slim tails. The wings do not bulge outward along the trailing edge like those of accipiters and most buteos, and their heads are relatively small. Harriers have slim bodies, lacking the "chesty" appearance of other raptors. Some buteos have lanky wings (see Swainson's Hawk and Rough-legged Hawk), but they are always broader than those of Harriers. Male Harriers are smaller and lighter than females, with proportionately shorter wings and tails, but this difference in size is usually apparent only in the field when both sexes are seen together. When the bird is gliding, its wings taper sharply at the tips and project well past the base of the wings, making them appear similar in shape to a large falcon; however, Harriers lack the broad head and chest and the tapered tail shown by Peregrine, Prairie, and Gyrfalcon. Perched, Harriers are slim with long wings and long tails, and the head appears small but blocky or squared.

Plumage: There are 2 ages of Northern Harrier that are safely differentiated by plumage: adult and juvenile. Adult males and females differ greatly in plumage, but juveniles are similar to adult females.

Adult males are unique among North American raptors in being strikingly white below with black wingtips and a black trailing edge along the secondaries. Adult males can have a gray bib that in combination with the dark head forms a hooded appearance. The upperparts of adult males are gray with faint, pale mottling on the upperwing coverts and scapulars, but they generally appear uniform grayish. Some males are washed with rufous on the chest and leggings, and brownish on the head and upperwing coverts. Second-year birds can be safely aged only by the presence of retained juvenile flight feathers, but retention is very uncommon since most undergo a complete molt in the first summer. In spring, Harriers are paler above because of plumage fading. All Northern Harriers have brilliant white uppertail coverts, commonly referred to as a "white rump." This field mark is helpful in identifying low-flying Harriers, as it can be seen at great distances. Confusing the white "rump" on Harriers with the white uppertail coverts or white tail of other raptors is a common mistake among birders. The tail on adult males is gray with a black tip, or with faint dark bands throughout. All adult males have lemon-yellow eyes.

Adult females are streaked brown on buff below and dark brown above with paler tan to rufous mottling on the upperwing coverts. Some adult females have limited streaking on the underbody while others can show a strong rufous tone on the underparts (especially in western North America). Both types can appear juvenile-like in the field. The topside of the flight feathers shows a slight grayish tone (especially the secondaries) that may contrast slightly with the darker brown upperwing coverts. The primary coverts on many adult females are washed grayish and barred darker; these are generally plain brownish on juveniles. Some adult females have distinct golden streaking throughout the head. Eye color on females changes from dark brown to yellow over the first 3 years.

1st-year (juvenile) Harriers are very similar in plumage to adult females but typically distinguished by their richer, rufous underparts, with faint dark streaking on the chest. The rufous tone below often fades to dull buff by spring, when separation from adult females can be more challenging. Juveniles have dark brown upperparts that are uniform in tone. The mottling on the upperwing coverts is rufous but often fades to buff by spring. The head of juvenile Harriers is dark brown with a pale, incomplete eyering. The topsides of adult females and juveniles are difficult or impossible to judge in the field without considerable experience. Juvenile sexes are similar, but males have pale yellow-green eyes compared with dark brown on females. The axillaries, underwing linings, and secondaries of adult females and juveniles are dark and contrast with the slightly paler primaries. The tail of adult female and juvenile Harriers is dark brown and indistinctly banded.

Melanistic Northern Harriers occur in North America, but they are exceedingly rare (5 sightings). Melanistic birds are completely blackish on the underparts with paler flight feathers, and blackish above, lacking the white uppertail coverts of typical Harriers.

Geographic Variation: One subspecies in North America: (*C. c. hudsonius*). Adult females in the West are slightly more rufous on the underbody than adult females in the East.

Molt: The first molt from juvenile to adult plumage is usually complete (April to November), after which birds attain an adult plumage that changes little. Rarely second-year birds retain a few secondaries or more often primaries. Adult plumage is replaced in an annual molt that occurs from May to October on breeding grounds prior to migration.

Similar Species: Distinctive if seen well, where shape, flight style, and the bold white "rump" in all plumages help identify it. The Harrier is often called a "chameleon" by hawk watchers because it can appear buteo-like in a soar and falcon-like in a glide when flying high overhead. Best distinguished from *Swainson's Hawk* by its longer tail, less pointed wings, and broad white rump. Told from similarly shaped *Rough-legged Hawk* by the dark flight feathers, white rump, and lack of blackish belly and carpal patches. Compared with all *buteos*, Harrier is slimmer overall (especially the body) and small-headed. Harriers are less stable in flight, often teetering back and forth while soaring much like a Turkey Vulture, and exhibit "floppier," more relaxed wingbeats than other hawks.

Status and Distribution: Harriers are widespread but uncommon breeders in open habitat, especially marshes and fallow fields. Northern breeders are migratory, wintering primarily in the Lower 48, rarely moving as far south as Panama. Frequently encountered during migration when they can occur in significant numbers at hawk watches (especially coastal and Great Lakes sites), or in winter, with concentrations of dozens of birds in areas with ample rodent populations. Sometimes tens to hundreds of birds might gather over an area, and these birds roost communally, often with Short-eared Owls. The overall population is stable, but perhaps decreasing as a result of habitat alteration and loss. In some states it is a species of concern, but it has no special status nationwide.

Migration: Northern Harrier has a long migration period, spanning the entire spring and fall seasons. Harriers move south from August through December and head north in spring as early as February, with some straggling through as late as early June. In fall, the peak for juveniles typically occurs from mid- to late September, whereas the peak for adults is often several weeks later. In spring, peak Harrier movements occur from early to mid-April; juveniles migrate throughout the spring, with a gradual peak from mid-April to early May. Flights occur later in fall at the southern range of their migration, and earlier at the northern part of their range; the opposite is true for spring migration.

Northern Harriers can be seen migrating from sunup to sundown and are even known to fly throughout the night. In North America, the daily high count (440) and seasonal high count (3177) for Harrier both occurred at Braddock Bay, NY, in spring. Cape May Point, NJ, averages the most Harriers per season with about 1750. From east to west, Kiptopeke State Park, VA, Derby Hill, NY, Holiday Beach, ON, Whitefish Point, MI, Hawk Ridge, MN, Bountiful Peak, UT, the Goshute Mountains, NV, and Gunsight Mountain, AK, are all excellent sites to witness Harrier migration.

Vocalizations: Harriers are seldom vocal, but sometimes give a repeated, emphatic laughing *whew, whew, wee, wee, wee, wee, wee,* with 2 introductory notes, and a short series trailing off at the end. They are more vocal in small groups in winter, giving a high, whining call similar to the juvenile begging call. This "whine" is heard from adults during courtship as well.

Sharp-shinned Hawk *(Accipiter striatus)* SSHA page 44

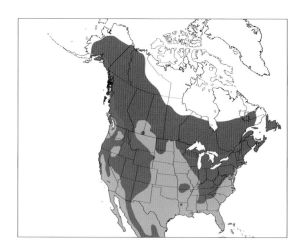

On a frigid winter day, a mass of songbirds anxiously feeds on seed strewn in a grassy area cleared of snow, their bustling chatter discernible through the living room window. At once, they freeze, pinning themselves low to the ground in response to alarm calls from nearby jays. From the corner of the yard a blue streak appears, seemingly materializing from thin air, moving swiftly toward the flock. The group scatters as a high-speed chase ensues. The small, compact hawk picks its target. It extends its long legs and talons outward and fans its long tail as it banks sharply and snatches a White-throated Sparrow from midair. The hawk disappears into the brambly thickets without moving a branch; the only evidence of the event is a plume of feathers softly floating to the ground.

Overview: Sharp-shinned Hawks are small hawks, with males being the smallest hawks in North America; however, females are considerably larger. They are strictly bird catchers, preying on small birds up to the size of a dove or quail. "Sharpies" (their familiar nickname) are agile hawks able to tail-chase songbirds through the most tangled thickets and reappear unscathed. They nest in secluded, dense coniferous woodlands, but winter in low-elevation edge habitat and suburban areas. They are regular at backyard birdfeeders in winter, when they are confused with the nearly identical Cooper's Hawk. Sharpies are common at most migration sites throughout North America.

Flight Style: Sharp-shinned Hawks are light-weight, buoyant, and highly maneuverable in flight, able to make abrupt turns in pursuit of prey or when harassing larger raptors. They soar frequently, especially on migration, rising quickly on winds or thermals. On days with minimal lift, their flight is direct, with extremely quick, snappy flaps interspersed with short glides. Sharp-shinned Hawks are unsteady in even moderate winds and share a similar flight style with American Kestrel; however, they appear more anxious than other raptors, making constant minor wing adjustments.

Size and Shape: L 24–34 cm (9–13 in), WS 53–65 cm (20–26 in), WT 87–218 g (3–8 oz)
Sharp-shinned Hawks are stocky overall with short, rounded wings and slim, long tails. In a soar, the wings bulge at the secondaries and taper slightly at the hands, while the wrists are pushed forward. In a glide, Sharp-shinneds are compact with a small head that projects only slightly past the wrists. The body is short and "chesty." Sharp-shinned Hawks' tails are narrow, especially at the base, and short compared with those of Cooper's Hawks and Northern Goshawks. The tail is typically square-tipped when closed (male) to slightly round (mainly females). Occasionally males have notched tails, with the central tail feathers shorter than the outer tail feathers; this is atypical for Cooper's Hawk and Northern Goshawk (beware of molt and feather damage when assessing tail shape). Even though females are larger than males, judging size in the field can be difficult from a distance or without comparative experience. But a Sharp-shinned Hawk with captured prey nearly as large as itself, such as a Mourning Dove, jay, or quail, is almost always a female; males usually take smaller birds. When perched, Sharp-shinned Hawks appear small, with long tails, short wings, and small heads, and may be overlooked as passerines at first glance.

Plumage: Adults and juveniles differ in plumage, and adult males and females differ slightly, though the juvenile sexes are similar.

Adults are barred rufous on white below with white undertail coverts. The upperparts are gray-blue with a blackish blue head and rufous cheeks. The tail is banded black and gray-blue with a narrow white tip. Adult males are more vibrant rufous underneath, especially on the flanks, and paler blue above (mantle and upperwing coverts) than females. Adults have orange eyes (typically second-years) that become dark red as they age. Older males typically have the darkest red eyes, while even older adult females may retain an orange-red iris.

1st-years (juvenile) are buffy below with thick, reddish brown or brown streaking on the underbody, often denser on the flanks. The streaking is variable, as some first-years, especially males, are narrowly streaked and show pale faces. They are brown above with rusty fringes on the back and upperwing coverts. The tail is banded black and gray with a narrow white tip. Juveniles have yellow eyes (rare aberrant birds may have darker brownish eyes; cf. Merlin).

Geographic Variation: There are 2 subspecies of Sharp-shinned Hawk in North America, but plumage differences are minor, and subspecies are probably not safely assigned under field conditions. The widespread *A. s. velox* breeds across the majority of its range in North America. Western birds average slightly smaller than eastern birds. The heavily marked subspecies *A. s. perobscurus* breeds on the Queen Charlotte Islands and possibly adjacent mainland British Columbia, but more study is needed regarding this. Some winter on the breeding grounds, but the full winter range is poorly known. Birds of this subspecies have been recorded as far south as southern California in winter.

Molt: Juvenile Sharp-shinneds retain their brown plumage for about 1 year, beginning their first molt during the late first spring and early summer. From June to August, second-year birds have a notable mix of new adult and retained juvenile feathers. By fall they are indistinguishable from adults under field conditions, even if they have retained some number of juvenile feathers on the rump, upperwing, or flight feathers. Adults undergo a complete molt each year from May through October. Most replace all the flight feathers during this subsequent molt, but occasionally a few are retained. Birds in the West tend to retain flight feathers, while eastern birds typically replace all their flight feathers each molt cycle. In the montane West, some Sharp-shinned Hawks complete their flight feather molt in September to early October during migration.

Similar Species: Sharp-shinned Hawks are most easily confused with Cooper's Hawks, and to a lesser extent with Northern Goshawks. They are marginally smaller than male *Cooper's Hawks* (often difficult to judge on lone birds), but also differ in shape and flight style, and slightly in plumage. Sharp-shinned Hawk has shorter, more rounded wings, and a shorter, narrower tail than Cooper's. The white tail tip is typically narrower on Sharp-shinned, and often absent on worn spring birds. Sharp-shinned is rounder-headed and big-eyed compared with the large, square head, and small-eyed look of Cooper's. Adult Sharp-shinned lack the pale nape shown by Cooper's.

Juvenile Sharp-shinned is typically more heavily marked below, with reddish brown, thick streaks, as opposed to the thin, chocolate brown streaks of Cooper's (beware of heavily marked juvenile Cooper's, especially in the West). Juvenile Sharp-shinned Hawks rarely show the tawny-headed appearance of juvenile Cooper's. In flight, Sharp-shinned Hawk soars on flat wings, typically pressed forward at the wrists, creating a short head projection. Cooper's soars with a slight dihedral, and holds its wings straight out from the body, imparting a more "cross-like" shape. Cooper's is distinctly longer-tailed.

Sharp-shinned Hawk is told from *Northern Goshawk* by its greatly smaller size and buoyant, unsteady, hurried flight characteristics; Goshawks appear stable in flight, even in strong winds. Adult Goshawks are distinctly gray above and whitish gray barred below. Juvenile Goshawks are superficially similar in plumage to Sharp-shinned Hawk, but Goshawk has dark chocolate, teardrop-shaped streaking below, often continuing through the undertail coverts. Goshawk has a pale upperwing bar formed by buffy markings on the upperwing coverts (Sharp-shinned sometimes has white spots on the upperwings), and a pale tawny nape, absent on Sharp-shinned. Goshawks' tail has wavy dark bands with pale highlights compared with the plainer banded tail shown by Sharp-shinned. The silhouettes of Sharp-shinned and Goshawk can be similar at a distance, but note Goshawk's distinctly broader body and back; longer, wider tail; and longer, broader wings that taper more sharply toward the tips.

Status and Distribution: Sharp-shinned Hawks are fairly common across most of the Lower 48 during migration, especially at raptor migration hotspots, and at winter backyard feeders, but they are shy and retiring breeders, rarely encountered by birders during summer. Sharp-shinneds winter primarily from the U.S.–Canada border to Central America. They breed from May through August in high-elevation coniferous forest and remote wood-land from Alaska through Canada, south into the Lower 48. Perhaps stable in North America, but their breeding areas are remote, creating difficult survey conditions. Recent migration counts at many sites show a general decline, but count numbers are difficult to assess because of many variables and biases. Unfortunately it, along with many other raptors, is still persecuted by humans in some areas for its bird-hunting habits.

Migration: Sharp-shinned Hawks are short- to long-distance migrants. Juveniles move somewhat earlier in fall (September) and later in spring (April through May). During migration, Sharp-shinned Hawks can be encountered almost anywhere, but the largest concentrations occur at raptor migration sites.

Considerable numbers can be seen in fall at Cape May Point, NJ, Hawk Mountain, PA, Hawk Ridge in Duluth, MN, Kiptopeke, VA, Wasatch Mountains, UT, Goshute Mountains, NV, Manzano Mountains, NM, Marin Headlands, CA, and Corpus Christie, TX. In spring, significant concentrations can be seen along the Great Lakes, the Atlantic Coast, and along the Rocky Mountain foothills. Peak fall migration period is mid-September to November; peak spring migration period is mid-April to mid-May.

Vocalizations: Typically silent away from breeding grounds; both sexes give an alarm call—the female's is slightly lower-pitched—a repeated, descending *kil, kil, kil, kil, kil.* Also gives a series of high-pitched "chirps" when agitated.

Cooper's Hawk *(Accipiter cooperii)* **COHA** page 48

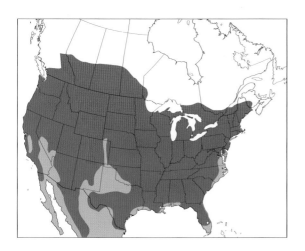

It's late September, and a group of birders has assembled on a ridgetop to watch the fall hawk migration. This is peak migration time for many raptors, an ideal chance to hone identification skills, and to compare species side by side. As the flight kicks into gear, hawks pass by consistently, sometimes at a rate of dozens per minute. Many of the accipiters are easily identified, showing all the characters typical of each species. But heated discussions arise about others. One bird in particular passes by at eye level, giving a view in which field marks and proportions are more difficult to judge. Did the head project far enough beyond the wrists? Was the tail long and rounded enough? Was it stable in flight? Honestly, it

was hard to tell! Some say they are confident it was a Cooper's, while others swear it was a "Sharpie." Who is correct, and how could one know with certainty? Each group makes its argument based on assessment of the traits essential for an accurate identification. But these traits are generally subjective, and opinions vary between observers! Regardless of how many books, articles, or information is published about accipiter identification, this age-old ID problem will never be put to rest. The truth is, it takes years of practice to gain the ability to accurately distinguish Sharp-shinned Hawks from Cooper's Hawks in the field...*lots of practice*! And even then, sometimes it's still impossible.

Overview: Cooper's Hawks are the most common nesting accipiter across much of the Lower 48, found in forest but also in more open, suburban habitats. Cooper's Hawks have always inhabited backyards with birdfeeders during winter, but they have now adapted to urban living year-round (especially in the West), sometimes using manmade structures for perches, and nesting in neighborhoods and parks and on golf courses, usually in large trees. Significant numbers of Cooper's Hawks occur at many hawk migration sites, where they can be frequently seen soaring and gliding. This is when their overall shape is best assessed.

Flight Style: Cooper's Hawks are steady fliers, adept at soaring, and they are also capable sprinters, bursting quickly into high-speed tail chases with dramatic twists and turns. They soar with wings held straight out from the neck, often with a slight dihedral (Sharp-shinned and Goshawk hold their wings flatter), and like all accipiters, glide on slightly bowed wings. Cooper's are often direct and steady in flight with stiffer, more powerful wingbeats than those of Sharp-shinned. Beware of Cooper's courtship display flight, which consists of slow, exaggerated, owl-like wingbeats, often causing it to be mistaken for Northern Goshawk. During courtship, all accipiters flare the undertail coverts outward, extending them beyond the base of the tail as a fluffy white triangle.

Size and Shape: L 37–47 cm (14–19 in), WS 70–87 cm (28–34 in), WT 302–678 g (10–24 oz)
Cooper's Hawk is a medium-sized hawk (about the size of a crow), larger than Sharp-shinned Hawk but smaller than Northern Goshawk. Female Cooper's are notably larger than males (as with most raptors, but particularly so in the accipiters). When identifying accipiters, use size with caution. Male Cooper's Hawk is only slightly larger than female Sharp-shinned Hawk; female Cooper's Hawk is only slightly smaller than male Goshawk. Cooper's Hawks from the West average smaller than those in the East, and western males are especially confused with Sharp-shinned Hawk.

Shape is generally a better indicator than size. Cooper's is rangier overall compared with the other accipiters, having proportionately longer, narrower wings. Its tail tip is usually rounded when closed, with a bold white tip, and is of generally even width throughout its length. Cooper's holds its wings nearly straight out from the body while soaring, accentuating its larger-headed appearance compared with Sharp-shinned. In fact, the head of Cooper's projects farther out from the wings than Sharp-shinned in all postures. Cooper's Hawks that are actively molting tail feathers or have worn tail feathers (mostly in spring) can exhibit square-tipped tails with little to no white at the tip. When perched, Cooper's Hawks appear medium-sized, but slim with a long tail.

Plumage: There are 2 distinct age classes of Cooper's Hawk that are easily distinguishable with sufficient views: adult and first-year (juvenile). Cooper's Hawks attain adult appearance after their first molt, which begins at about 1 year old. Some second-year birds, especially in the West, retain a few juvenile flight feathers that can be visible in the field under ideal conditions (high resolution photos!), but this is not a consistent plumage shared by all second-years.

Adults have rufous (on white) barring below, with bright white undertail coverts. Adults are blue-gray above with a blackish cap and a paler nape; adult Sharp-shinned Hawk lacks the paler nape and thus lacks a distinct cap. Adult males are typically more vibrant in color and more finely barred on the underparts, and have bluer upperwing coverts than females. Adult males have gray cheeks, but often have rufous cheeks in their second year, similar to most females. Adult males acquire dark blood-red eyes as they age; females have orange-red eyes even as older adults, rarely attaining eyes as dark as males; however, most second-year Cooper's of both sexes have orange-yellow eyes.

1st-years are whitish buff below with thin, chocolate-brown streaking, sometimes limited to the breast and upper belly. Cooper's Hawks typically show the least prominent streaking of the accipiters, but plumage varies among individuals, with some being heavily streaked throughout the underbody (especially in the West). The upperparts are brown to slate-brown with pale buff-rufous fringes on the back and upperwing coverts, and a contrastingly tawny head. The eyes are yellow-green (usually bright yellow in Sharp-shinned and Goshawk) turning yellow-orange by spring.

Geographic Variation: Monotypic, but western birds average smaller than eastern birds, and juveniles average more heavily marked underneath in the West.

Molt: Juveniles undergo their first molt mainly from May through August, after which they acquire adult plumage. In the second year, some birds retain a few juvenile rump feathers or upperwing coverts (worn, faded, and brownish), and a variable number of juvenile flight feathers, ranging from none to several throughout the wings and tail. Older adults typically molt from June through September, and often show 2 ages of adult flight feathers since they fail to complete a full molt each cycle, particularly birds from the West.

Similar Species: Cooper's Hawk is most easily confused with Sharp-shinned Hawk and Northern Goshawk. Cooper's is told from *Sharp-shinned Hawk* by its larger size, different shape, and slight plumage differences. Shape and flight style characteristics are more helpful than plumage in most cases, but plumage is often helpful on perched birds, especially when they are seen near backyard feeders. Cooper's Hawk is lankier overall, with longer, narrower wings and a longer, more broad-based tail than Sharp-shinned. In flight, the head of Cooper's projects farther out from the wings than Sharp-shinned in all postures. When soaring, Cooper's flies with a shallow dihedral, whereas almost all Sharp-shinneds hold their wings more level. The flight style of Cooper's is overall stable, with stiffer, more powerful wingbeats than Sharp-shinned. The white tail tip is typically broader on Cooper's, especially on fall birds in fresh plumage. Perched, Cooper's is square-headed and small-eyed, and adults of both sexes show a dark blackish gray cap and contrasting paler nape. Adult Sharp-shinned lacks the pale nape and capped effect shown by adult Cooper's.

Cooper's Hawk differs from *Northern Goshawk* by its smaller size and slimmer shape. The silhouettes are similar at a distance, but Goshawk has a distinctly broader body, tail, and back, with broader wings that are more tapered at the tips, and often pressed forward at the wrists when soaring and gliding. Plumage differences are more obvious on adults than on juveniles. Adult Goshawk is distinctive, with gray upperparts, a black head with a bold white eyeline, and gray-barred underparts. Juveniles are very similar in plumage to Cooper's, but Goshawk has broader, teardrop-shaped dark brown markings on the underbody, usually extending through the undertail coverts (very rare on Cooper's). The topside of juvenile Goshawk has pale (buff to tawny) mottling along the upperwing coverts (usually absent or white when present on Cooper's), a pale tawny nape, and a fairly distinct facial disklike pattern similar to a Harrier. The tail of Goshawk has wavy dark bands with pale highlights on top, lacking in both Sharp-shinned and Cooper's.

At times, Cooper's Hawk can appear similar in flight to *Northern Harrier* since the two are similar in size and both have long tails; however, Harrier has longer, narrower wings and a slimmer body, and it flies in a buoyant, teetering manner with deep, easy wingbeats.

Hybrids: Hybrid accipiters are rare, but there are 2 known records of Cooper's Hawk x Northern Goshawk hybrids, both captured in the East at raptor migration stations. Since Cooper's is undergoing a range expansion, it makes sense that it might pair with Northern Goshawk, and possibly even with Sharp-shinned Hawk on the northern periphery of its range. More study is needed to determine the extent of hybridization in accipiters, and distinguishing one given a typical field view would be nearly impossible.

Status and Distribution: Cooper's Hawk is fairly common overall, but much less common in the northern Unites States and essentially nonexistent north of south-central Canada. It winters widely throughout the breeding range, but withdraws from the northern limits and migrates as far south as Central America. Reports indicate that Cooper's are increasing, especially in the East and North. Recent migration counts at many sites show a general increase, but these numbers are difficult to assess because of the variable nature of hawk counts. Cooper's Hawk is still persecuted by humans in some areas for its bird-hunting habits.

Migration: Cooper's Hawk is a fairly common migrant at most hawk migration sites throughout the United States. The biggest fall concentrations occur along the East Coast and the Kittatinny Mountains, and in the West at the Marin Headlands, CA, and in the Intermountain West at the Goshutes, NV, from late September to early October. Spring migration occurs mainly from mid-March to early May, with the most significant concentrations found along the southern shore of Lake Ontario. Juveniles migrate earlier in fall and later is spring than adults, typically by a few weeks.

Vocalizations: Cooper's Hawk is generally silent away from the breeding grounds. Both sexes give an alarm call, with the female's being slightly lower-pitched: an even, husky, laughing *kek-kek-kek-kek-kek*; they also make a sapsucker-like mewing, sometimes heard on migration or in winter. Fledglings make a high-pitched, rising, whistled *sweeee* when begging for food.

Northern Goshawk *(Accipiter gentilis)* **NOGO** page 54

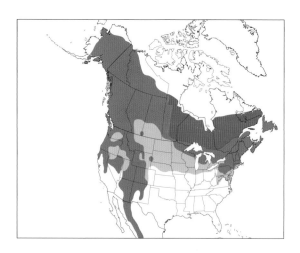

It's been a good summer. Easy living…just relaxing in the nest while Mom and Dad brought squirrels, woodpeckers, jays, and anything else they could find to keep me from begging. But now I'm an outcast, first pushed out of the nest, and now out of their territory. It's September and temperatures are falling. I need to figure out how to survive on my own. I'm well equipped though, at least based on what I've seen by Mom and Dad. Big and strong but also agile, built to outmaneuver prey, with long, powerful talons: everything I need to make it in this world. But putting to use what I've got is a whole 'nother ball game.

I take a breath, shuffle nervously on my perch, and settle into the hunt. I'm alert now, piercing eyes scanning the boreal forest for any sign of movement. A young Ruffed Grouse ambles out into view below. Instinct kicks in, and I bob my head excitedly, zeroing in on its position. I can do this. I drop silently from my perch, and with a few quick wingbeats I'm barreling straight for it, rapidly closing the distance, using my long tail to maneuver through small openings in the forest as I descend. I break into the clearing just feet from the ground; the Grouse finally sees me, leaps in a panic, and I bank sharp left, slam on the brakes…Wham! We fall together to the ground in a heap of feathers and dirt. I immediately realize the grouse is no match for my power, and it goes quietly, quickly. I'm the baddest thing in this forest now. I can get used to this…

Overview: Northern Goshawk is a powerful predator that nests in boreal and high-elevation mixed forest (usually conifers) across northern and western North America. Goshawk is notoriously aggressive toward humans and other intruders that approach its nest. Its fierce demeanor is legendary, causing some researchers to require helmets and leather jackets to avoid talon strikes while working near Goshawk nests. It is the largest and scarcest of the North American accipiters, making it much sought after by birders—a perfect recipe for frequent misidentification. It is seldom encountered, usually staying hidden in the forest. At a few hawk migration sites, it can occasionally be seen in good numbers with other migrant hawks. Goshawk moves south into the Lower 48 and U.S.–Canada border region in numbers roughly every 10 years in response to prey population cycles. Unlike the other accipiters, Goshawk eats mainly mammals, including squirrels and hares, but is equally adept at chasing birds such as Flickers, Jays, and other birds of similar size. Grouse, ptarmigan, and birds larger than itself are also fair game, occasionally pursued into the thickets on foot!

Flight Style: In flight, Goshawk is steady and powerful with wingbeats that are stiffer, more labored, and more elevated on the upstroke than the similar Cooper's Hawk. Male Goshawks have quicker wingbeats than females, making them trickier to distinguish from Cooper's, but usually the wingbeats are slower than other accipiters, giving Goshawks a somewhat buteo-like appearance when flapping. Goshawks soar with wings held flat and glide on gently bowed wings.

Size and Shape: L 53–66 cm (18–24 in), WS 102–117 cm (38–45 in), WT 677–1214 g (24–43 oz) Northern Goshawk is a large bird; females approach the size and bulk of a Red-tailed Hawk, but males are significantly smaller and can be confused with female Cooper's Hawk. Cooper's Hawks (and sometimes even Sharp-shinned Hawks) can be perceived as large in the field, so great care should be taken when judging accipiters by impression of size alone. Wing shape is often a good feature for separating Goshawk from Cooper's and Sharp-shinned Hawks. The wings of Goshawk are broad but tapered toward the tips, appearing stocky in a soar and more falcon-like in a glide. Males have slimmer, more tapered wings than females, especially in adults, but this can be difficult to notice without practice. Juveniles show a gentler S-shaped trailing edge to the wing, and a more prominent wedge-shaped tail. The tail of Goshawk is very long and fairly broad, but when closed its tip can be rounded, wedge-shaped, or squared. All Goshawks have broad chests, and when viewed head-on, they have a bulky profile.

Plumage: Northern Goshawk shows 2 age classes: juvenile and adult. *Adult* Northern Goshawks of both sexes are pale grayish white below with faint, dark barring on the underbody. The flight feathers are slightly darker, sometimes creating a two-toned appearance below, but adults generally appear pale overall in flight. The head and body can appear bright white in direct sunlight. *Adult males* are bluish above with darker flight feathers and slightly more vibrant in color than *adult females*, which are more uniformly gray-blue above; rarely, females are slaty-brown above. All adults lack mottling on the upperwings. In spring when birds have faded plumage, the bluish upperside of Goshawk can appear very pale in certain instances (direct sunlight), especially on males. The head on both sexes of adult Goshawk is blackish with a bold white eyebrow. *2nd-year* birds may be more coarsely barred with blackish below than older adults, and usually have orange to orange-red eyes that get progressively darker red with age, especially males. Many retain a varying number of juvenile body and flight feathers, but they are often indistinguishable from older adults in the field.

1st-year (juvenile) Goshawk is buff below with broad chocolate brown streaking continuing through the undertail coverts and buff-mottled underwing coverts. Most are heavily streaked, but some are more lightly streaked and can appear paler overall underneath. Almost all juvenile Goshawks have streaking or barring on the undertail coverts, but this is often difficult to see on flying birds, especially distant ones. Juveniles have pale-fringed upperwing coverts, scapulars, and mantle, typically showing pale mottling along the upperwing coverts that forms a narrow buffy "bar" when seen at a distance from above. Some Cooper's Hawks may show mottling or fading (in spring) on the upperwings, but it is rarely as prominent as on Goshawk, and it generally appears as distinct white spots and not a tawny buff wing bar. Juvenile Goshawks have pale cheeks (along with the pale eyebrow), which can

make them look pale-headed in the field. Juveniles often have a prominent Harrier-like facial disk, unlike other accipiters. The tail has brownish and black bands, often with thin, pale, wavy lines separating the bands, and a bold white tip. The eye is yellow, or more rarely orange-yellow.

Geographic Variation: There are 4 described subspecies in North America, and up to 7 worldwide. North American forms include *atricapillus* of the boreal forest, *striatulus* in western North America, *laingi* in coastal British Columbia (Queen Charlotte Islands), and *apache* in mountains of the Southwest. Differences among the subspecies are marginal, though, and most authorities now recognize just 1 form in North America, *A. g. atricapillus*, with clinal geographic variation. Size generally decreases from southwest to northwest (Queen Charlotte Islands birds average smallest), and dorsal coloration is darkest in the Southwest and Pacific Northwest.

Molt: Juveniles undergo their first molt during the first spring and summer, after which they acquire adult plumage, but they often retain a varying number of juvenile body and flight feathers that help identify them as second-year birds. Montane breeders in western states and Canada on average retain more juvenile feathers through the second year. Adults molt once a year from April through November, but almost always retain feathers from the previous year.

Similar Species: Adult Northern Goshawk is fairly distinctive, but juveniles are frequently misidentified, or perhaps over-identified by eager birders. Juvenile Goshawk is most often confused with juvenile *Cooper's Hawk* (especially females), and to a much lesser extent with Sharp-shinned Hawk. Northern Goshawk is heavily built for an accipiter, and is stockier overall with broader wings that show more tapered hands than those of Cooper's Hawk. Goshawk soars on flatter wings (Cooper's often soars with a dihedral) and displays heavier wingbeats. When gliding, Goshawk droops its wings slightly more than Cooper's, giving Goshawk a longer-handed look, a trait that can be seen at eye level. On perched birds, note Goshawk's rather small-headed look, accentuated by its broad shoulders; Cooper's is more slimly built. The buff-mottled upperwings of juvenile Goshawk are unique, but beware of white spotting or mottling on some Cooper's and Sharp-shinned Hawks. Goshawk also tends to have a tawny nape and Harrier-like facial disk. If the upperside of the tail can be clearly seen, look for the wavy, uneven banding of Goshawk with pale "highlights," compared with the more evenly banded tails of Cooper's and Sharp-shinned.

Goshawk is also confused with *buteos* such as juvenile Broad-winged and Red-shouldered Hawk in flight because of its size and stocky structure. But the wings of Goshawk are broader and more tapered at the tips compared with the straighter trailing edge of buteos. The tail of Goshawk is significantly longer, and truly accipiter-like. Juvenile Goshawk is almost always more heavily marked underneath than juvenile Broad-winged and Red-shouldered Hawk, especially the underwing coverts.

Adult Goshawk is similar in shape and plumage to *adult gray-morph Gyrfalcon*. Both are grayish above and pale below, but Goshawk shows a blackish head, white eyebrow, and darker back. Gyrfalcon always shows longer wings that taper to a sharper point, with black tips to the outer primaries. The wingbeats of Gyrfalcon are stiffer and shallower and more continuous than those of Goshawk.

Hybrids: Accipiter hybrids are exceptional, but 2 known Goshawk x Cooper's Hawk hybrids have been documented, both captured during fall migration: one in Tennessee and one in Pennsylvania.

Status and Distribution: Goshawk is generally uncommon to scarce in most areas. It is a northern breeder in the East, typically not seen south of Pennsylvania during summer, but is known to nest throughout the mountainous areas of the western states. Across the boreal forest, it is widespread but never dense, and like many of the boreal forest predators, birders can cover hundreds of miles without seeing one.

Migration: Some Goshawks are year-round residents (especially adults), but many migrate south, and mid- to high-elevation nesting birds move to lower elevations. Goshawk migration takes place mainly from February to May in spring, and October to December in fall. In the eastern half of its range, Goshawk invades into the south roughly every 10 years, when large numbers pass relatively few northern hawk watches in fall. Hawk Ridge in Duluth, MN, sees the biggest Goshawk flights in North America. The Goshute Mountains, NV, are also a significant site for Goshawk. As a spring migrant, it is most easily observed at hawk-watch sites along the southern shores of the Great Lakes and at some mountainous western sites.

At most sites, seasonal totals for Goshawks number in the tens, with some sites counting birds in the low hundreds during good years. Invasion years can bring thousands past Duluth and increase numbers elsewhere; indeed, Duluth has counted more than 1000 birds in a day during peak migration on invasion years! Peak years at Duluth were 1972 (4963), 1982 (5819), 1992 (2040), 2000 (1101), and 2001 (1107). The 10-year annual cycle held up well in the '70s, '80s, and '90s, but then shifted up a few years in the 2000s with peak numbers in 2000 and 2001.

Vocalizations: Goshawks are quite vocal on the breeding grounds, giving a loud, screaming *kak-kak-kak…* when disturbed or territorial. The call is slower, harsher, and deeper than that of Cooper's.

Red-tailed Hawk *(Buteo jamaicensis)* **RTHA** page 60

Red-tailed Hawk *(Buteo jamaicensis)* **RTHA** page 60

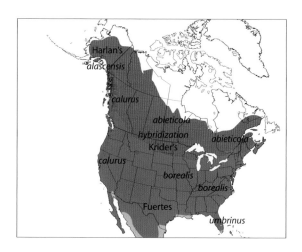

A stiff west wind blows perpendicular to the long ridgeline disappearing on the horizon. Ominous gray snow squalls drift across the wintry sky, and intermittent sunbeams slowly roam patches of open country in the distance. It's November here on the ridgetop, and I can't escape the arctic wind. I'm buffeted, chilled, and need to take cover behind the tallest boulder just to hold my binoculars steady.

I scan the bumpy horizon, pan slowly across the skyline…not a bird in sight. The conditions are right for birds to move today, but these late November flights are made up of the "big birds": Red-tails, Red-shoulders, Goshawks, eagles, and a few Rough-legged Hawks. These big birds are fickle; they don't get up early…they wait for the air to warm up, and for lift to become optimal. It's 11 a.m., and my toes are freezing, nose running, body quivering, glasses fogging—why am I still here? Any normal person would be long gone, warm under a blanket, next to a fireplace. But I stick it out because the reward of a parade of Red-tails can't be seen from my living room…only up here on the mountain.

A distant bird, a mere speck, finally comes into view. It's gliding southwest along the spine of the ridge, approaching slowly, but it hasn't moved a muscle in doing so, not a single flap, tilt, or adjustment despite the strong wind—giving no hint of what it could be. But wait, these are all good clues to its identification…stable in flight even in these strong winds, and not a big flapper. These traits suggest an eagle, but it appears too small and stocky for that. As it approaches, its slightly bowed, broad wings and wide chest become more apparent. The bird, once a dot on

the horizon, now glides directly overhead and a full suite of field marks are revealed: dark patagial marks and wrist commas, distinct bellyband, and reddish backlit tail. Adult Red-tailed Hawk—no doubt about it. Others like it materialize over distant knolls, and soon a procession of birds is heading my way. The steady west wind creates a constant source of lift for these southbound travelers, allowing mile after mile of nearly effortless flight. I find a nook between some rocks and settle in as one after another passes by. The cold wind and snow squalls are now just an afterthought…all of a sudden I'm feelin' warm.

Overview: The Red-tailed Hawk is perhaps the most common and familiar raptor in North America, and a favorite among birders. Even nonbirders recognize their voice, as Red-tailed Hawks are stars among birds; Hollywood chooses to play their primeval scream in the background of every movie or commercial that even remotely relates to nature. Found in a wide variety of open and semiopen habitats, Red-tails are frequently encountered along roadsides, where their hulking form is hard to miss. Red-tails usually hunt in clearings, weedy fields, semiopen woodland, and agricultural areas, but are much less common in tracts of extensive woodland, where they exploit openings in the forest or boggy areas.

Red-tailed Hawks are generalists, in terms of both the habitats they occupy and the animals on which they prey. Small rodents are typical prey items, but Red-tails also take birds, reptiles, and just about anything else of like size that makes itself visible. Red-tails hunt efficiently from the air, often hovering and kiting from mid- to high elevation, as well as from a perch, typically a roadside power pole or tree. They can also stoop at high speeds to surprise, flush, or overtake prey.

Although they show great variation in plumage, the vast majority of them look very similar, and becoming familiar with Red-tailed Hawks is greatly helpful toward identification of other buteos, since it is a good baseline against which to compare other raptor species. In many areas the typical light-morph is most widespread and common. The greatest diversity of variation is found on the southern Great Plains during winter and in western Canada during the breeding season.

Flight Style: Red-tailed Hawks are stable in flight, even while aloft in strong winds. They soar in wide circles on a slight dihedral and glide on flattish to slightly bowed wings, when they appear particularly stocky. In a glide, the wingtips protrude slightly past the trailing edge of the wings, but project well past the trailing edge in a steep glide. The wingbeats are stiff and somewhat shallow, but fluid and notably heavy when compared with those of smaller buteos. Juveniles typically have "floppier" wingbeats than adults, accentuated by their longer, narrower wings. Smaller Red-tails often have quicker wingbeats than larger ones, and this can be obvious at times.

Size and Shape: L 45–55 cm (17–22 in), WS 110–141 cm (43–56 in), WT 710–1740 g (1.5–3.8 lb)
Red-tailed Hawk is the quintessential buteo, smaller than an eagle, but a good bit larger than many buteos, including Broad-winged, Gray, and Red-shouldered Hawks. Adult Red-tailed Hawks are stoutly built, with broad wings and relatively short, rounded tails. Juveniles are rangier overall with narrower wings, longer tails, and a more exaggerated dihedral. Red-tailed Hawks in the West are longer-winged than in the East, with Harlan's being the most variable in shape; some look compact overall and similar to Eastern, whereas others are lankier overall, and built more like Westerns. Regardless, subspecies are impossible to determine based on wing shape alone, since Red-tailed Hawks can vary in shape between individuals. When perched, Red-tails are bulky and the wingtips do not reach the tail tip.

Plumage: Red-tailed Hawk is probably the most variably plumaged raptor in North America, with adults ranging from completely blackish below to nearly completely white (see Geographic Variation). Despite this, across the majority of its range, most Red-tailed Hawks are light-morphs, showing the classic field marks for the species, including dark patagial bars and heavy bellyband, and on adults, a red tail. That said, in terms of plumage variation there is a complete cline from light to dark (even within certain subspecies), but most birds are easily assigned to either light-morph or dark-morph, based on their general appearance.

Red-tails have 2 ages, adult and juvenile, but the sexes are similar. They attain adult appearance by the second fall, but they very often retain 3–4 outer primaries and a few secondaries (which are browner and faded), sometimes rendering these second-year birds identifiable in the field. Spring birds have notably faded heads and often uppersides (especially on the Great Plains), causing potential confusion when trying to identify individuals to subspecies (especially Krider's).

Adults have completely red tails with multiple black bands or lack tail bands altogether (tail can be whitish to blackish in Harlan's), dark eyes, a dark well-defined trailing edge to the wings, often a golden head that contrasts with the brown upperside, and a streaked or barred bellyband. The eye color may take several years to change.

1st-years (juveniles) have brownish tails with narrow blackish brown bands, a poorly defined dusky trailing edge to the wings, pale squarish wing panels on the upperside of the outer primaries, pale yellow eyes, and often mottling on upperwings and scapulars. Juveniles show a brown head and streaked bellyband.

Geographic Variation: The Red-tailed Hawk is widespread across North America, Central America, and the Caribbean, occupying a diverse array of habitats, and as such has developed substantial geographic plumage variation. Overall there are roughly 15 subspecies, 7 of which occur in North America. There are 3 main groups: Eastern (*B. j. borealis*), Western (*B. j. calurus*), and Harlan's (*B. j. harlani*) are generally distinctive, and in most cases identifying birds as belonging to one of these groups is relatively straightforward, but some individuals are impossible to identify to subspecies. Krider's (*B. j. kriderii*) is likely a subspecies in transition, now mixing with Eastern, Western, and Harlan's, its characteristics so muddied that only the most extreme birds are identifiable to subspecies. We treat it here with Eastern, as it most closely resembles that subspecies in most plumage features, and most often intergrades with it on the northern Great Plains. All other races in North America are indistinct in plumage from Eastern and Western, and are possibly just variations of these races. Subspecies differences are marginal on juveniles but more apparent on adults.

Eastern birds are known to occur only as light morphs (but data on boreal forest breeders throughout Canada are very limited); Western and Harlan's occur as light or dark morphs with a continuum of plumages between them. Dark morphs do occur within the Eastern range during migration and winter, but these are likely vagrant birds of western origin. Intergradation between the 3 main subspecies occurs in many areas where ranges bump up against each other. There is little variation from the eastern edge of the Great Plains eastward compared with west of the Great Plains.

The Alaska race (*B. j. alascensis*), Fuertes race (*B. j. fuertesi*), and Florida race (*B. j. umbrinus*) are the other proposed races in North America. Little is known of *alascensis*. It is presumably an uncommon resident or short-distance migrant through southeast coastal Alaska and northwest British Columbia. It is generally more rufous below than typical light-morph Westerns, but often impossible to distinguish from Westerns that occur from northern Washington to British Columbia. So far as is known, the Alaska subspecies occurs only as a light morph. It is possible *alascensis* is simply a form of the Western race, but more study is needed to determine this. Fuertes is a common resident from southern Arizona to southern Texas north through Oklahoma. It is characterized by its minimal or lack of a bellyband, and a faint rufous wash to the leggings and underwing coverts. Fuertes overlaps greatly in plumage and range with the Eastern and Western races, but is possibly a form of the Eastern subspecies rather than a distinct subspecies. The Florida race is uncommon within peninsular Florida. It is heavily marked underneath and often has multiple tail bands similar to those of many Western birds. Little is known about the extent of its plumage variation, or its exact range, and more study is needed.

Eastern birds breeding across much of their range are characterized by buffy undersides, lightly marked underwings and bellybands, whitish throats (often), and a red tail with few to no bands. Juveniles often have a light to moderately marked bellyband, lightly marked underwings, and pale throats. The form known as *abieticola*, breeding across the boreal forest of Canada, is usually considered a form of the Eastern race that often shows more heavily marked undersides, a dark throat, and multiple tail bands, but more study is needed on this enigmatic and scarce form. *Abieticola* from western Canada may be Eastern x Western intergrades, as they are difficult to identify to race, and they occur within the range of both subspecies.

Krider's *(B. j. kriderii)* has been lumped with Eastern in most literature, but it is generally distinctive. Krider's is an uncommon breeder on the northern Great Plains from central Alberta to South Dakota, and winters mainly from the southern Great Plains to the Mississippi River Delta and the Gulf Coast. Krider's is rare in winter across the Southeast to Florida. Characterized by a striking overall white appearance, adults often show a mostly white head and tail (often with pinkish tip), and nearly unmarked underparts, with very faint patagial marks and bellybands, and extensive white mottling on the upperwings. Juveniles have whitish tails with narrow dark bands. Krider's has yet to be documented west of the Rocky Mountains, so consider a Red-tailed Hawk west of the Rockies with a whitish tail likely to be a light-morph Harlan's. Harlan's are often darker-headed, with whitish cheeks and supercilium. They are dark brown on top and lack mottling on the upperwing coverts. Juvenile Harlan's and Krider's can be nearly identical and are distinguished with great care in the field.

Western Red-tail is extremely variable in plumage, occurring in light (common) and dark morph (about 10% of the overall population) with a multitude of variation between. Typical *light-morph adult Westerns* are characterized by a rufous-tinted ground color, heavily marked underwings and bellyband, broad patagial bars, darkish throat, and a red tail, often with multiple black bands. Western birds with lightly marked bellies and underwing coverts can still exhibit broad patagial bars and dark throats. Juvenile light morphs often have a streaked throat and heavily marked undersides. Western light morphs do not approach the pale extreme of Eastern, but there are many Westerns that are inseparable from Easterns. Previous literature considers dark-morph adults with slightly paler rufous-brown chests or juveniles with fully streaked underbodies to be "rufous-morphs" (or "intermediate-morphs"), but here we lump those with dark morphs, as they are dark overall.

Dark-morph adult Westerns are dark brown on the belly and underwing coverts, with a dark rufous-brown chest that is slightly paler than the belly. A small percentage (5–10%) of dark-morph adults are uniformly brown underneath. Juveniles are heavily streaked underneath, sometimes with slightly less prominent streaking on the chest, or solid brownish on the underbody. Both types of dark-morph adults and juveniles can appear uniformly dark at a distance. The flight feathers and tail patterns of light and dark morphs are similar.

Harlan's Red-tails have the most highly variable

plumage of any of the subspecies, with a complete cline from ghostly white to completely black below. Unlike the other subspecies, where light morphs predominate, light-morph Harlan's make up only about 12% of the population. Most Harlan's are dark-morph types with white mottling on the chest. Completely dark birds underneath are less common.

Adult Harlan's are particularly distinctive, and best identified by their uniquely patterned tail, often having whitish, grayish, brownish, or blackish mottling or streaking versus the typical even, transverse banding shown by other subspecies. Some adult Harlan's show an almost completely reddish tail with limited mottling at the base, making them difficult to distinguish from other subspecies (these may be intergrades). Dark-morph adult Harlan's usually have grayish or whitish tails with a broad, blackish, smudgy tip. A few dark adults have black-and-white banded tails, but these are uncommon, and many may actually represent intergrades with Western or Eastern Red-tails. Adult light-morph Harlan's often have whitish or grayish tails with a broad, blackish or rufous tip. Many adult Harlan's (especially light morphs) lack banding in the secondaries and primaries; this absence is very rare on other races. Juvenile Harlan's have a whitish yellow eye that changes to the adult brown more slowly than in the other races.

Dark-morph adult Harlan's are blackish or brownish on the underbody with white mottling on the chest. Often, they are whitish on the throat or crown, unlike Western adult dark morphs. Solid dark types are generally blackish overall, but some can be brownish and virtually identical to Westerns. Some adult dark-morph Harlan's have a rufous chest similar to dark-morph Westerns. Dark-morph Harlan's show several traits lacked by dark-morph Westerns, such as whitish throats and white-streaked heads. A few adult Harlan's show white spots on the leading edge of the wings near the neck, and they are the only dark buteo known to do so.

Dark-morph juveniles range from being completely streaked below, mostly blackish or brownish with variably streaked white breasts, to solidly dark underneath. Like adults, juvenile Harlan's can be black on the underbody, but most are otherwise brownish and generally indistinguishable from Westerns by body plumage alone. Although juvenile dark-morph Harlan's are similar to Westerns, they are often distinguished by other traits such as these: the outer primaries are banded at the tips; the tail bands are broader, usually wavy, and with unique white spots on the inner webs that give the tips a "spiked" look; the upperwing coverts and primaries are more "spangled" black and white and generally more bold and extensively patterned; and the head and throat are often white-streaked. Note that other races can have wavy tail bands, but they lack the white spots on the tips shown by Harlan's.

Light-morph Harlan's are strikingly snow-white below, with only some showing buffy underwing and leg feathers. They often have well-demarcated, moderately marked bellybands, appearing much like Easterns in this respect. The uppersides of all morphs of adult Harlan's are dark brown to slate-brown (usually darker than Eastern and Western) with white mottling limited to the scapulars. The head often shows white markings around the eyes and white streaking on the crown, with some having lots of white in the head, making Harlan's confusable with Krider's, especially whitish-tailed Harlan's; however, adult Harlan's of all morphs lack the extensive whitish mottling and rufous tones on the upperwings shown by Krider's. Also, adult Harlan's rarely lack a bellyband. Juvenile light-morph Harlan's have whitish wing panels and often extensive white mottling along the upperwing coverts, also appearing Krider's-like at times. But juvenile Krider's often have a whitish tail with narrow, dark bands throughout and show a buffy wash (not snow-white) to the underside; the tail of juvenile light-morph Harlan's is usually brownish gray in ground color, and either has bold, dark banding or is partially or fully mottled, similar to adults.

Molt: Because of its large size, the Red-tailed Hawk does not typically undergo a complete molt each year. Juveniles begin their first molt in the spring and continue into early fall. They usually replace P 1–7, and most of the secondaries in the first wing molt, but occasionally birds can molt all their flight feathers in one molt period. All, or nearly all, the body feathers are replaced as well. Once adult, Red-tails undergo an incomplete molt annually, usually occurring from spring to fall, but it can be suspended during breeding. Some flight feathers can be grown during migration and winter, especially in western populations. Adults usually have multiple visible generations of adult flight feathers in the primaries and secondaries. The timing and extent of molt vary between populations, generally with northern birds retaining more feathers than southern birds.

Similar Species: Since Red-tailed Hawk is generally the default identification for birders unsure of a large raptor, almost every other hawk around is mistaken for it! No other adult light-morph buteo shows a combination of dark patagial bars and a brick-red tail, but these things are not always easily visible in the field. Rufous and dark-morph Red-tailed Hawks, especially juveniles, are more easily confused with other buteos. Certain plumage features usually separate Red-tail from other similar buteos, but wing shape and flight style are often the key to distinguishing birds in the field.

Adult light-morph *Ferruginous Hawk* can have a reddish tail, but only rarely does it approach being fully red. Regardless, the rufous upperwing coverts, whitish primary panels, and dark rusty leg feathers of adult Ferruginous Hawk are not shown by adult Red-tails. Juvenile light-morph Ferruginous Hawks can look similar in plumage to Red-tailed Hawks from below, especially Krider's. Juvenile Ferruginous can have dark spotting on the lower belly and sides, but they lack a full bellyband and dark patagials, appearing particularly white underneath. They also have a white tail base and whitish primary panels above, but these are darker on the upperwing coverts and scapulars. Also note, Ferruginous Hawk has longer and more pointed wings than Red-tailed, with a bulkier body, and smoother, more languid wingbeats. Ferruginous usually glides and soars with a distinct modified dihedral, whereas Red-tail has a shallow dihedral. Ferruginous are also more buoyant and teetering in flight.

Dark-morph Ferruginous Hawks are similar in plumage to dark-morph Red-tailed Hawks, but dark Ferruginous never show reddish tails and often have pale primary panels. They also lack heavily banded flight feathers and show a faint dark trailing edge to the wings and limited black on the primary tips, making their wings look fairly whitish below.

Swainson's Hawk is often confused with Red-tailed Hawk. All Swainson's Hawks have dark flight feathers and slimmer, more pointed wings. They are also more buoyant and teetering in flight, and typically hold their wings in a stronger dihedral. From above, all Swainson's lack mottling on the upperwings and scapulars; juveniles can have pale-fringed coverts, but they do not have the pale mottling shown by Red-tails. Dark morphs are similar between the two, but dark Swainson's still have dark flight feathers, unlike Red-tail.

Red-tailed Hawk is told from *Rough-legged Hawk* by its stockier build in all postures. Rough-legged Hawks have slimmer wings and a slightly longer tail, making them more Harrier-like in structure than Red-tailed. They also fly with a modified dihedral or pronounced dihedral, and are more buoyant and teetering in flight than Red-tail. Light-morph Rough-legged Hawks (except some adult males) have a solid blackish belly and carpal (wrist) patches, and more lightly banded flight feathers. They also show a white-based tail with a dark distal half. Dark-morph Rough-legged and Red-tailed Hawks are similar in plumage, but Rough-legged often shows a dark brown body with blacker belly and carpals, never shows an orange-rufous chest, and the tail is never wholly reddish like that of adult Red-tail. Many adult dark-morph Rough-leggeds actually have a blackish tail with several bold white bands, and juvenile dark-morph Rough-leggeds essentially lack banding on the tail.

At a distance, Red-tailed Hawk can be confused with *Golden Eagle*, especially juvenile dark morphs; however, Red-tail is always stockier in build with shorter wings and tail and a smaller head. Red-tail never shows the white wing patches of immature Golden Eagles, or the dark flight feathers shown by all Golden Eagles. Golden Eagles soar in slow, lazy circles with a prominent dihedral, as opposed to the tighter-soaring, flatter-winged Red-tailed. The wingbeats of Red-tailed Hawks are also faster and stiffer than the labored wingbeats of Golden Eagles.

Hybrids. Red-tailed Hawk hybrids are rare, but Red-tails have hybridized with Red-shouldered Hawk in the Northeast, and Ferruginous and Swainson's Hawk in the West. Records of Harlan's Red-tailed Hawk x Rough-legged Hawk exist as well. There are also reports of Harris's Hawk breeding with Red-tailed Hawk.

Status and Distribution: Red-tailed Hawk is common throughout most of its broad range, from Alaska to the East Coast to Central America. The Canadian Great Plains to the western Canada/Alaska boreal region is a melting pot where Eastern, Western, Krider's, and Harlan's meet and interbreed, producing intergrades that are impossible to classify to subspecies with certainty. Eastern and Western Red-tailed Hawks have been documented in central Alaska on migration, and one Eastern to date has been documented breeding there with a Harlan's. The true status of Red-tailed Hawk subspecies in the

Northwest is yet to be determined, and more study is needed in these remote regions.

The Eastern race is a widespread breeder from the East Coast to the east side of the Rocky Mountains from Texas and as far north as Alaska. The exact extent of its northwestern range is unknown. Eastern birds winter mainly in the United States and parts of southern Canada and northern Mexico. The Eastern race is seen throughout most of North America on migration but is rare in Alaska and west of the Rocky Mountains.

Western Red-tailed Hawks are common across much of the West, from the Pacific Coast east to the western Great Plains, south to New Mexico and north to southern Alaska. They winter mainly in the western United States and Mexico, east to Texas, and sparingly into the Mississippi River Valley and the Gulf Coast states. They are rare visitors to the East Coast and Alaska on migration, but are regular in the western Great Lakes region, and rare in the eastern Great Lakes region during migration.

Never common, Harlan's Red-tailed Hawks are widely scattered and somewhat scarce (perhaps just well-spaced away from roads) throughout their massive breeding range from western Alaska through the Yukon, Northwest Territories, and northern Alberta. Light-morph Harlan's were recently discovered breeding in the Turtle Mountains, ND, on the border with Canada, but the extent to which they breed on the northern Great Plains is still unknown. So far only light morphs are known in summer from the northern Great Plains. They winter in small pockets throughout the West, but are most common on the southern Great Plains in winter (still relatively uncommon in comparison to other subspecies), becoming rare toward the Mississippi River delta. A few reach the Southeast, and rarely, Florida. Legitimate records in the Northeast are surprisingly few. They are very rare visitors to the East Coast during fall migration with records from Cape May, NJ, and Kiptopeke, VA.

Migration: In spring, Red-tailed Hawk migration takes place mainly from March to May, and from October to December in fall. Northern populations augment residents across the Lower 48 during fall and winter. Large movements of Red-tails are noted at Great Lakes hawk watches in fall such as Hawk Ridge, MN, Lake Erie Metropark, MI, and Hawk Cliff, ON; and in spring at Derby Hill, NY, Braddock Bay, NY, Whitefish Point, MI, and Brockway Mountain, MI. Large concentrations of Red-tails are seen through the northern Great Plains, such as at the Pembina Valley hawk watch in southwest Manitoba, and along western mountain ranges, such as the east and west sides of the Rocky Mountains, the Goshute Range, NV, and the Cascade Range along the West Coast. But much of the West is still to be explored in regard to Red-tailed Hawk migration sites. Moderate numbers move down the Appalachian ridges in fall at places such as Hawk Mountain and Bake Oven Knob, PA, and along the East Coast. The Harlan's race of the Red-tailed Hawk is scarce at most migration sites, but several thousand can be seen at Gunsight Mountain, AK, in April. In fall, notable numbers of Harlan's move through the Yukon, especially at Teslin Lake migration watch.

Vocalizations: Red-tailed Hawks are generally silent away from the nesting territory, but sometimes call during encounters with other raptors on migration or in winter. The raspy, loud *krréeeeeerrr* call can be heard in the background of innumerable Hollywood movies and commercials, frequently behind an image of a Bald Eagle or other species! Juveniles give a high-pitched repeated begging *whee, whee, whee, whee.*

Swainson's Hawk *(Buteo swainsoni)* SWHA page 70

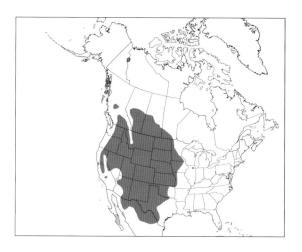

It's mid-September, time to think about moving on for a pair of Swainson's Hawks that have made an Alberta prairie their summer home. Winter transforms this land into an icy, frigid province, and the resources that allowed the adults to raise a brood of three young are all but exhausted now, forcing the family to move south. They are heading far away, in search of a similar habitat on another continent and in another hemisphere. Over the course of the next two months they will travel more than 7000 miles, chasing the summer they have left behind in the North. Along the way they'll gather with thousands of their own kind, soaring high on thermals generated by the warm tropical sun. They'll move south across the Great Plains, through Texas, then coastal Mexico, across Panama, and finally over the high Andes down into the verdant grassland of Argentina. A long journey lies ahead, but the pair will be back here next spring to raise another family and start the cycle again. The pair soar higher over the barren prairie, set their wings, and head south…the northern prairie drifting away behind them.

Overview: Swainson's Hawks are birds of western open country, nesting in a wide variety of habitats, including grassland, agricultural areas, riparian corridors, and scattered pinyon-juniper woodland. They typically nest in large trees with a broad expanse of surrounding open country, but they can also be found in relatively treeless expanses of prairie, and in these places they can nest in very small trees or on power poles, even on the ground in rare cases. Swainson's Hawks are territorial on the breeding

grounds, but forage over shared territories where densities are high. They capture mainly rodents and insects but also eat small birds.

Swainson's Hawks tend to congregate outside the breeding season in places where foraging resources are plentiful, and they can be abundant around active agricultural areas, especially flooded fields (particularly alfalfa) where mice are forced out of their burrows in search of drier ground. It is not uncommon to see large groups on the ground and following tilling tractors that turn up rodents and insects. During migration and winter they are also gregarious, forming large groups, with kettles of thousands occurring in Texas and at points farther south (e.g., Veracruz, Mexico; Panama) during migration.

Flight Style: Swainson's Hawks are elegant, amazing aerialists with an incredibly light, buoyant flight. They teeter from side to side in Harrier-like fashion in strong winds, but can be surprisingly flat-winged in lighter winds. They flap somewhat like a Harrier as well, having deep, easy wingbeats, but usually with more stiffness and power. Adults especially can flap with shallower, almost Red-tailed Hawk-like wingbeats. Swainson's Hawks spend lots of time in the air, especially in windy conditions, when they hover and kite at medium height while hunting. Swainson's Hawks soar with a slight to strong dihedral, but glide with a modified dihedral. When the bird glides at eye level, the wings appear drooped and Osprey-like, but are shorter and more pointed.

Size and Shape: L 43–55 cm (17–22 in), WS 120–137 cm (47–54 in), WT 595–1240 g (1.3–2.7 lb) Swainson's Hawks are large buteos, similar in size to Red-tailed Hawk, but with slimmer wings that appear pointed at all times. Their wing shape is most similar to that of Broad-winged Hawk, but is overall longer and more elegant. When they glide overhead, the wingtips of Swainson's Hawks appear very falcon-like, projecting well past the back edge of the wings, creating an M-shaped silhouette. Juveniles are slightly lankier overall than subadults and adults because of their narrower wings, especially evident in the secondaries. Juveniles also have slightly longer tails than adults.

Plumage: Unlike many large buteos, Swainson's

Hawks take 2 full years to acquire adult plumage and have 3 distinct age classes: first-year (juvenile), second-year (subadult), and adult. The first- and second-year sexes are identical, but adult sexes can differ slightly in plumage, though there is some overlap. Swainson's Hawks have a complete range of plumages from light to dark below, with many having a strong rufous component to the body and underwings. We've simplified this variation into 3 categories below: light, rufous, and dark. The best plumage field marks for identifying Swainson's Hawks include the dark flight feathers contrasting with the paler underwing coverts (on all but the darkest birds), two-toned upperside with paler upperwing coverts and blackish flight feathers, and dark bibbed chest (light-morph adults). Light-morph Swainson's Hawks have pale uppertail coverts that contrast with the tail and rump.

2nd-years are similar to juveniles below, but they have adult-like uppersides and flight feathers, including the tail. The body plumage is either nearly identical to juveniles or is intermediate between juvenile and adult. This progression is most easily recognized on intermediate/dark morphs. A few subadults have an adult-like body plumage and are difficult to tell from adults in the field. In fall, Swainson's Hawks that appear juvenile-like but with symmetrical wing or tail molt are subadults (see Molt). Second-year birds typically have a dark head, but the head can be paler by the second spring because of fading. The eyes are mixed amber and brown.

Light-morph adults are whitish underneath with dark flight feathers, appearing strongly two-toned in flight. The dark flight feathers have a broad, slightly darker trailing edge. Swainson's Hawks have a dark brown or rufous chest or "bib" that is apparent at considerable distances. Adult males tend to have grayer faces and paler rufous bibs, whereas females average browner on the face and bib, but there is some overlap in plumage between the sexes. The tails of all Swainson's Hawks appear somewhat pale underneath with a prominent dark tip that is broader than on juveniles. Adults have dark brown eyes, usually attained by the third year. Adults are dark above with a slightly paler brown back and upperwing coverts, imparting a two-toned appearance, though less prominently so than when seen from below. The two-toned upperside of all Swainson's Hawks is often more pronounced in spring, when the upperwing coverts can be faded. Adults usually show unmarked dark heads with pale throats.

Light-morph juveniles are creamy-buff to pale rufous below, variably spotted/streaked darker, usually most concentrated on the upper breast sides. The colorful wash on the underbody usually fades to whitish in winter. They may be moderately streaked on the underbody (and even heavily streaked on the chest and appear bibbed like adults) but are lightly marked on the underwing coverts, again showing the two-toned underwing very prominently. The dark flight feathers have a diffuse, dusky trailing edge to the wing, and are somewhat paler than those of adults, making them less distinctly two-toned when seen from below. Juveniles can have dark or pale heads in fall, but by spring the head is almost always pale because of fading and wear. Juvenile Swainson's of all morphs are dark above with pale-fringed upperwing coverts, lacking the pale primary panels shown by most other juvenile buteos. In spring, these pale fringes are often absent due to wear. The eyes of juvenile Swainson's Hawks are pale amber.

Rufous-morph adults are either wholly dark rufous underneath or show a rufous-barred belly and darker brown bib. The underwing coverts are highly variable, ranging from whitish with rufous mottling to solidly rufous. The underwing coverts are often paler than the body and flight feathers, and stand out as the palest area on the bird when seen from below, usually causing the two-toned appearance typical of Swainson's to be visible. Rufous adults also have pale undertail coverts similar to those of all light morphs. The flight feathers and upperparts are identical to those of light morphs.

Dark-morph adults are uniformly dark brown to blackish brown on the underbody, lacking any contrast between the chest and belly. The underwing coverts are usually slightly paler and rufous-toned, but in some cases can be completely dark, erasing any of the two-toned appearance typical of this species' underwings. The topsides of dark Swainson's Hawks are similar to those of light-morph birds, but are often a shade darker overall and show dark (or sometimes pale) uppertail coverts. Even the darkest birds usually show paler undertail coverts, and only in very rare cases are the underparts wholly dark.

Rufous/dark-morph juveniles are grouped together since it is not completely known which types of heavily marked birds transition into which adult types. It is likely that uniformly, moderately streaked birds become rufous-morphs as adults, and that the darker extreme, heavily streaked dark juveniles become dark-morph adults. Darker examples appear fully dark on the underbody and underwing coverts at a distance, but when seen well, they show faint buffy streaking throughout the body. First-spring intermediate/dark-morph juveniles are surprisingly pale-headed as a result of bleaching and wear, and these are frequently misidentified, usually as Rough-legged Hawks or Krider's Red-tailed Hawks. The flight feathers and upperside are identical to those of juvenile light-morph birds.

Geographic Variation: Swainson's Hawks are monotypic, but California breeders (Central Valley) average a higher proportion of dark morphs (80%) than in other regions and have more extensive molts, earlier spring migration timing, and earlier breeding schedules. Some California breeders have remained on breeding grounds year-round in recent years. The proportion of dark morphs varies elsewhere, with the lowest proportion of dark morphs on the Great Plains (~5%).

Molt: Molt timing differs between California breeders and Great Plains breeders, with California breeders molting earlier and generally more extensively than those breeding elsewhere. First-year birds may undergo a limited molt during their first winter in which a few body and head feathers are replaced, but their first flight feather molt takes place from March through September, with California birds usually replacing all the flight and tail feathers; Great Plains and Intermountain West birds often retain a few outer primaries and a few secondaries. During the first molt, the general body plumage changes to an intermediate stage between juvenile and adult, usually still with a streaked appearance below. In the second spring/summer, a near complete molt results in the adult appearance. Subsequent molts are incomplete, with adults using stepwise molt to replace flight feathers during summer, usually suspending for migration, and then sometimes continuing on the winter grounds. More study is needed to understand the complexities of Swainson's Hawk molt patterns.

Similar Species: Swainson's Hawk has one of the most distinctive shapes of any North American raptor: elegant and slim, with long, pointed wings, often raised in a smooth dihedral. Dark morphs are dark overall, similar to eagles and vultures, but their size, shape, and flight style are very different.

Likely to be confused only with other buteos, especially juvenile and immature *White-tailed Hawk*.

Swainson's are told from White-tailed by their slimmer overall build, darker flight feathers (especially secondaries), darker tail with wider bands, and slightly narrower wings and hands. Juvenile White-tailed usually has a distinctive bold white chest patch, very unusual on dark juvenile Swainson's. Juvenile White-tailed averages blacker overall than Swainson's, and usually shows a pale grayish wash to the upperside of the tail.

Swainson's is told from other buteos by its dark flight feathers, slimmer proportions, and more pointed wingtips; however, *Broad-winged Hawk* is sometimes confused for Swainson's Hawk. Adults are distinct, but juveniles of both species are similar in plumage. Although Broad-winged Hawks show pointed wings in all postures, the wings are stockier and held flat when soaring. Broad-winged Hawks also lack the dark flight feathers of Swainson's, but this can be tough to distinguish on some backlit juvenile Swainson's Hawks.

Swainson's Hawk is sometimes misidentified as *Northern Harrier* since both are slim-winged, buoyant, and fly with a dihedral. Swainson's Hawk is larger overall with a shorter tail, heavier body, larger head, and more pointed wings. When coursing low over a field, Swainson's is more stable than Harrier, and displays stiffer wingbeats.

Hybrids: Exceptional with Red-tailed Hawk and Rough-legged Hawk. Possibly hybridizes with Ferruginous Hawk based on anecdotal reports, but no confirmed records to date.

Status and Distribution: Swainson's Hawks are fairly common breeders across much of their range from northern Mexico to central Canada and west to California's Central Valley. They are generally local in the northern part of their range and rare in Alaska. Swainson's Hawks become uncommon along the eastern Great Plains with a few pairs breeding east to Illinois.

Migration: Swainson's Hawk is a long-distance migrant, wintering primarily in Argentina, but with recent rare but regular populations wintering in Florida, Texas, and California. It is a rare migrant along the Great Lakes and to the East Coast in spring and fall. Swainson's Hawks can be seen in large kettles on migration, especially along the Texas coast (and Veracruz, Mexico) and in smaller groups throughout parts of the West. Spring migration generally takes place from March to May, and from September through November in fall. California breeders arrive from late February to March and depart from September to early October.

Vocalizations: Swainson's Hawk's call is a classic raptor scream, but is higher-pitched and more drawn-out than that of Red-tailed Hawk. Juveniles give a high-pitched, repeated, begging call, *whiw, whiw, whiw, whiw.*

White-tailed Hawk *(Geranoaetus albicaudatus)* **WTHA** page 76

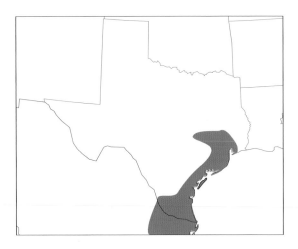

My goal is to see White-tailed Hawks, so I travel to the coastal prairies of south Texas where they are common. I have studied the literature on this species' varied plumages, and I am prepared as well as I can be. I have also read stories about the so-called Firehawk, the name referencing White-tailed Hawk's habit of keying in on distant plumes of smoke that signal burning sugarcane fields. White-tailed Hawks are attracted to these fires because the advancing flames send rodents and insects scurrying for escape, in the process becoming easy targets for hunting predators.

It's midmorning, and speeding down the highway, I notice a black plume of smoke rising to the east: my new target. I use the patchwork grid of Texas roads to work my way closer to the blaze, hoping to get near enough to spot some hawks. As luck would have it, a dirt road allows close access, and I park my car on the roadside adjacent to the flames. Smoke and ash rise high into the air, and I feel the heat even at a safe distance. Glancing skyward, I see my strategy has paid off, as out in front of the slowly advancing fire are at least 15 White-tailed Hawks.

I watch as they hover and kite overhead, some hanging motionless in the rising smoke and ash, just high enough to escape being burned by the intense

heat. Occasionally one stoops onto a prey item, then carries it off to a nearby spot on the ground for consumption. The strikingly plumaged adults are easily identified, and even the more variable subadult plumages are generally distinctive. But the young of the year are highly variable, and it takes me longer to get a handle on them, to get used to all their permutations. By the time I leave in the afternoon, more than 50 White-tailed Hawks have gathered at this field, along with a host of other buteos, including Swainson's and Red-tailed Hawks. All in all, a wonderful study of the "Firehawk" of south Texas.

Overview: White-tailed Hawks are striking raptors restricted in North America to the coastal prairie of south Texas. They hunt mostly small vertebrates, including rodents, birds, and reptiles. White-tailed Hawks habitually forage in burning sorghum and sugarcane fields, where they catch rodents and insects fleeing the flames. In addition to burning fields, White-tailed Hawks congregate near tractors actively tilling fields, where they hover, kite, and pounce from above. White-tailed Hawks also perch-hunt from utility poles and other manmade structures.

Flight Style: White-tailed Hawks are steady in flight, and soar in wide, lazy circles like other large buteos. They often hold their wings in a modified dihedral. Their direct flight is with stiff, deep wingbeats, similar to those of Red-tailed or Swainson's Hawk.

Size and Shape: L 46–58 cm (18–23 in), WS 126–135 cm (50–53 in), WT 880–1235 g (1.9–2.7 lb)
White-tailed Hawks are large buteos, roughly comparable in size to Red-tailed Hawk and Swainson's Hawk. Combining some structural elements of both of those species, White-tailed Hawks have broad wings and short tails (adults) like Red-tailed, but have relatively tapered wingtips like Swainson's. Juveniles are much lankier overall, shaped more like

a Swainson's Hawk, but with notably broader-based wings. Perched, they are bulky with long wings that extend past the tail in all ages, a good field mark.

Plumage: White-tailed Hawks have the most complicated and unusual age-related plumage progression of the buteos. They acquire adult appearance at about 4 years old, resulting in 4 identifiable age classes. Minor sex differences exist in adults.

Adults have gray backs with colorful rufous upperwing coverts, clean white underparts with grayish flight feathers, and a short white tail with a broad, black, subterminal band. This gives them a distinctive two-toned appearance when seen from below. Males average paler overall than females, with grayer heads and wings, but the differences are not always obvious.

1st-years (juveniles) are markedly different from adults, ranging from solidly dark below to very pale-breasted with a dark belly and mottled underwings. Juveniles have uniformly fresh flight feathers lacking molt contrasts, and the upperwing coverts are evenly pale-edged.

2nd-years have variable underparts and look much like similar-plumaged juveniles, but they have darker heads and throats (some retain a hint of paleness on the ear coverts), a bold dark trailing edge to flight feathers, and a grayish tail with a narrow subterminal band. Most second-year birds retain juvenile P9–10 in the first wing molt.

3rd-years are adult-like, but with darker heads and throats, and a slightly narrower tail band. Most are darker gray overall than adults, bordering on slate-gray; many have barred flanks.

Geographic Variation: There are 3 subspecies of White-tailed Hawk, but only 1, *G. a. hypospodius*, occurs in North America. It is larger than the other forms, and lacks the dark-morph adult plumage found in the two South American forms: *G. a. colonus* in the north, and *G. a. albicaudatus* in the south.

Molt: White-tailed Hawks attain full adult appearance by the fourth year (third summer/fall), the longest plumage maturation of any North American buteo. Juveniles have an absent or limited molt of head and body feathers during the first winter, and look generally the same until the first spring/summer, when they undergo a nearly complete molt. Most second-years retain juvenile outer P9–10. Over the second spring/summer they molt again, but

many retain P5–8 from the previous molt, which are now older than the surrounding feathers that have been replaced. During the third spring/summer, a nearly complete molt results in adult plumage. As a large raptor, White-tailed Hawks have a stepwise molt strategy to replace the flight feathers, with not all feathers being replaced each year. Adults often have 3 waves of primary molt occurring simultaneously.

Similar Species: Adults are distinctive and nearly impossible to mistake for any other raptor, but subadults and juveniles can be surprisingly confounding, and they are often confused with Swainson's, Short-tailed, and Red-tailed Hawks. Dark juveniles are most similar to *Swainson's Hawks*, but they differ in having broader wings with paler secondaries, a notably paler tail with narrower bands, and a white blotchy patch on the breast. Swainson's are usually evenly streaked below, lacking the white blotch on the breast, but some White-tailed Hawks lack the white breast patch, and very rarely some second-year Swainson's Hawks can show a similar breast pattern.

Extremely pale juvenile White-taileds can approach juvenile light-morph *Red-tailed Hawk* in plumage, showing a white chest and contrasting dark belly, but note White-tailed Hawk's darker, more finely barred flight feathers and narrower, more tapered wings.

When gliding high overhead, third-year White-tailed can be confused with light-morph *Short-tailed Hawk*. Compared with Short-tailed, White-tailed Hawk is larger, with a whitish tail and a moderately wide black tail band. They also have longer, wider wings and darker primaries, and they soar and glide with a stronger dihedral.

Status and Distribution: White-tailed Hawk is fairly common and conspicuous, but local within its restricted range, breeding in widely spaced pairs. It is a scattered, rare vagrant outside the breeding range north to Louisiana; reports from Arizona are unverified but possibly correct. White-tailed Hawk is listed as endangered in Texas.

Migration: Movements are poorly understood and mostly local. Probably no true migration occurs, but instead perhaps just seasonal movement or postbreeding dispersal within its general range. When White-tailed Hawks move locally, they form large winter concentrations near optimal foraging resources.

Vocalizations: White-tailed Hawks are vocal on the breeding grounds when agitated and during aggressive encounters. Typical call is a husky, up-slurred scream followed by repeated, 2-note phrases, *rrrreeer, K-reer, K-reer, K-reer, K-reer.*

Ferruginous Hawk *(Buteo regalis)* **FEHA** page 78

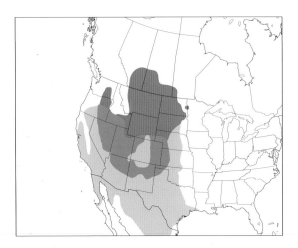

Across a bright, treeless prairie, a stiff wind bends the grasses as dust kicks up, and tumbleweeds roll along in perpetual motion. The horizon line draws on forever; the sky above is cobalt blue dotted with puffy white-and-gray clouds. Over a distant hilltop is a large hawk, kiting and soaring effortlessly for its size. As the bird banks around, its overall whiteness is striking. It takes another turn, and the topside is revealed, with bold white primary panels and a white tail glowing in the sky, all highlighted by the strong afternoon sun. The bird readjusts and sets its long wings in a glide, hands tapered to blunt points. Its head-on profile is unusual, with a robust body and raised wings that flatten at the wrists. As the hawk glides overhead, its colorful rusty leggings form a V on the lower belly, contrasting with its otherwise stark white plumage. The bird floats off to the west on steady wings, kiting motionless, periodically surveying the ground below, all the while its brilliant white plumage flashing in the sun.

Overview: Ferruginous Hawks are birds of western open country, favoring large expanses of prairie, grassland, and agricultural areas (winter). They nest in barren areas of the West and the northern Great Plains, where they use single trees, cliffs, power poles, and even the ground as substrates. Infrequently seen throughout the West during migration, Ferruginous Hawks are best looked for during winter, when they can be found across a broader range of habitats, and even in more populated areas where ground squirrel, prairie dog, or mouse populations are high. Ferruginous Hawks often perch on power poles, fence posts, and the ground (especially hilltops), where they scan for prey from places with a commanding view of their surroundings. They hunt in flight as well, equally adept at stooping from a height, surprising prey in low-elevation direct flight, or hovering and kiting for short periods. In certain areas in winter, Ferruginous Hawks roost in groups of up to 100 birds, sometimes with Rough-legged and Red-tailed Hawks.

Flight Style: Ferruginous Hawks are buoyant fliers, soaring in wide, lazy circles with wings held in a shallow to pronounced dihedral. When gliding, they hold their wings above the body but flatten along the "hands," forming a modified dihedral, as they teeter side to side similar to Northern Harriers, but much less wobbly. Ferruginous Hawks have labored, stiff wingbeats that are slightly quicker on the upstroke (somewhat owl-like), being somewhat heavier and less choppy than those of Red-tailed Hawk, but not quite as fluid as Swainson's Hawk. At times, Ferruginous Hawks have shallow wingbeats during powered flight over flat lands, especially when chasing prey.

Size and Shape: L 50–66 cm (20–26 in), WS 134–152 cm (53–60 in), WT 880–2030 g (2–4.5 lb)
Ferruginous Hawks are unmistakably large and bulky; they are on average the largest of the North American buteos. When perched, structural features include a broad chest and shoulders, small head, and long wings and tail with the wingtips nearly reaching the tail tip. In flight, Ferruginous Hawks have long, fairly broad wings with hands that taper to a point, appearing beautifully angular. The wings are slimmer than those of Red-tailed Hawks but not quite as narrow or pointed as Swainson's Hawks. When the bird is gliding, the wingtips extend well past the trailing edge of the wings, making them appear M-shaped overhead, similar to Swainson's Hawks, but slightly less pronounced.

Plumage: Ferruginous Hawks are polymorphic, occurring in light (common) and dark morphs (rare). All share similar flight feathers, being largely whitish and lacking distinct barring, with limited black on the tips of the outer primaries compared with most other buteos. The yellow gape of all Ferruginous Hawks is prominent compared with other buteos. There is sexual dimorphism in size, with females larger than males, but there is individual size variation. The eyes are pale yellowish in juveniles, changing to brownish in adult, but it takes several years longer than other buteos for eye color to fully change.

Light-morph adults are particularly striking white below, with rufous leggings forming a V across the lower belly. They have dark wrist "commas" and rufous-marked underwing coverts, with some lightly marked and others nearly fully rufous. Some adult light morphs have faint to moderate dark rufous barring on the belly, others have a dark wash on the breast, or both. Some heavily barred individuals are perhaps light x dark intergrades, but more study is needed. Light morphs (often second-years) can be less vibrant in color overall and show fainter rufous leggings. Adult males average grayer-headed than the browner heads of females.

From above, light-morph adults are brownish gray with brilliant rusty-orange upperwing coverts that contrast with the grayish flight feathers and the obvious white primary panels. The tail is whitish, reddish, or grayish mottled and lacking bands. Some individuals have nearly completely reddish tails (rare variant) or gray tails (typically dark morphs). Regardless of color, the tails of all adults appear whitish from below, but when fanned, typically appear whitish or pinkish and sometimes translucent. Light-morph birds of all ages often appear "hooded" because of the contrast between the bright white throat and body, and dark head. However, grayer-headed adults may appear pale-headed in the field.

Light-morph juveniles are stark white underneath similar to adults, but lightly spotted brown on the legs and belly, and with faint dark wrist commas, but may appear mainly unmarked below in the field. Some juveniles show fairly mottled underwing coverts, but this is rare and much less distinct than on adults. The tail of juveniles appears pale overall from below when folded, but when spread the white base and dark distal third is more obvious, and may show faint broken bands. The dark trailing edge to the wings on juveniles is slightly less distinct than that of

adults. All light-morph juveniles are uniform brown (slightly more warm-brown compared with other juvenile buteos) above with bold white primary panels and a white base to the tail.

Dark-morph adults show a dark rufous-brown tone to the underbody and underwing coverts with a slightly darker grayish brown chest, and pale flight feathers. Rarely, they are entirely blackish underneath. Dark-morph adults are brown to slate-brown above with much less vibrant rufous tone on the upperwing coverts than on light morphs, and faint grayish primary wing panels that are less obvious than those of light-morph birds. The dark trailing edge of the wings is slightly bolder on adults than on juveniles. The topside of the tail is typically grayish, or grayish with whitish or rufous mottling.

Dark-morph juveniles are brownish on the underbody and underwing coverts with a slightly paler chest (often giving a rufous-bibbed effect), and nearly identical to adult dark-morph body plumage. From above, dark-morph juveniles are warm brown with paler primary wing panels, similar to juvenile light morphs. Some dark-morph juveniles lack the white base to the tail shown by light-morph juveniles, while the tail of others is identical to that of light morphs. Juvenile dark birds with white tails will show a dark tip on top; dark adults lack a defined tail tip.

Geographic Variation: Ferruginous Hawks are monotypic, and occur only in North America. Dark morphs are more common on the Canadian prairie (7–9%) than farther south.

Molt: The first molt takes place during the first spring and summer (March to October), after which most birds are indistinguishable from adults. Unusual for such a large buteo, the first molt is usually complete, with all flight feathers replaced. Adults undergo a variable molt from April to October, sometimes replacing all the flight feathers, but usually a few primaries are retained, resulting in a stepwise molt pattern thereafter. Some Ferruginous Hawks molt slowly during fall migration, finishing the replacement of their outer primaries while heading south, sometimes carrying over to the winter grounds.

Similar Species: At a distance, Ferruginous Hawks can deceive even the most skilled observers, especially when seen at eye level along a ridge, when their silhouette can be mistaken for a Swainson's Hawk,

Red-tailed Hawk, Rough-legged Hawk, Northern Harrier, or even a Turkey Vulture.

Ferruginous Hawks are most easily confused with other buteos, especially dark-morph Rough-legged Hawk and the pale prairie-breeding Krider's Red-tailed Hawk. They are distinguished from *Krider's* by their longer-winged shape with strongly tapered hands, stronger dihedral, bold rufous upperwing coverts and leggings (adults), and brownish head. Juvenile Krider's show pale wing panels above, but they are typically not so prominent as on Ferruginous Hawk. Juvenile Krider's also have extensive pale mottling on the upperwing coverts, which are dark on Ferruginous Hawk.

Juvenile dark-morph Ferruginous Hawk is most easily confused with dark juvenile *Rough-legged Hawk*. Both show uniform dark plumage strongly contrasting with paler flight feathers. Compared with Rough-legged Hawk, Ferruginous Hawk is more heavily built and has longer, more pointed wings, a stouter body, and broader tail. Rough-legged Hawk is much more likely to hover while hunting. The wingbeats of Rough-legged Hawk are deep and fluid, whereas Ferruginous is a bit stiffer and less even-paced. Dark Rough-legged shows more heavily barred flight feathers below, a broader dark trailing edge to the wings (adults), and dark topside with weaker pale primary panels (juveniles). Juvenile dark-morph Ferruginous Hawk can show a white tail base; dark-morph Rough-legged Hawk lacks a white tail base. Adult dark Ferruginous has a primarily whitish or grayish tail, whereas dark Rough-legged has a blackish tail dorsally with multiple whitish tail bands or a dusky tail with a blackish tip.

Hybrids: At least 1 (but possibly 2) Ferruginous Hawk and Red-tailed Hawk mated pairs occur in Utah's West Desert.

Status and Distribution: Ferruginous Hawk is a widespread but uncommon breeder in grassland and shrub-steppe habitats across the northern Great Plains and Intermountain West. During migration, it can be seen more broadly across the West, but no large concentration points are known. In winter, Ferruginous retracts from the northern portions of its range, moving south into the southern Great Plains, western United States, and north-central Mexico, stretching east to the Texas coast; exceptionally farther east.

Ferruginous Hawk may be decreasing in North America because of conversion of grassland nesting habitat to big agriculture and invasion of cheat grass. It is not easily monitored because of its remote nesting areas and lack of concentrations during migration. In summer it avoids the most populated areas, breeding in remote grassland, shrub-steppe habitats, and near smaller, open rural areas or farming towns.

Migration: Ferruginous Hawks are short- or medium-distance migrants. There is no true peak time period for Ferruginous Hawk migration, which spans the entire spring and fall seasons. Adults arrive back at their breeding grounds in spring (mainly March through April) before juveniles. Some adults are resident. Fall flights occur from September through November. Dinosaur Ridge, CO, and the Wasatch Range in Utah are the most reliable sites to witness Ferruginous Hawk migration. The Goshute Mountains, NV, are a fairly reliable site as well.

Vocalizations: Typically silent away from breeding grounds, Ferruginous Hawks occasionally vocalize during aggressive encounters with other raptors. Their primary call is a quavering, descending, muffled *kreeeeer!* Female's call is lower-pitched.

Rough-legged Hawk *(Buteo lagopus)* **RLHA** page 82

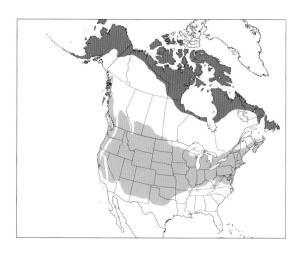

An open field that bustles with rusty tractors throughout the summer has now gone silent. The winter's snow transforms this place into a serene, beautiful landscape, with a lone ice-crusted tree as its centerpiece. Atop the tree on the highest branch sits a large hawk, bending the tiny limb under its body weight. It takes flight, and a bold plumage pattern is revealed. The white-based tail, black wrists, and black belly help make for an easy identification. But it's not the mystery of identification that is so appealing about the Rough-legged Hawk; it's the species' grace and beauty, as well as the fortitude with which it hunts.

Suspended in midair as if held by invisible strings, the Rough-leg hangs over the field searching for prey. Facing directly into the strong wind, its wingtips bend upward, and its back feathers ruffle. As it surveys the scene, its head stays steady, unmoving, while the body and tail adjust with the wind. It barely needs to flap, but when the wind gusts diminish, the hawk switches from kiting to hovering, flapping its wings hurriedly to keep stationary. With one quick turn the hawk folds up and slams into the ground… *Wham!* The vole it was after must have seen it coming and ducked under ground in the nick of time, as this time the hawk comes up empty. The hawk again takes flight, moving from one location to the next as it seeks food. Stoop…missed again. This game of "hawk-and-mouse" goes on for hours, and I wonder if the hawk will catch what it needs for the day.

Rough-legged Hawks come from the Arctic, visiting the Lower 48 only in winter. And juveniles such as this bird need to be capable of surviving on their own, or this first winter will be its last. But Rough-legs are survivors, adapted to harsh weather—their feathered legs and feet are evidence of this. They come from a place where Harlan's Hawks, Gyrfalcons, Snowy Owls, polar bears, caribou, and arctic foxes are its neighbors—rough company. *Wham!* The Rough-leg slams into the ground again, shuffling its feet in the tall grass…does it have prey this time? The hawk lifts up, carrying a white-footed mouse in its talons, and flies to the top of the lone tree, where it quickly eats its meal before starting the process all over again.

Overview: Rough-leggeds nest in the Arctic on cliffs or sometimes on the ground, but are most often seen by birders during migration and winter. They are widespread throughout North America in winter, but are far more common in the northern states. Often found hovering at medium elevation in search of prey over farmland or marsh, or perched on roadside poles or fence posts, Rough-leggeds are also comfortable perching on the ground. Unlike other large buteos, they frequently perch on the smallest twigs at the very top of trees and shrubs, looking impossibly large for such frail branches. Rough-leggeds are the only regularly occurring dark-morph buteo across much of the East. They are well adapted for cold weather, having small bills and feet compared with other large buteos, mainly to keep bare-part exposure to a minimum. Rough-legged Hawks roost in large groups, sometimes with Ferruginous and Red-tailed Hawks in winter.

Flight Style: Because of the cold climate they occupy, Rough-legged Hawks are able to rely less on thermals for soaring and more on powered flight, and are thus more Harrier-like in flight style. They are buoyant and languid in flight, able to gain lift and to stay aloft easily. Rough-leggeds soar with a dihedral and teeter a bit, but they don't come close to the "wobbliness" of Harriers. They also migrate in conditions most raptors wouldn't (e.g., snow and rain), similar to Harriers. When gliding, they hold their wings in a modified dihedral, only rarely appearing drooped or flat-winged. Rough-leggeds possess great stamina, and they are able to hover for hours at a time in search of prey, surveying the landscape, moving from one area to the next. They are also able to kite, so in strong winds they can stay aloft without flapping at all. The wingbeats of Rough-leggeds are floppy and loose like those of Harrier, but deeper and somewhat stiffer.

Size and Shape: L 46–59 cm (18–23 in), WS 122–143 cm (48–56 in), WT 745–1800 g (1.6–4 lb)
Rough-legged Hawks are large buteos. Females are larger than males, with the largest females weighing as much as the largest Ferruginous Hawks. But unlike most large buteos, Rough-leggeds appear delicate, with small feet and a small bill. They possess long wings and somewhat long tails. In several ways they resemble a cross between the stocky Red-tailed Hawk and the lanky Northern Harrier. Male Rough-leggeds are slimmer-winged than females, but distinguishing sexes by shape alone can be very difficult, especially without much practice. Luckily there are plumage differences to consider. When perched, Rough-legged Hawks are bulky, but their smaller bill compared with that of most other buteos is sometimes evident. They often sit at a slight angle when on trees, as opposed to more upright when sitting on utility poles.

Plumage: Rough-legged Hawks have 2 basic plumages, juvenile and adult. They attain their adult plumage after the first molt at about 1 year old, but the plumage differences between the sexes can take up to 2 years to develop. Second-year males attain a plumage that can look similar to adult females, though some can also look like older adult males, so sexing second-year birds is usually not possible. Most second-year birds of both sexes retain a few juvenile outer primaries and a few secondaries, which are shorter, paler, and more worn than the adjacent adult feathers. Usually these retained outer primaries are obvious in winter, allowing second-years to be safely aged. Third-year birds show typical adult plumage, and the sexes are usually safely distinguishable at this age (light birds only). The eyes of adults are dark brown; the eyes of juveniles are pale yellowish to yellow-brown.

Adult male light-morph plumage varies from white underneath with dark mottling throughout the body and underwings, lacking an obvious bellyband and carpal patches, to white underneath with only a dark bib on the upper chest and faint carpal patches. Adult males tend to have barred flanks and leggings, but some females also show this. Males tend to be grayer above than females and show mul-

tiple black tail bands, but there is overlap in plumage between adult females and males, and some birds are not safely sexed in the field.

Adult female light morphs are buffy below with solid blackish bellies and wrists, and a white tail with a well-defined blackish tip. They also show a well-defined dark trailing edge to the wings. Some adult females are heavily mottled blackish on the underwing coverts, and have dark mottled bellies. Adult females are brown on the upperside with grayish and rufous mottling mixed in, with pale, streaked heads.

1st-year light morphs (juveniles) are similar to adult female light morphs, with a blackish belly and wrist patches. Juveniles differ from adult females in having a smudgy tail tip, bold, pale windows in outer primaries, and a diffuse, gray trailing edge to flight feathers. Light-morph juveniles are brown above with pale mottling along the upperwing coverts, and paler, sometimes whitish heads. The pale primary panels and white tail base are distinct when seen from above and are notable at a great distance. Sexes are identical in juvenile plumage.

Adult male dark morphs can be uniformly black underneath or brownish like females. Blackish adult males show a dark gray-blue cast to the upperside and neatly banded tails. But some males can show female-like multiple, crooked, narrow white bands. Some adults (especially males) show a small white patch on the back of the head that juveniles typically lack.

Adult female dark morphs are wholly dark brown below with slightly darker wrist patches and bellies. The flight feathers of adults are more boldly banded than those of juveniles, giving the underwings a silvery appearance at times (especially males). Adult females can show dark tails with a broad, black tip, or have multiple, crooked, narrow white bands, but all dark morphs lack the white base to the tail of light morphs.

1st-year dark-morph Rough-leggeds are similar to adult female dark morphs, but are slightly paler overall with a dusky trailing edge to the wings and a fainter dark tail tip. The upperside is dark brown lacking any mottling, and shows pale primary windows and a grayish brown tail with very faint, narrow, gray inner bands. Juvenile dark-morph birds have slightly paler eyebrows and cheeks than adults, but females in their first adult plumage often share this head pattern.

Geographic Variation: There are 3–4 described

subspecies of Rough-legged Hawk, with 1 occurring throughout North America (*B. l. sanctijohannis*), and 1 vagrant from Asia (*B. l. kamtschatkensis*). Subspecies differ mainly in size and plumage, as well as in frequency of dark birds, but extensive overlap between Alaskan and Asian breeders suggests that many birds are not diagnosable to subspecies. The Old World forms lack a complete dark morph, but dark morphs are common in North America. The Asian form is tentatively recognized as occurring in the western Aleutians, but more study is needed. Migration data suggest a higher incidence of dark-morph birds occurring in the western portion of the species' range, but breeding studies are needed to determine whether this is the case.

Molt: Juveniles undergo the first molt at about 1 year old, mainly from April through September, through which they attain adult plumage. These second-year birds typically have 2–4 outer primaries and a few secondaries retained. These retained flight feathers are paler, shorter, and often worn at the tips. In the second spring/summer, another partial molt takes place, and light-morph adults usually attain more obvious sex-specific plumage characteristics at this age. These third-year birds can still be aged by molt pattern, usually showing a block of fresher inner primaries and fresh P7–10, with retained second-year middle primaries, but this can be impossible to see in the field. Adult primaries may have pale bases that give adult birds the appearance of having pale wing panels like juveniles, but these panels (or windows) are less distinct in contrast and width. Subsequent molts occur mainly from March through September but are incomplete, involving most of the body feathers and some flight feathers. Like most other large raptors, Rough-leggeds use a stepwise molt strategy to replace their flight feathers.

Similar Species: Light-morph Rough-legged Hawks can be readily identified by their unique plumage characteristics, but dark morphs can be a bigger challenge, as they are frequently confused with other dark-morph buteos, especially Ferruginous Hawk and Harlan's Red-tailed Hawk.

Dark-morph *Ferruginous Hawk* is very similar in plumage to dark-morph Rough-legged Hawk, especially juveniles! However, Ferruginous has a larger bill and gape, heavier build, more sharply tapered wingtips with less extensive black on the underside of the tips, and paler flight feathers overall. Rough-legged Hawks have a slight bulge along the back edge of the secondaries, lacking the more angular look of Ferruginous Hawks. When seen well, dark-morph Ferruginous Hawk will not show the darker wrist patches and belly of juvenile dark-morph Rough-legged Hawk. Tail pattern can be remarkably similar on juveniles, with dark-morph Rough-legged showing a dark tail with slightly paler, narrow bands, and dark-morph Ferruginous showing a dark tail with slightly darker, narrow bands, but on flying birds this is often impossible to note.

Dark-morph *adult Harlan's Red-tailed Hawks* and adult Rough-leggeds can be very similar in plumage. Most Harlan's have white streaking on the chest, and some have white streaks on the crown and throat, traits that dark Rough-leggeds do not show. But solidly dark Harlan's are often confused with Rough-legged. The tail pattern varies greatly on adult Harlan's, but most are mottled grayish or reddish, which dark-morph Rough-leggeds do not show; however, some Harlan's can have all-dark tails or banded tails similar to Rough-legged. Dark-morph adult Harlan's with banded tails show mostly whitish tails with narrower dark bands; on Rough-legged the tail is black with narrower white bands. Adult Harlan's have either heavily banded, completely mottled, or plain, unbanded flight feathers; the flight feathers on Rough-legged are often faintly banded. Rough-legged also has feathered tarsi, a good trait to use for perched birds. Red-tailed Hawks of all races are stocky-chested and broader-winged than Rough-legged. Red-taileds soar on flat wings or with a slight dihedral, and they glide with less of an exaggerated modified dihedral than Rough-legged Hawk.

Northern Harrier and Rough-legged Hawk are similar in shape, but show obvious plumage differences. Harrier's don't show a pale head, black belly, and black wrist patches. Rough-leggeds hold their wings in a dihedral or modified dihedral similar to Harriers (but slightly shallower), and are similar in profile; however, Rough-legged Hawks have bulkier chests and broader wings, and they teeter in flight much less than Harriers.

From overhead, *Swainson's Hawks* appear M-shaped in a glide, similar to Rough-legged Hawks, but they show slimmer, more pointed wings. Bibbed adult male Rough-leggeds can be mistaken for Swainson's Hawks, but Rough-legged Hawks always show pale flight feathers compared with the dark flight feathers of all Swainson's Hawks.

Zone-tailed Hawk and adult male dark-morph

Rough-legged Hawk are superficially similar in plumage, but Zone-tailed has a different tail pattern and more finely banded flight feathers. Zone-taileds are often confused with Turkey Vultures because of their wobbly flight style and strong dihedral; Rough-leggeds rarely give the impression of being a Turkey Vulture!

Hybrids: Extremely rare with Swainson's Hawk and Harlan's Red-tailed Hawk.

Status and Distribution: Rough-legged Hawks breed in northern Alaska and northern Canada, and winter sparsely throughout most of North America, excluding the deep South, where they are a vagrant. Rough-leggeds are generally uncommon, but can be locally common in winter in areas of high food concentrations, especially on the Great Plains and in agricultural valleys of the Intermountain West. They are much less common farther east and toward the Pacific Coast, where scattered individuals occur. A few winter every year in coastal saltmarshes along the East Coast, but numbers vary annually. Likewise, winter numbers vary around the Great Lakes, ranging from just a few in typical years, to hundreds in "irruption" years. Like many Arctic predators, Rough-leggeds are somewhat cyclic in their breeding success and closely tied to prey populations, which causes irruption years to occur. During these irruptions, larger numbers are noted at hawk watches.

Some stay north of the U.S.–Canada border region in winter, especially in the eastern portion of their range. Rough-leggeds rarely oversummer south of the Arctic, but when they do, they are almost always first-summer nonbreeders.

Migration: Rough-leggeds are medium- to long-distance migrants, moving north in spring from February to May, and south in fall from mid-September through December. Fall migration appears to be slightly earlier in the West, but in general the migration interval is similar across the Lower 48. In spring, Brockway Mountain, MI, Derby Hill, NY, Braddock Bay, NY, and along the southern shore of Lake Superior are good sites to see Rough-legged Hawks. Gunsight Mountain, AK, sees up to 40% dark-morph birds in spring, an unusually high percentage. But Whitefish Point, MI, (spring count) leads all sites as far as total numbers of Rough-leggeds, with counts as high as 526 in a day, and 2886 in a season. In fall, Hawk Ridge, MN, and sites along the northern shoreline of the Great Lakes, such as Hawk Cliff, ON, see consistently high numbers annually.

Vocalizations: On the breeding grounds, adults give a pure-toned, descending scream, similar to Ferruginous Hawk but more drawn-out and higher pitched. They are generally silent in winter but do call during aggressive encounters or territorial disputes in areas of high raptor concentrations.

Red-shouldered Hawk *(Buteo lineatus)* **RSHA** page 88

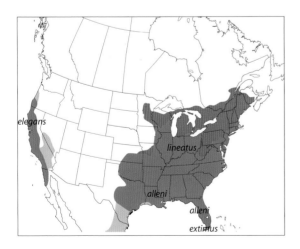

Along a damp trail draped in cathedral oaks and maples, streaks of light break through the canopy, dappling sun across hanging Spanish moss. The surrounding woods are alive with singing birds. Suddenly, a piercing scream—a repetitive, descending, *keeyar-keeyar-keeyar*—echoes through the swamp, stopping you in your tracks. Motionless, you wait. Again the scream rings out just as a large hawk flies in from the shadows and perches on a thick, mossy branch just 30 feet away, its breast brilliantly barred reddish. As you lift your binoculars, the hawk is unnerved by your movement and takes flight. With hurried wingbeats, it flies away, displaying its stunning rusty shoulders and crisply patterned black-and-white flight feathers before disappearing into the canopy. The hawk's compact build, long tail, and flight style leave you wondering whether you've just seen a large accipiter, but you've just had a typical encounter with a Red-shouldered Hawk.

Overview: Red-shouldered Hawks are medium-large buteos, only slightly smaller than Red-tailed Hawks. In the East, they are found in mixed riparian or swampy mature woodlands. In the West, they are found in oak woodlands, riparian areas, and suburban areas with large eucalyptus groves. Often noisy, Red-shouldered Hawks are frequently detected by ear. Red-shouldered Hawks are wary in the East, but during the breeding season they can be conspicuous and vocal while performing courtship displays above the canopy. More confiding in the West and in south Florida, they often perch in the open on pole tops and on roadside wires. They hunt primarily from low to medium-height perches for amphibians, reptiles, mice, and small birds.

Flight Style: While soaring or gliding, Red-shouldered Hawks are steady, strong fliers. In a soar, the wings are held fairly flat but arch slightly forward instead of straight out from the body, at some angles giving the appearance of a slight dihedral. In a glide, the wings are held slightly bowed. When flapping, the wingbeats are quick and stiff, similar to those of Broad-winged Hawks but somewhat "wristy" and more fluid in comparison.

Size and Shape: L 38–47 cm (15–19 in), WS 92–107 cm (37–42 in), WT 460–930 g (1.1–1.9 lb) Red-shouldered Hawk is a medium- to large-sized hawk, smaller than Red-tailed Hawk but larger than Broad-winged Hawk. When perched, Red-shouldered Hawks appear slimmer overall than Red-tailed Hawks and more Cooper's Hawk-like, but with a shorter tail. Red-shouldered Hawks have somewhat broad wings that are slightly squared at the tips (but tapered in a glide), and a longer, slimmer tail than Red-tailed Hawk. The tail is often rounded at the tip. When soaring overhead, Red-shouldered Hawks often look smaller-headed than Broad-winged and Red-tailed Hawks.

Plumage: All Red-shouldered Hawks have pale, translucent, crescent-shaped panels near the wingtips. These pale crescents are obvious from above and usually obvious from below (especially when backlit) but can be inconspicuous in poor lighting. Adult males average paler overall than females; juvenile sexes are similar. Females are slightly larger than males.

Adults are striking, being brilliant rufous underneath with faint white barring and fine dark streaking on the body, appearing orangey overall at a distance. The flight feathers (including the tail) are boldly banded black and white. From above, adult Red-shouldered Hawks are brownish with rufous "shoulder" patches, and the boldly banded flight feathers are obvious at this angle. By spring, some adults can be paler than usual because of fading, especially on the head and underbody.

1st-years (juveniles) are pale below with variable dark streaking, typically evenly dispersed across the body. The tail is dark with narrow pale banding and a wider dark subterminal band. The upperparts are brown, with some showing faint to bold rufous shoulder patches, which are generally much less distinct than on adults.

Geographic Variation: There are 4 subspecies of Red-shouldered Hawk: Eastern (*B. l. lineatus*), California (*B. l. elegans*), Southeast/Texas (*B. l. alleni/texanus*), and Florida (*B. l. extimus*), but not all Red-shouldered Hawks are identifiable to subspecies. General trends include larger size and darker overall coloration in northern breeders; southern birds tend to be paler on the head and underparts, and slightly smaller in size. Some authorities suggest that the California subspecies is a distinct species on the basis of genetic differences from other Red-shouldered Hawks; its range is also disjunct from the 3 eastern subspecies. Birds of southeast Texas (ssp. *texanus*) are usually subsumed under *B. l. alleni*, but more study is needed to determine whether they are distinct enough to warrant subspecies status.

Eastern adults are darker overall than other subspecies, with brownish heads and more coarsely barred underparts, often with fine black streaks intermixed. Eastern juveniles are streaked below but less heavily marked in general than other subspecies.

California adults are richer and more vibrant in color overall than other subspecies. California juveniles are more adult-like, with dense rufous-brown barring below, a rufous streaked breast, rufous underwing coverts, and brighter rufous shoulders. The flight feathers, and especially the tail, are adult-like.

Florida adults are uniquely pale-headed (especially males), and paler rufous below, generally lacking dark streaking on the barred underparts. Juveniles are more heavily marked below, often with barred bellies and flanks. Southern peninsular Florida birds are the palest of all the Red-shouldered Hawks, often with a whitish-gray head, pale back, and lightly marked underparts.

Southeast/Texas juveniles are variable with some looking similar to Florida juveniles and others similar to Eastern, but Southeast/Texas adults are not distinctly pale like Florida birds, being more like Eastern adults. Southeast/Texas birds may not be safely assigned to subspecies on plumage alone.

Molt: Juveniles undergo a complete molt (or near complete) from April through August, resulting in adult plumage. Adults undergo a complete molt (or near complete) mainly from May through August.

Similar Species: Juvenile Red-shouldered and *Broad-winged Hawks* can appear extremely similar to each other, especially when perched. Juvenile light-morph Broad-winged Hawks range from heavily marked to almost unmarked underneath, but moderately marked birds are extremely similar in appearance to juvenile Red-shouldered Hawk. Often, juvenile Broad-winged Hawks are more heavily streaked on the sides of the chest, whereas Red-shouldered Hawk is more evenly streaked throughout the underparts. On perched birds, note the plainer head pattern of Red-shouldered, the more "banded" appearance of the secondaries, and the dark tail with narrow pale bands (pale with variable-width dark bands on juvenile Broad-winged). The dark subterminal tail band on Broad-winged Hawk is often more distinct than on Red-shouldered Hawk. In flight, the best way to distinguish these two species is by overall shape. Broad-winged Hawk has a stocky body and wings, and always shows pointed wingtips. Red-shouldered Hawk pushes its wings slightly forward when soaring, while Broad-winged Hawk holds its wings straight out from the body. In a glide, the wingtips of Red-shouldered Hawk protrude farther past the trailing edge of the wings than those of Broad-winged Hawk. When held closed, the tail of Red-shouldered Hawk is broader and more similar to larger buteos, whereas the tail of Broad-winged Hawk is narrower and more similar to that of an accipiter.

Plumage of adult Red-shouldered and Broad-winged Hawk is similar as well. Adults of both species are rufous-barred below with black-and-white banded tails, but the tail bands of Broad-winged Hawk are broader and more evenly spaced, with only 1 or 2 broad white bands typically visible on soaring birds. Adult Red-shouldered Hawk is more vibrant in color, especially the underwing coverts, and also lacks the dark-bibbed chest sometimes shown by adult Broad-winged Hawks.

Juvenile Red-shouldered Hawks are similar to juvenile light-morph *Red-tailed Hawks* in plumage. Both are pale below with dark streaking, but Red-tailed Hawk has streaking concentrated on the belly, imparting a clean white-breasted look not typically shown by Red-shouldered. In flight, Red-shouldered Hawks are flatter-winged; Red-tailed soar with a slight to moderate dihedral. Also note the bold dark patagial marks shown by Red-tailed Hawk, whereas Red-shouldered is generally plain or lightly marked on the underwing coverts. When soaring, Red-tailed Hawks hold the wings straight out from the body, as opposed to the slightly pressed forward wings of Red-shouldered Hawk. The wingbeats of Red-shouldered Hawks are quicker and more accipiter-like than those of Red-tailed Hawks.

Hybrids: Red-shouldered Hawks rarely hybridize, but 4 Red-shouldered x Red-tailed Hawk hybrids are known from New England, 1 from Kentucky, and 1 specimen from California. A mated Red-shouldered Hawk and Red-tailed Hawk is documented hybridizing in Kentucky.

Status and Distribution: The Red-shouldered Hawk is uncommon to fairly common as a breeder throughout the eastern part of its range, but declining in certain areas (e.g., New Jersey). Eastern birds breed across the Midwest, New England, and into the Canadian border region. Northern populations are migratory, but it is mainly resident elsewhere. It is common in peninsular Florida and California. The California subspecies is uncommon in Oregon and rare in southern Washington. The California subspecies appears to be expanding north and east, with increasing records from Washington, Arizona, Nevada, Utah, and New Mexico.

Migration: Northern populations are migratory, wintering mainly in the Southeast. Red-shouldered Hawks are seen during migration in small numbers at many eastern hawk-watching sites, but at spring Great Lakes hawk watches, daily high counts peak in the high 100s (e.g., Braddock Bay and Derby Hill, NY, along Lake Ontario). Spring migration occurs typically from mid-March through April. Fall migration occurs mainly from late September through November. In spring, adults move about a month earlier than juveniles; in fall juveniles move south 2–4 weeks earlier than adults. On the West Coast, migrants are seen at hawk watches such as the Marin Headlands and Point Loma in September and October, but western movements are perhaps postbreeding dispersal as much as true migrations.

Vocalizations: Red-shouldered Hawks are highly vocal year-round, especially during the breeding season from February through April. Call is a piercing, descending, slightly nasal, repeated *keeyar-keeyar-keeyar*! A lower, softer *kak-kak-kak* is heard year-round, but more often during breeding.

Broad-winged Hawk *(Buteo platypterus)* **BWHA** page 92

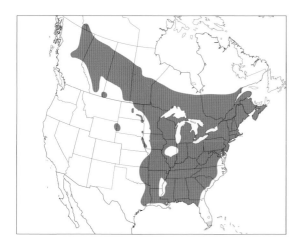

There's energy in the air—like static electricity. Conditions for hawk migration are perfect: passing cold front, northwest winds, and puffy clouds sprinkled across a bright blue sky. Expectations are high. Cars from the surrounding states fill the lot as a throng of hawk watchers gather at the lookout. Noon arrives, but only a handful of birds have traversed the ridge. Dissatisfied, murmured grumblings can be heard from newcomers, but old hands like "Broad-wing Charlie" just sit and wait, scanning the sky, anticipating what's to come. The anticipation of a big Broad-winged flight is like no other moment in birding. Will it happen, and how big will it be?

The first significant group of hawks begins to appear on the horizon, circling together in the distance, gathering lift on mounting thermals. Reaching the top of the thermal, they break off toward the south in loose lines. Then it happens. Someone spots a mass of birds developing to the north, swirling kinetic energy. In the distance thousands of birds spiral skyward, creating a dark tornado-like vortex known to hawk watchers as a "kettle." Adrenaline

rushes through the crowd. The north wind pushes the dynamic kettle closer. More hawks stream into the bottom from the north, rise up through the spinning column, and then leave from the top gliding south. The hawk-counter's clicker keeps a rapid pace as the birds pass overhead, counting them by 10 or even 50 at a time now. Newcomers wonder how it's possible to count such a huge flight, and how clusters of circling birds don't run into each other. The flight picks up to a steady pace until near darkness. It's uncertain exactly how many Broad-winged Hawks passed overhead today on their way south toward the coastal bend of Texas, then Mexico, and finally on to the wintering grounds in tropical South America. One thing is certain: witnessing a big flight of Broad-winged Hawks is one of the most thrilling events in hawk watching.

Overview: Broad-winged Hawks breed in deciduous woodland throughout North America but are generally secretive. They hunt mainly reptiles and amphibians from a perch below the forest canopy. During the breeding season, they may soar in mid-morning above the treetops, when they are more easily detected. During migration they are very conspicuous, moving south past hawk watches in September and October, especially in the eastern United States and Texas, where they often form large kettles. Spring migration is generally more dispersed, but large numbers are seen along the southern shores of the Great Lakes in mid-April to mid-May.

Broad-winged Hawks roost communally at night in semiopen or dense forest during migration, usually away from people, and their secretive nature makes them hard to detect. During winter, Broad-winged Hawks inhabit semiopen areas and forest edge, and they are often seen perched on snags in clear-cut tropical forest from where they perch-hunt. Occasionally they are seen on roadside wires.

Flight Style: Despite their small size, Broad-winged Hawks are steady fliers except in the most extreme winds. They soar in tight circles compared with larger raptors and flap in a quick, snappy manner similar to Red-shouldered or Cooper's Hawks, but somewhat stiffer or "choppy" in comparison.

Size and Shape: L 34–42 cm (14–17 in), WS 82–92 cm (32–36 in), WT 308–483 g (11–17 oz) Broad-winged Hawks are small, chunky, compact buteos. They have stocky wings with pointed tips in all postures, and a bulky head and chest. The tail is narrow and usually square tipped, appearing somewhat narrow and long when closed. Gliding overhead, the wings are angular, with the tips barely projecting past the trailing edge. Broad-winged Hawks usually hold their wings flat or with a very slight dihedral in a soar, and slightly drooped when gliding. When perched, they often appear small but stocky with short wings and large heads.

Plumage: Broad-winged Hawk occurs in a light or dark morph (no intermediates known so far) with 2 distinct age classes: adult and juvenile (first-years). Male and female plumages overlap, but overall plumage of adults and juveniles is variable, especially in light morphs. Eye color of juvenile is pale yellow-brown to pale brownish, turning darker brown as adults.

Adult light morphs are dark brown above including the head, and pale underneath with a rufous-barred chest (and sometimes belly). The barring on some adults is faint and inconspicuous on distant birds, while others show a nearly solid rufous chest. A few second-year Broad-winged Hawks show juvenile-like body plumage but have adult flight feathers. The adult flight feathers have a conspicuous dark trailing edge to the wings; the trailing edge on juveniles is more diffuse. The underwing coverts of adults and juveniles are essentially unmarked or lightly marked on the patagials. The tail is distinctly marked with several white bands between thicker black bands.

1st-year light morphs (juveniles) are whitish below with extreme variation from almost completely unmarked to heavily streaked below. Most show streaking that is limited to the sides of the breast. Some juveniles even show a streaked belly

similar to that of Red-tailed Hawks (but lack other Red-tailed Hawk characters). Rarely, juvenile Broad-winged Hawks are lightly barred underneath, similar to adults. The tail is pale with a few narrow bands, a broad dark subterminal, and faint pale tip. From underneath, the tail looks pale with a dark tip. Some juveniles have wide dark bands that are more adult-like, but the bands are less contrasting black and white. Juveniles are slightly paler brown above than adults and typically show some pale mottling on the upperwing coverts. The primaries show a faint, paler rectangular wing panel, which looks translucent from below in most situations. Many juveniles have a pale-streaked crown, a pale face, and a whitish supercilium, and often a bold dark malar.

Adult dark morphs are wholly blackish underneath on the body and underwing coverts. They are similar to light morphs on the upperside, but are slightly darker overall. The flight feathers are identical to those of light-morph adults. Dark-morph birds are rare, especially in the East. Be careful, birds can appear uniformly dark underneath when they are shadowed or backlit, but true dark morphs show a blackish underbody and wing coverts that contrast with the paler flight feathers in all conditions.

1st-year dark morphs (juveniles) are typically dark brownish on the body and underwing coverts, with most showing faint, tawny streaking/mottling throughout the underbody, appearing solidly dark at a distance. Some show more prominent tawny streaking below, but this is uncommon. The flight feathers are identical to those of light birds in most respects, but juvenile dark morphs have a darker trailing edge to the wings and can be similar to adults, but always less bold. The topside is slightly darker overall with less mottling than on light-morph juveniles, and the head typically lacks the pale areas shown by many light-morph juveniles.

Geographic Variation: There are 6 subspecies of the Broad-winged Hawk, but just 1 occurs in North America, *B. p. platypterus*, which breeds across the eastern half of North America and in parts of the West, and winters to South America. Five other forms are endemic to different islands throughout the West Indies. Subspecies differences are based on general coloration and size; the island forms are generally smaller. There is plumage variation and overlap in all subspecies. Dark morphs occur but are found primarily in the western United States and Canada. They are rare in the East on migration.

Molt: The first molt of Broad-winged Hawk begins typically during first spring, mainly in mid-April, and continues through August, after which most birds are indistinguishable from adults. Some birds rarely retain an outer primary or two (or secondary) through the second year. Adults usually undergo a complete molt cycle each year, mainly from May through September.

Similar Species: Adult Broad-winged Hawks are distinctive but sometimes confused with adult *Red-shouldered Hawks*, since both have banded tails and are rufous on the underparts. One main difference is that Red-shouldered Hawk is paler underneath with a rufous wash throughout the underwing coverts; Broad-winged Hawks are darker rufous on the breast with paler underwing coverts. Adult Red-shouldered Hawk has prominent black-and-white banding on the flight feathers that is most visible in flight, but also visible on perched birds. Adult Broad-winged Hawks lack clear banding of the flight feathers. On the topside, adult Red-shouldered Hawk has rufous shoulder patches and whitish, comma-shaped panels across the base of the outer primaries. The tail has narrow white bands compared with the broad white tail bands of adult Broad-winged Hawk.

Juvenile *Red-shouldered Hawk* can be very similar in plumage to juvenile light-morph Broad-winged Hawk, especially when perched. Both are pale underneath with varying amounts of streaking on the underbody, with Red-shouldered being more evenly streaked throughout. Juvenile Red-shouldered also has pale comma-shaped wing panels similar to those of adults, which all Broad-wingeds lack. From late April through June, Broad-winged Hawks (especially juveniles) molt primary feathers, and this sometimes gives the appearance of comma-shaped wing panels, but once you're aware of this, it is easy to tell the "gap" in the wing of Broad-winged from the translucent wing panel of Red-shouldered Hawk. The wings of Red-shouldered Hawk are longer and never pointed at the tips like those of Broad-winged. Broad-winged Hawks are stockier when perched, with shorter legs, usually show a bolder head pattern than Red-shouldered, and have plainer secondaries (usually clearly banded in Red-shouldered). The wingbeats of both species are snappy, but Red-shouldered's are shallower and looser.

Juvenile *Gray Hawk* and juvenile light-morph Broad-winged Hawk are similar in plumage and size, but there are several differences between the two.

The dark tail bands of juvenile Broad-winged are equal in width and space throughout the tail with a broader subterminal, whereas the dark bands of juvenile Gray Hawk become narrower toward the base. Gray Hawk also has a pure white supercilium and cheek patch, and is typically whiter on the uppertail coverts. Gray Hawk shows less pointed wingtips and lacks the pale primary wing panels shown by Broad-winged; instead, its flight feathers are very pale and finely barred, lacking the dark-tipped primaries of Broad-winged. Body plumage of both species is similar and varies among individuals. Gray Hawk tends to have a more defined dark central throat stripe, but some Broad-wings also show this.

Short-tailed Hawk is similar in shape and size, but all Short-tailed Hawks have grayish flight feathers, whereas Broad-winged Hawks have much paler, whitish flight feathers that are usually less heavily banded. In terms of behavior, Broad-winged is much more likely to be seen perch-hunting from the forest edge, and it does not kite like Short-tailed. Juvenile light-morph Short-tailed Hawks are generally lightly marked below, but be careful, because body plumage can be nearly identical to that of the palest variant juvenile Broad-wings. Juvenile dark morph Short-tailed Hawks are heavily streaked tawny below, with a rare all-blackish variant. Broad-winged is the opposite, with dark juveniles being mostly blackish with faint-looking, tawny streaking. Short-tailed Hawk is longer-winged when perched, with the wingtips just about reaching the tail tip.

Status and Distribution: Broad-winged Hawks are fairly common across much of the East, but are significantly less common in the West. They nest in deciduous and boreal forest from eastern North America to western Canada. They are uncommon west of Minnesota, and nearly absent throughout the Great Plains. Dark morphs are known to breed primarily in Alberta with few summer records elsewhere and are presumed rare even within their restricted range; however, much remains unknown about the distinct range and occurrence of dark Broad-wingeds. Migration counts in the western United States average a ratio of about 1:20 dark-morphs to light-morphs, but there is almost no breeding data with which to compare this ratio. There are no breeding records of dark morphs east of the northern Great Plains (one in North Dakota). Broad-winged Hawks winter mainly from southern Mexico to northern South America, but a few spend the winter in southern

Florida, Louisiana, Texas, and California. They arrive on their breeding grounds in late April through May, and depart from their territories in late August through October.

Migration: Broad-winged Hawk migration is spectacular, and the famously large flights of legend are dictated by several dynamics. Broad-wings generally move on a broad front, and they can be seen just about anywhere throughout the East during migration, but they utilize thermals and ridge updrafts to keep them aloft and to save energy. When birds come together seeking means of lift during optimal weather conditions, groups of thousands can form. At a few locations where weather and topography combine to "funnel" these groups together, massive concentrations can occur. Not surprisingly, most of these locations are established hawk watches.

Spring migration in North America occurs primarily from April through May, with the peak typically in mid- to late April. Of course, the southern United States sees Broad-wingeds about a week or two earlier in spring and later in fall than northern United States and Canada. Adult flights peak at least 2–4 weeks earlier than juvenile flights (which occur into June). The southern shore of the Great Lakes is the best site to see Broad-winged Hawks in the spring.

The bulk of fall migration occurs from mid-August through October, with the peak from mid- to late September. The northern shores of the Great Lakes, including Hawk Cliff in ON, Hawk Ridge, MN, and the Appalachian Mountains in the eastern United States (including Hawk Mountain, PA), and Corpus Christi in south Texas are reliable sites to see large numbers of Broad-wings. Lake Erie Metropark in southern Michigan (just south of Detroit) sees the biggest numbers in North America, second only to Veracruz, Mexico. There is no significant difference between timing of major movements of adults and juveniles in fall, but some juveniles linger in the north long after the adults are gone. November and December records are almost always juveniles. Dark morphs are extremely rare in the East on migration (only a handful of records), but they are much more common in the West, especially at sites such as the Goshute Mountains, NV, Marin Headlands, CA, and Dinosaur Ridge, CO.

Vocalizations: Broad-winged Hawks are vocal mainly on the breeding grounds, when listening for their call is a good way to find these relatively secretive birds. The common call is a high, thin, drawn-out, two-part whistled *ps-eeeeee*.

Gray Hawk *(Buteo plagiatus)* **GRHA** page 98

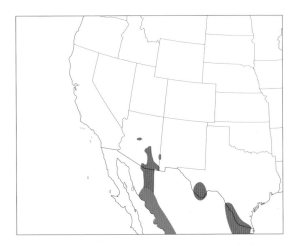

Morning sun beats down through a gallery forest of cottonwoods lining a small river in Arizona. Walking quietly along the leaf-strewn path, you observe many

of the birds you've come here to find. Tropical Kingbirds twitter from the shady spots, and a dashing male Vermilion Flycatcher catches your eye, moving like a flame toward an unseen insect. The river's edge is full of sound, but one in particular is unfamiliar and striking: a repeated mournful whistle. Thinking you've stumbled upon a tropical rarity, you begin your search, tiptoeing toward the sound. The bird goes silent. A minute later it sounds off again, *pooEEEeer, pooEEEeer, pooEEEeer, pooEEEeer.* Where is this bird? What is this bird? You imitate the call as best as you can, and within seconds a hawk bursts out of the cottonwoods and lands on a thick branch nearby. The bird before you is unmistakable—an adult Gray Hawk, but that can't be what you heard, can it? You're stunned as it calls again, responding to your whistles with its own unusual voice, a sound not at all what you'd expect from a raptor.

Overview: Gray Hawks are medium-sized, striking buteos restricted to a few areas in the Southwest. They nest in large trees (usually cottonwoods) along rivers and dry creek beds in Arizona, New Mexico, and south Texas. They sometimes forage in mesquite woodland adjacent to these riparian areas, but in general are not prone to wander. Gray Hawks perch-hunt, and while they soar readily and often quite high on midmorning thermals, they typically do not stoop on prey from a height. Instead they sit quietly in the shady areas of large cottonwoods waiting to pounce on lizards, small mammals, birds, and insects. Adults are simply remarkable and unlikely to be confused with any other North American raptor, but juveniles are more variable and frequently confused with juvenile Broad-winged and Red-shouldered Hawks. From below, Gray Hawks often appear very pale when soaring, with few notable field marks (but see tail pattern). Unlike many buteos, their underwings are very plain and unmarked.

Flight Style: Gray Hawks soar on flat wings in steady circles. Their direct flight uses snappy accipiter-like wingbeats, which are generally faster than other buteos. Unlike some buteos, Gray Hawks are not aerial raptors and they do not kite or hover, instead preferring to perch-hunt.

Size and Shape: L 36–46 cm (14–18 in), WS 82–98 cm (32–38 in), WT 378–660 g (13–23 oz)
Gray Hawks are medium-sized raptors, but they are small for a buteo, roughly similar in size and structure to Broad-winged and Red-shouldered Hawks. They appear generally slim of build when perched, but compact overall in flight, with tapered wingtips.

Plumage: Gray Hawk sexes are similar, but the 2 age classes differ markedly. Gray Hawks attain adult appearance in the first summer/second fall.

Adults are striking: they are the only all-gray North American raptor with fine barring below, a boldly banded black-and-white tail, and dark brown eyes.

1st-years (juveniles) are overall brown above and variably marked dark brown on buff below, with a notably striking head pattern combining a white check, dark malar, dark eyeline, and white supercilium; most have a dark central throat stripe. The tail pattern is unique, with many broad, brown bands that become narrower near the base. The flight feathers are finely barred, even the outer primaries, and these are largely translucent in flight on both juveniles and adults.

Geographic Variation: Gray Hawk taxonomy is still evolving, but recent studies show that 2 species are involved. Gray Hawks occur north of Costa Rica (including the entire range of the species in the United States), and Gray-lined Hawks (formerly lumped with Gray Hawk) occur from southwest Costa Rica south through the termination of the species' range in South America. There are no North American records for Gray-lined Hawk.

Molt: Being a small buteo, Gray Hawks usually have a complete molt each year, similar to Broad-winged and Red-shouldered Hawks. Juveniles undergo their first complete molt during the late first spring/summer and become adult-like by the second fall. First-summer birds are obvious when transitioning into adult plumage, replacing the brownish juvenile feathers with the grayish adult ones. Subsequent molts are generally complete, mainly from June to October.

Similar Species: Adults are unmistakable if seen well; note the combination of unique gray plumage, finely barred gray underparts, and boldly banded black-and-white tail. Juveniles are told from juvenile *Broad-winged Hawk* by their more distinct head pattern with bold pale cheeks, shorter wings (cf. primary projection when perched), a longer tail with progressively narrow bands toward the base, and lack of a dusky trailing edge to evenly translucent flight feathers (vs. pale panels on juvenile Broad-winged). Juvenile Gray Hawk is told from juvenile *Red-shouldered Hawk* by its bolder head pattern and the lack of pale crescents on the outer primaries.

Status and Distribution: Gray Hawks are generally uncommon and found locally in a few riparian areas of southeast Arizona, New Mexico (rare), and south Texas. They can be relatively easy to find in the places where they do occur because of their vocal habits and their propensity for sitting on relatively exposed perches. Gray Hawks are a rare vagrant north of their mapped range (1 Kansas record).

Migration: Most Arizona birds withdraw from the breeding range during winter, but Texas birds appear to be resident (Big Bend and lower Rio Grande Valley).

Vocalizations: Quite vocal, especially in early morning. Common call is a repeated mournful whistle, highest in the middle, *pooEEEeer*; some variations are more drawn-out and less rising. Also a drawn-out scream, longer, lower, and more pure-toned than Red-tailed Hawk.

Short-tailed Hawk *(Buteo brachyurus)* **STHA** page 100

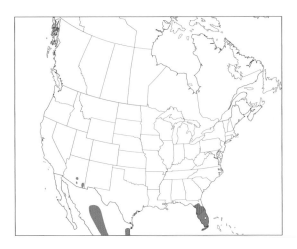

It's hot for a late fall day in south Florida—almost tropical. In the shade of an isolated pine hammock, the thick chip notes of dozens of Palm Warblers fill the scattered palmetto understory. In the blue, beyond the obvious vultures, is a distant speck, motionless against the bright sky. It's compact with broad wings. The white body and underwings contrast strongly with the darker flight feathers. It is persistent in its kiting behavior, with wingtips curled slightly upward. At once, the bird turns hard on a wing, folds up, and plummets into the nearby grove of pines. Songbirds scatter in all directions. A few seconds later, a Short-tailed Hawk emerges and flies overhead, carrying one of the songbirds that failed to avoid its high-altitude sneak attack.

Overview: The Short-tailed Hawk is mainly a tropical raptor, with a small population in Florida, as well as a few nesting pairs in Arizona. In Florida, Short-tailed Hawks breed in tracts of swampy forest bordering open areas, becoming more concentrated toward the southern end of the state in fall and winter. But in Arizona, Short-tailed Hawks have been found only at higher elevations, nesting in pine forest on the mountainous "sky islands" of the southeastern corner of the state. Throughout its tropical range, however, Short-tailed Hawk is a habitat generalist, and it can be expected almost anywhere. Short-tailed

Hawks are only rarely seen perched and typically do not sit on roadside wires or poles like other small buteos. In all plumages, note Short-tailed Hawk's broad wings with relatively tapered tips and dark flight feathers that contrast with paler outer primaries. On light morphs, note the pale underwing coverts that contrast strongly with the dark flight feathers.

Flight Style: Short-tailed Hawks are aerial hunters, frequently kiting high overhead in search of prey. They often hang motionless while hunting but do not hover like some other buteos, turning abruptly on one wing and falling into a stoop, pouncing on birds, rodents, and reptiles. Generally distinctive in flight, Short-tailed Hawks soar with flat wings, with the wingtips characteristically upturned. Even when kiting they have a rather flat-winged profile, with only the wingtips flared upward. Short-tailed Hawks fly with even-paced, smooth wingbeats, somewhat between a Broad-winged Hawk and a Red-tailed Hawk.

Size and Shape: L 39–44 cm (15–17 in), WS 83–103 cm (33–41 in), WT 342–560 g (12–20 oz)
Short-tailed Hawks are small for a buteo and most similar in size and shape to Broad-winged Hawk. Their wings are broad, but somewhat pinched-in at the base, and strongly tapered at the tips. Despite the name, Short-tailed Hawks do not often appear to have especially short tails; instead they appear fairly typical in length compared with most buteos. When the bird is seen head-on, though, the tail can appear quite short in relation to the broad wings.

Plumage: Short-tailed Hawks are dimorphic, occurring in light and dark morphs, but with no intermediate plumages reported so far. Dark morphs slightly outnumber light morphs in Florida, but all Arizona breeders have been light morphs to date. Ages differ, with first-years (juveniles) distinguishable from adults throughout the first year. The sexes are similar and not distinguishable from each other in the field. All Short-tailed Hawks share similar flight feathers that are mostly dusky grayish with the outer 3–4 primaries notably paler. The tail pattern is variable, ranging from lightly to heavily banded, but always with a wider dark subterminal band.

Adult light morphs are clean buff to white below. The tail has a broad dark subterminal band and several ill-defined and variable inner bands. The inner primaries and secondaries are grayish with a distinct, dark trailing edge, and the outer primaries have paler bases. The topside is dark brown, lacking any mottling, appearing similar to adult Swainson's Hawks in this respect.

Adult dark morphs are dark brown above with wholly blackish underparts. The flight feathers are similar to light-morph adults.

1st-year light morphs are brown above and buffy below with variable brown streaking (sometimes absent) on the sides of the upper breast, a more diffuse dark trailing edge to flight feathers than on adults, and translucent primaries. The tail pattern is similar to adults, but the subterminal band is often narrower and less defined.

1st-year dark-morphs are variably dark below, but typically show extensive tawny streaking on the body and underwing coverts; rare examples are completely dark. Most birds show light speckling on the belly and underwings. The flight and tail feathers are similar to those of light-morph juveniles.

Geographic Variation: Two subspecies of Short-tailed Hawk have been described, but only one occurs in North America: *B. b. fuliginosus* ranges south through Panama, and is told from the nominate form of South America by its generally paler upperparts and brighter rufous neck sides.

Molt: Juveniles undergo their first molt beginning in the first spring and continuing through early fall. Being a small buteo, Short-tailed Hawk usually replaces all its flight feathers in a single year. Adult plumage is attained by the second fall, but in rare cases a few juvenile primaries and secondaries can be retained until the second complete molt, which occurs during the second summer. Adults usually have a complete molt each year from April to September.

Similar Species: The biggest source of confusion is *Broad-winged Hawk*, which shares a similar shape and size. All Short-tailed Hawks have darker grayish flight feathers, whereas Broad-winged Hawks have much paler, whitish flight feathers that are usually less heavily banded. In terms of behavior, Broad-winged is much more likely to perch-hunt on the forest edge, and it does not kite like Short-tailed. Juvenile light-morph Short-tailed Hawks are generally lightly marked below, but be careful; body plumage is often separable from Broad-winged but can be nearly identical to the palest variant juvenile Broad-wingeds. Juvenile dark-morph Short-tailed Hawks are heavily streaked tawny below, with a rare all-blackish variant. Broad-winged is the opposite, with dark juveniles being mostly blackish, and only rarely do they show distinct tawny streaking. Short-tailed Hawk is longer-winged when perched, with the wingtips just about reaching the tail tip.

Also beware of confusion with *Swainson's* and *White-tailed Hawks*. Though larger and rangier, both can have similar plumage to Short-tailed, and both have dusky grayish flight feathers. Be especially careful with third-year White-tailed Hawks gliding high overhead; they can be surprisingly similar and have a similar dark-hooded appearance.

Hybrids. Short-tailed Hawk possibly hybridizes with Swainson's Hawk, but more study is needed. A bird that has overwintered in Tucson for several years seems to show intermediate characters, and it is fond of perching on power poles (atypical for Short-tailed Hawk; typical of Swainson's Hawk). It seems this bird could be a hybrid, but it may be a variant of Short-tailed.

Status and Distribution: Short-tailed Hawks are fairly common in Florida, especially from central Florida south to the tip. They are still quite rare in Arizona, but records are increasing in the state. Elsewhere in North America it is strictly a vagrant, with the largest number of records coming from south Texas.

Migration: Short-tailed Hawk movements are generally poorly understood. Florida birds breed largely in the central portion of the state, and then move south in fall and winter to concentrate in the southern third of the state. Relatively few birds move north of typical Florida breeding areas in winter. Arizona breeders presumably disperse or migrate south, but lack of winter birding coverage in the high-elevation habitat where they breed makes certainty impossible. In Texas, Short-tailed Hawks are rare vagrants, but in recent years they have occurred with increased frequency, perhaps suggesting an overall range expansion to the north. Hawk watchers should be on the lookout for this species at all migration sites across the South, especially in south Texas and Arizona, but also in New Mexico.

Vocalizations: Mostly vocal during nesting, Short-taileds give a drawn-out *keeeeer*. They also make other typical buteo calls around the nest when agitated or delivering prey.

Harris's Hawk *(Parabuteo unicinctus)* **HASH** page 102

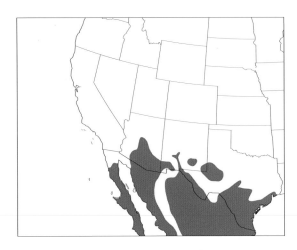

I sit shoulder to shoulder with five members of my group, bonding before the hunt. As a youngster, I've taken the easy assignment so far, spotting prey while perched atop the shoulders of my siblings, and only once did I initiate a pursuit. But today I want to prove my mettle and make the kill with my own two feet. Our quarry is rabbit, desert cottontail to be specific. Over the past nine months I've learned the tactics used to catch these wary animals, and I've learned our group is more successful hunting together than any one of us could be alone. Pack mentality. We have to share the spoils, but we catch more too.

Three of my companions break off from different saguaro tops and scan the mesquite brush intently for movement. I'm sitting next to mama, the hardest-hitter of our bunch. She can accelerate like lightning, turn on a dime, and anticipate a rabbit's movements better than any of us. One of the pack drops from the air into the dense mesquite; a rabbit flushes. Adrenaline flows and instinct takes over. I burst off my perch as fast as I can, sending the rabbit coursing down trails only it knows, dashing for the next thicket. I close the distance, cornering around thorny cholla and saguaro—moves made easy by my long, maneuverable tail. Around the next opening, I'm within 10 feet of my quarry…this is it! Out of nowhere a sinister black shape streaks in from the right,

tackling the rabbit and rolling over in a dust cloud. I break off, circle back, and fly into the dust-up, but mama has already made the kill. My job is done for today. I'm learning, and I'll get another chance to prove myself soon.

Overview: Harris's Hawks are distinctive raptors of the arid Southwest. Closely related to the buteos, Harris's Hawks are now in their own genus but have been lumped with the buteos at times in the past. Harris's are found in open to semiopen habitats with well-spaced perches, usually tall cacti (atop the thorns), power poles, or trees, and are frequently found in surprisingly suburban areas, such as around Tucson. Harris's Hawks are generally social during both nesting and winter, and their hunting tactics are among the most complex and unique of any bird. Hunting groups usually consist of a pair of dominant adults assisted by several immature or adult birds, often offspring of the adults or even birds from other nesting pairs. These groups cooperatively hunt prey year-round, sharing the catch, but Harris's Hawks are also capable of hunting alone. Harris's Hawks are known to practice "back-standing," where one hawk perches atop another to gain a better view of the territory. Although most North American Harris's Hawks breed in spring, in some cases they can breed year-round when food is plentiful. Generally confiding, they often allow close approach.

Flight Style: Harris's Hawks soar steadily on flattish or bowed wings, and glide on bowed wings with the tips curled upward. When flapping, the wingbeats are even and heavy, somewhat recalling a Red-tailed Hawk. They are impressive sprinters as well, accelerating quickly at the first sign of prey.

Size and Shape: L 46–59 cm (18–23 in), WS 103–119 cm (40–47 in), WT 568–1203 g (1.3–2.6 lb)
Harris's Hawks are large raptors, similar in size to a Red-tailed Hawk, but are shaped somewhat like an oversized accipiter. They have long, broad wings

and a very long tail that is always white-based. The wings are not quite as stocky as an accipiter, and this masks the tail's real length. When perched, they appear large and bulky, similar to a Red-tailed Hawk, but with a much longer tail.

Plumage: Formerly called the "Bay-winged Hawk" because of its striking rufous upperwing coverts, Harris's Hawk has two distinct plumages: juvenile and adult. *Adults* are solidly blackish brown overall with rufous underwing coverts and rufous uppertail coverts. *1st-years* (juveniles) are variably streaked below, sometimes with a more solid breast, and finely banded flight feathers. Both ages have a blackish tail with a conspicuous white base, but adults have a bolder white tip than juveniles. Sexes are similar in plumage, but females average larger than males.

Geographic Variation: There are 2–3 subspecies described range-wide, with 1 or 2 occurring in North America. But the 2 described North American races are weakly differentiated at best, and most authorities treat them as conspecific. Western breeding *P. u. superior* is named for its larger size, but it is not consistently larger than the eastern breeding *P. u. harrisi*. Plumage differences are not field-diagnosable.

Molt: The extent of molt in juveniles over the first winter is unknown, but probably limited if present at all. Molt timing is hard to discern because of year-round breeding, but most are on typical spring breeding schedules. Juveniles undergo a partial molt mainly from February to November, with up to 4 outer primaries and a few secondaries retained, resulting in a stepwise replacement of flight feathers thereafter. Adults undergo a partial molt mainly from March to December.

Similar Species: Harris's Hawks are not easily confused if seen well. But their white tail base invites confusion with the superficially similar adult female and juvenile *Northern Harrier*. Note the Harrier's warmer brown plumage, more languid flight style, and lankier overall structure. Perched Harris's Hawks are told from dark-morph buteos by their rufous upperwing coverts, and the long, white-based tail with a graduated, bold white tip.

Status and Distribution: Harris's Hawks are fairly common residents across their relatively restricted U.S. range. They are rare north and west of the mapped range. Juveniles and some adults possibly engage in some northward postbreeding dispersal, but more study is needed. Harris's Hawks are frequent escapees from falconry and the pet trade, and these birds confuse the natural occurrence of Harris's Hawks in California and elsewhere outside the normal range.

Migration: Essentially nonmigratory, but periodic irruptions bring birds north of their typical range, occasionally with several birds reaching southern California and even rarely as far north as southern Utah. The cause of these events is not yet known. Any Harris's found out of range should be looked at carefully for signs of captivity, as they are frequently kept by falconers.

Vocalizations: The typical call is a short series of harsh *kak, kak, kak, kak* notes. Harris's also give a high, hoarse scream, and a somewhat corvid-like, drawn-out raspy *krrrrrr*. Begging juveniles give a repeated high-pitched *whew, whew, whew, whew*.

Common Black-Hawk *(Buteogallus anthracinus)* **COBH** page 104

White-and-gray puffy clouds drift overhead, carried north by a mounting south wind. It's mid-March, and the cottonwood trees along this stretch of the Santa Cruz River in southeast Arizona bend in the breeze, already in full leaf. The morning birding is good, and a group of birders have "ticked" several life birds, many of which are specialties of this region. But now everyone is looking for one more bird: the Common Black-Hawk. The date is right for Black-Hawks to be returning to their breeding sites from Mexico. These birds follow the north–south riparian corridors that stretch across the border, like green highways winding through the desert, leading back to the shady, cottonwood-lined creeks of Arizona they call home.

The group scans the treetops from a bridge, looking off to the south. A few Gray Hawks are up now, soaring, calling, and courting. A group of vultures begins to rise above the cottonwoods, but there is a different bird among them. Similar in shape to a Black Vulture and overall dark, with flat, wide wings, and a short tail—is it the bird the group is seeking? It banks, and a glimpse of white can be seen on the tail from above. A Black-Hawk! As the kettle drifts closer, the Black-Hawk breaks away, following the river and gliding directly overhead. As it passes, its identity becomes clearer. The group is elated as they watch the hawk pass, but in the distance someone has spotted two more suspicious specks drifting their way…

Overview: Common Black-Hawks are a specialty bird of the Southwest. In flight, adults are unmistakable, but perched birds can be more challenging.

Their general coloration closely matches another Southwest specialty, the Zone-tailed Hawk. But most problematic are juvenile birds, which are very different from adults, having a plumage pattern similar to several other juvenile buteos with which they are often confused.

Common Black-Hawks are generally shy and retiring during the breeding season, nesting along perennial streams lined with cottonwoods throughout the desert Southwest. There are relatively few places where birders can access their nesting areas, most of which are in Arizona. Black-Hawks soar briefly in midmorning (the best chance to see one), but then return to the gallery forest canopy, where they quietly perch-hunt amphibians, reptiles, and fish. Occasionally they hunt on the ground, even wading in shallow water with their long legs.

Flight Style: When soaring, Black-Hawks do so on flat wings, lacking the shallow dihedral shown by Black Vulture. They soar in wide, steady circles, and their direct flight is with stiff, labored wingbeats.

Size and Shape: L 51–56 cm (20–22 in), WS 102–133 cm (40–52 in), WT 630–1300 g (1.4–2.9 lb) Common Black-Hawks are large raptors, roughly the size of a Red-tailed Hawk. They are generally distinctive, as their stocky, wide-winged shape and short tail render adults in flight nearly unmistakable. Adults are more similar in shape to Black Vulture than to any of the dark buteos. Juveniles are lankier, with narrower wings and longer tails, and are much more likely to be misidentified or passed off as a streaky-plumaged buteo. The shape difference between juvenile and adult Common Black-Hawk is the most dramatic age-related difference in any North American raptor species. On perched Black-Hawks, the wingtips nearly reach the tail tip, especially on adults, and the bill is less sharply curved than on most other raptors.

Plumage: Common Black-Hawk shows 2 plumages, first-year (juvenile) and adult. There is no appreciable difference between the sexes as juveniles or adults, but as with many raptors, females are slightly larger. Black-Hawk attains its adult plumage by the second fall.

Adult Common Black-Hawks appear completely black below with dark, finely banded flight feathers, an extremely broad, dark trailing edge to the wings, and a single bold, white tail band that creates a white-rumped look from above. The upperside is otherwise blackish, including the head, often with a bluish sheen, but the cere and flesh in front of the eye are pale. Adults also have pale bases to the outer primaries that may be visible at times.

1st-years show dark streaking below, finely banded flight feathers, a bold face pattern, and multiple wavy white tail bands with a black tip that are striking from above and sometimes from below. The upperwings are dark brownish black, showing pale panels on the inner primaries that are visible from above and below. By the first summer, 1-year-old birds look intermediate between juvenile and adult, as they are molting from the streaky juvenile plumage to the solidly dark plumage of adults.

Geographic Variation: There are 3–4 subspecies of the Common Black-Hawk throughout its range, but only 1 subspecies occurs in North America: *B. a. anthracinus*. The North American form averages larger and darker overall than the southern forms. The Mangrove Black-Hawk (*B. a. subtilis*) has at times been considered a separate species, but is currently considered a mangrove-inhabiting subspecies of Common Black-Hawk. The recently split Cuban Black-Hawk (*B. gundlachii*) is endemic to Cuba, but has occurred once in Georgia as a vagrant (probably not naturally, though).

Molt: Black-Hawks undergo their first molt in late first-spring/summer, and look mainly adult-like by the second fall. Second-year birds often retain a few juvenile secondaries and outer primaries, but plumage is otherwise adult-like. After the second molt, they are not distinguishable from older adults. Adults usually have a partial molt, similar to many large buteos, where not all the flight feathers are replaced each year. Thus, adults often have multiple generations of primaries and secondaries, replaced in a stepwise fashion.

Similar Species: In flight, adult Black-Hawk is easily confused with *Black Vulture* at a distance, which shares a similar shape, but note Black Vulture's all-dark wings with pale outer primaries, narrow-based

black tail (lacking a white band), and smaller, naked head. Common Black-Hawk soars on flatter wings, with just the tips of the primaries upturned.

Adult *Zone-tailed Hawk* and adult Common Black-Hawk are very similar in plumage, but their shapes in flight are nearly opposite as raptors go. Perched, they are much more difficult to tell apart. Black-Hawk is told from Zone-tailed Hawk by its stockier build, longer legs, bare yellow facial skin, and less sharply hooked bill. On perched Black-Hawks, the wingtips nearly reach the tail tip, especially on adults; the tail tip of Zone-tailed Hawk extends well beyond the wingtips.

Juvenile Black-Hawks are fairly distinctive, but there is possible confusion with streaky juvenile buteos, especially juvenile *Red-tailed* and *Swainson's* Hawks. Note juvenile Common Black-Hawk's relatively broad wings and more finely banded flight feathers. Common Black-Hawk has a distinctive tail pattern unlike that of any other juvenile buteo, showing narrow, wavy black-and-white bands.

Status and Distribution: A rare breeder throughout its U.S. range, Black-Hawks are generally hard to find, known from only a few breeding areas. The bulk of the population nests in Arizona, with smaller numbers breeding in New Mexico, southwestern Utah, and locally in west Texas. In winter a few birds are usually found along the lower Rio Grande in south Texas, but breeding is not known from this region. Black-Hawk is an exceptional vagrant away from known breeding areas or south Texas.

Migration: Little is known about Common Black-Hawk migration, but spring migrants are observed in southeast Arizona beginning in early March, arriving on breeding grounds there in mid-March. Peak spring migration of adults appears to be the second half of March. Birds leave the nesting areas in fall from September to October, with almost all departing for more southerly wintering locales.

Vocalizations: Black-Hawks are quite vocal on the breeding grounds. Their call is a series of short, emphatic whistles, rising and slowing down toward the end, recalling an Osprey: *whi-whi-whi-whi-whée whée whée.*

Zone-tailed Hawk *(Buteo albonotatus)* ZTHA page 106

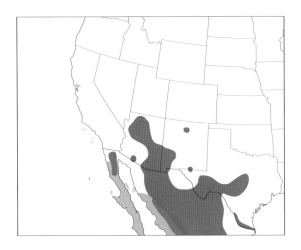

Every morning we vultures gather here over the grassland, an aerial biker gang, cruising together, looking for trouble, seeking out last night's casualties. We are 55 strong, floating on the wind in unison, but there's a pecking order here, and not just any poser can join the group. Another of our kind joins the mass from below, now spinning in a dark vortex on the horizon. The newcomer is a fine example, soaring with wings raised, swaying back and forth, letting the wind guide his direction. As he rises through our ranks, closer inspection reveals something's *off* about this stranger. He's too small to be one of us. His head is covered with black feathers and his tail seems to have a white band. Wait…he's not one of us…but he sure looks like it!!! Before we can take a closer look, the *infiltrator* drops from the sky in an amazing stoop, snatching a quail right off the ground …the thing never saw it coming. Wow…none of us can do that. Well, he's not one of us, but I guess this guy's OK after all. Maybe we'll get some of his scraps.

Overview: Zone-tailed Hawk is a large raptor of riparian woods, mountains, canyons, and arid hills of the Southwest. Zone-tailed Hawks are consummate aerialists, spending most of the day hunting on the wing, usually in association with kettles of Turkey Vultures, but also on their own. They are thought to mimic Turkey Vultures in order to prey on animals that have become conditioned to the vulture's harmless presence, one of few cases of evolutionary mimicry in birds. While this relationship has not been scientifically proven, Zone-tailed Hawks are closely linked to Turkey Vultures through all aspects of their

lives, nesting in close proximity to vulture roosts, and even roosting with them during the nonbreeding season. Zone-tailed Hawks hunt birds, mammals, and reptiles, usually captured through spectacular aerial stoops, but they sometimes perch-hunt in the morning prior to the development of optimal soaring conditions.

Flight Style: At a distance, Zone-tailed Hawks are difficult to distinguish from Turkey Vultures without practice, but when seen together the two are more noticeably different. Zone-tailed Hawks often soar with their tails closed, swaying in a buoyant, wobbly manner much like that of Turkey Vulture, especially on ridge updrafts. They glide with a modified dihedral like Turkey Vultures, but exhibit slightly quicker, stiffer wingbeats, and are more agile overall by comparison.

Size and Shape: L 48–56 cm (19–22 in), WS 121–140 cm (48–55 in), WT 610–1080 g (1.3–2.4 lb) Zone-tailed Hawks are one of the largest buteos but slightly smaller and more compact than Turkey Vultures, with slimmer bodies and slightly narrower wings and tails. Females are considerably larger than males. In a moderate to steep glide, the wings of Zone-tailed Hawks taper more toward the tips, and in a shallow glide, they show a straighter trailing edge to the wings, especially when facing away. When perched, they are slimmer than Common Black-Hawk, with longer tails.

Plumage: There are 2 age classes: adult and first-year (juvenile). The sexes of juveniles are identical, but adult males and females differ slightly in tail pattern. It is possible that second-year birds have mostly adult female-like tail characteristics, but more study is needed. Zone-tailed Hawks take 1 year to attain adult plumage. First-year and adult Zone-tailed Hawks have dark eyes.

Adults are black below with contrasting grayish flight feathers that are heavily banded with a bold dark trailing edge. The tail has 1 prominent white band when closed and seen from below. When the tail is spread, adults show 2–5 inner bands, but this varies between individuals, and tail pattern overlaps between the sexes. Males average fewer inner tail bands than females. Males often have a slightly bluer cast to the back and chest than females. Some second-years retain a few juvenile secondaries and outer primaries, but are otherwise indistinguishable from adults.

1st-years are similar to adults but have fine white spotting on the breast, finely banded flight feathers out to the tips, and a finely banded tail with a wider black subterminal band. The flight feathers lack the bold dark trailing edge of adults, making first-years more similar to Turkey Vulture than adults. The pale inner primary panels are visible from above and below, but are not as striking or obvious as on many other juvenile buteos.

Geographic Variation: Zone-tailed Hawk is currently considered monotypic. Birds from eastern Panama and South America are sometimes treated as a distinct subspecies, but evidence is lacking to support this.

Molt: Juveniles undergo their first molt during the first spring and summer, after which they are usually indistinguishable from older adults, but some may retain a few outer primaries through the second year. Adults usually do not replace all the flight feathers in a single year, thereby developing stepwise molt patterns in the primaries and secondaries like many other large buteos. Molt generally takes place from May through October, but some birds possibly finish on the winter grounds.

Similar Species: Zone-tailed Hawk is often confused with and passed off as *Turkey Vulture*, which it closely resembles in flight. It shares Turkey Vulture's teetering flight and strong dihedral, but Zone-tailed's wingbeats are quicker and stiffer, and they are able to make quicker, more agile turns and stoops than vultures. Zone-tailed Hawks also differ in that they are smaller, larger-headed, and square-tailed, and they have slightly narrower wings. Plumage differences from Turkey Vulture include banded flight feathers with a bold dark trailing edge (adults), a yellow cere and feet, and different tail patterns. Since Turkey Vultures spend a considerable amount of time on the ground, the tips to their tails are often worn; the tail tip on Zone-tailed Hawk usually lacks significant wear.

Zone-tailed is very similar to *Common Black-Hawk* in plumage, but the two differ drastically in shape. In flight, Zone-tailed Hawk is much longer and narrower-winged than Black-Hawk, with a longer tail. When perched, Zone-tailed is even more likely to be confused with Black-Hawk. Zone-tailed Hawk is distinguished by its slimmer build with longer wings and tail, gray (vs. bright yellow) lores, grayish tail bands dorsally, and shorter legs.

Juvenile Zone-taileds are told from other dark buteos in flight by their finely banded flight feathers, including the primary tips, and bold yellow cere. Their shape is also more Turkey Vulture-like than other juvenile buteos.

Status and Distribution: An uncommon breeder in its U.S. range, Zone-tailed Hawk withdraws south in winter. Most leave Arizona, but a few winter in south Texas. Zone-tailed Hawk is rare in southern Utah, and exceptional elsewhere outside the mapped range. It arrives on the breeding grounds in mid-March, departing from August through September. Despite this species' limited range in the United States, it is more broadly distributed throughout the tropics, where it occupies more diverse habitats, but is never common.

Migration: Migration for Zone-tailed Hawks is mainly from March through April in spring and throughout September in fall, but is generally poorly understood compared with most other species. Zone-tailed Hawks are not seen in numbers at any North American hawk watch, and thus we know relatively little about their migratory habits. Some birds "overshoot" their breeding grounds in spring and can be seen into central California and Colorado. Zone-tailed Hawks often migrate with vultures, especially in Veracruz, Mexico, where they are seen in greater numbers than anywhere else.

Vocalizations: A harsh, drawn-out, agitated scream *kreeaaaaar!*

Snail Kite *(Rostrhamus sociabilis)* SNKI page 110

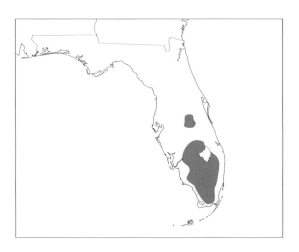

Creeping along the mud floor of this freshwater wetland, I move only millimeters per second with my one, massive, contracting foot…I guess the term "snail's pace" is accurate, but I don't appreciate it. I just want to be left alone to munch on algae and plants, but instead I'm under constant pressure, looking out for things that want to eat me. You might think snail life is all smooth sailing, but there are predators to avoid, and I don't see very well. These darn Limpkins, turtles, alligators, fish, and raccoons are all around me, just dying to find me. Even these human beings with the ugly toes who wade into my waters like to prop my gorgeous shell up on their bookshelf. But it's not these things I'm most afraid of; it's the Snail Kites…*they specialize in eating me*! I'd like to trust my camouflaged shell to keep me from being spotted, but whenever I feel a ripple in the water, I retract into my shell or hide in the mud as fast as I can. Those kites are deadly accurate, though, and they can see me from way off in the distance or way up in the sky…God, they make me nervous. *Pluuuurrrppp—* what's that splash? I'm in the air…in the clutches of a Snail Kite! A skinny, curved bill grabbing me…*I'm kite fooooooooooooood.*

Overview: Snail Kites are distinctive birds of freshwater marshes, drainage ditches, and flood channels in Florida. They occur where apple snails (large freshwater snails) can be found, and their bills are specially adapted to sever the muscle that holds the snail to its shell, enabling them to feed on this otherwise difficult meal. Unlike the Osprey, Snail Kites do not plunge-dive for prey; instead, they forage over very shallow water and delicately pluck the snail from the water by extending just their legs and talons beneath the surface. Snails are then carried to a favored perch for consumption, sometimes remaining in the talons, but often transferred to the bill in flight. Snail Kites are gregarious, often nesting in loose colonies and roosting communally with herons, egrets, and vultures. In fall and winter, large roosts can form near good foraging areas, sometimes with more than 100 birds, but usually fewer than a dozen are seen in any given marsh.

Flight Style: Snail Kites generally fly slowly, deliberately, and quite low over marshes, with heavy wingbeats, accentuated by glides on deeply bowed wings. They make agile, quick direction changes when prey is detected. Snail Kites rarely soar at high altitude, but when they do, confusion is possible with other raptors, especially the lankier juveniles that are less distinct than the adults.

Size and Shape: L 36–40 cm (14–16 in), WS 106–116 cm (42–46 in), WT 340–520 g (12–21 oz)
Medium-sized and distinctively shaped raptors, Snail Kites couple broad, rounded wings with slim bodies and long tails. Adults are stockier overall with wider wings than juveniles. Perched, they are slim overall, with long wings that reach the tail tip, and a long, narrow, sharply curved bill.

Plumage: Snail Kites differ by age and sex, and usually take 2–3 years to attain full adult plumage. In some cases, the plumage gets progressively darker in later years, but more study is needed to confirm whether this is individual variation or continued age progression. General plumage progresses from a streaky juvenile plumage where both sexes are similar, to an intermediate plumage in the second year where sexual characters begin to develop, to adult plumage in the third year. All ages show a distinctly white-based tail.
Adult males are dark overall, appearing black at a distance, but up close the upperparts have a dark charcoal-blue cast. The eyes, facial skin, and legs are all bright red, but the facial skin is less vibrant during the nonbreeding season. The flight feathers are mostly blackish, but some have minimal white mottling. *2nd-year males* are similar to adult males, but

typically have more prominently mottled flight feathers. The body of second-year males is mainly dark, but some have faint streaking. The head is darkish, usually with a paler throat. The eyes are orange-red.

Adult females are generally brownish overall, with a slaty blue-gray cast to the upperparts. The underparts are much like those of a juvenile but generally darker below and variably marked with tawny streaks. The head is usually dark with red eyes, but some have a semblance of the white markings retained from the bold juvenile head pattern. The flight feathers have a broad dark trailing edge (bolder than on juveniles), typically with whitish-based outer primaries. *2nd-year females* are similar to adult females, but usually have brownish eyes like juveniles, and a darker body and head than most juveniles.

1st-years (juveniles) have dark underparts with variable tawny streaks, fading to buff by winter/spring. They have a bold head pattern, with a dark streaky crown and ear coverts, and broad pale eyeline and throat. The eyes are dark brownish. First-spring males may average a grayer cast on the mantle, but the sexes are generally similar through the first year.

Geographic Variation: Three subspecies of Snail Kite have been described, but differences are marginal. The subspecies are generally differentiated by average size and wingspan. *R. s. plumbeus* occurs through the Florida range and is slightly larger and smaller-billed than other subspecies. In Texas, where Snail Kite is strictly a vagrant, the east Mexican form *R. s. major* is more likely than a wandering Florida bird. It averages slightly larger-billed than the Florida subspecies.

Molt: Juveniles undergo their first molt over the course of the first winter and spring, replacing head and body feathers, most or all of the tail, but usually no flight feathers. In the first summer, typically a complete molt occurs from March to August. Occasionally juvenile outer primaries and secondaries can be retained through the second year. During the second summer, a typically complete molt results in adult-like plumage. Some birds retain a few flight feathers and have a stepwise flight feather molt in later years.

Similar Species: Because of its distinctive shape and close association with water, Snail Kites are generally easy to identify within their limited U.S. range. Confusion is possible at a distance with adult female and juvenile Northern Harrier, which occupy the same habitat during migration and winter. But note Snail Kite's broad, rounded wings typically held cupped or strongly bowed. Harrier flies quite differently, with long, narrow wings held in a V, teetering from side to side. Snail Kite also appears heavier and more stable in flight than Harrier. When birds are up close, the plumage differences are obvious.

In south Texas where Snail Kite is an exceptional vagrant, beware of confusion with Harris's Hawk, which is widely distributed there. Harris's Hawk has a white tail base, but the overall plumage and shape (and to a lesser degree, flight style) are very different from Snail Kite.

Status and Distribution: Snail Kites are generally uncommon throughout their restricted Florida range. Even within range, their occurrence is local and heavily dependent on local water levels. In dry years, they may wander farther afield in search of suitable foraging habitat. It is a rare vagrant north of Florida, with records from Georgia and South Carolina. Snail Kites have occurred a few times in Texas, and these are likely wandering birds from eastern Mexico.

Migration: Mostly resident (nonmigratory) but nomadic, moving widely across the Florida peninsula in search of optimal foraging and breeding habitat. In fall a few are noted at the Florida Keys hawk watch, but these are mainly dispersing juveniles. In exceptionally dry years, they perhaps occur farther north than usual.

Vocalizations: Snail Kites are most vocal during breeding. Their typical call is a modulated, short, froglike laughing. Juveniles have a hoarse scream similar to that of many young raptors.

Hook-billed Kite *(Chondrohierax uncinatus)* HBKI page 114

You've made the trip here specifically to see a Hook-billed Kite—one of the most sought-after North American birds. Based on what you've read, a concerted effort is needed to see this bird; you are not likely to encounter it otherwise, unless you're extremely lucky. This particular location, the viewing platform at Santa Ana NWR along the Rio Grande in south Texas, offers a treetop-level view of the surrounding scrubby riparian thickets that border the river, the favored habitat of the Hook-billed Kite. Here, the kites quietly hunt for land snails by day and soar only briefly over the forest canopy on midmorning thermals. You wait, scanning the sky intently. A bird breaks the treetops and sets into a soar at eye level, but it is too flat-winged and lanky—it's a Cooper's Hawk. Scanning left, you notice a bird gliding toward you on the horizon. The unusual shape raises your eyebrows: bowed wings and peculiar wingbeats that are at once accipiter-like but also rather floppy. The bird tilts and you can see the distinctive wing shape that helps clinch the identification. Broad, rounded, and neatly pinched-in at the base, creating a distinct "paddle-shaped" wing. The bird is overall dark with boldly banded flight feathers, and the long tail is boldly banded black and white. It offers a quick but solid glimpse before it sinks into the trees, not to be seen again, a rather typical encounter with this enigmatic tropical species.

Overview: Hook-billed Kites are distinctive raptors of mainly tropical distribution, restricted in the United States to the riparian corridor along the lower Rio Grande in south Texas. Helpful hint: if you're not

in south Texas, you're not seeing a Hook-billed Kite! There are no North American records away from south Texas; even along the Rio Grande it is quite rare, and a concerted effort must be made to see it. Unlike the case with many south Texas specialty raptors (e.g., White-tailed Hawk), one is not likely to "bump into" a Hook-billed Kite during typical daily birding. Because of its habit of hunting quietly from perches within the canopy, it is typically encountered only in midmorning, when it soars briefly before disappearing into the forest at a favored feeding site. Hook-billed Kites feed almost exclusively on land snails, which they extract with their oversized, odd-looking bills. The ground beneath feeding sites can be strewn with snail shells. Elsewhere in its tropical range it can be found along forest edge, thorn forest, and in mangroves. Hook-billed Kites are rarely seen perched, but occasionally they can be seen sitting on open snags above the forest in early morning.

Flight Style: Hook-billed Kites usually fly relatively low over the treetops, with somewhat floppy wingbeats, yet at the same time can resemble an accipiter or small buteo. At times, they join kettles of soaring vultures and hawks, and they can be especially confusing when seen high overhead. The long, boldly banded tail is distinctive when seen at close range, but at a distance, Hook-billed Kite can be confused with soaring Cooper's Hawk, Red-shouldered Hawk, and Harris's Hawk. The wings are held bowed or flattish when soaring.

Size and Shape: L 43–51 cm (16–20 in), WS 87–98 cm (34–38 in), WT 215–353 g (8–12 oz)
Hook-billed Kites are medium-sized raptors, only slightly larger than Cooper's Hawks. In flight, they are generally distinctive if seen well; they have a long tail and broad, rounded wings that pinch-in near the body, creating an odd, paddle-shaped profile. At all angles, the wingtips appear rounded. When the bird is perched, note the large hooked bill accentuated by a smallish head, and unique face pattern with bold yellow-orange lores.

Plumage: Hook-billed Kites have plumage differences related to both age and sex, and there are generally 3 plumages to consider: adult male, adult female, and juvenile (sexes similar). Hook-billed

Kites usually attain adult appearance in about 1 year. Adults have whitish eyes; juveniles have dusky eyes.

Adult males are dark slate blue-gray above and below with coarse white barring underneath. The primaries are boldly banded, and the secondaries are largely dark. The tail is black with two whitish bands below, but from above it looks mostly gray. Dark-morph adults are similar, but these are exceedingly rare in Texas. On dark morphs, the underparts are entirely blackish, and the flight feathers are blackish with some white spotting on the outer primaries. The tail usually shows only 1 broad white band; a second white inner band is sometimes visible, but often obscured by the undertail coverts.

Adult females are slate-gray above, with rufous underparts coarsely barred with white. Females have a bold rufous face, throat, and collar, all set off by a distinct blackish cap. The flight feathers are overall heavily banded, and the tail has 2 whitish bands.

1st-year light morphs are much like adult females in overall pattern but lack the rufous tones. The upperparts are edged paler and neatly patterned. The mainly white underparts are marked with variable black barring, usually imparting a rather evenly barred appearance below. The sexes are similar during the first year.

1st-year dark morphs are similar to adult dark morphs, but the upperparts are edged paler and the flight feathers are evenly banded throughout.

Geographic Variation: Hook-billed Kite taxonomy is generally poorly understood, and more research is needed. There are 3 subspecies, but just 1 occurs in North America. *C. u. uncinatus* is found across the Texas range, averaging larger than the other subspecies, and lacks the brownish collar on males of the West Indies forms. It also occurs in a dark morph (though rare in Texas), and this morph is possibly lacking in other subspecies. There is substantial variation in bill size range-wide, but this is not reported in Texas birds, which all seem to have relatively smallish bills in comparison to birds elsewhere in the range. Bill size variation appears to be independent of age/sex and geographic range, and is perhaps best interpreted as polymorphism.

Molt: Because it is a secretive bird, the molt of Hook-billed Kite is generally understudied, and more research is needed. The general molt pattern appears to be as follows: juveniles replace some to most of the body feathers and a few tail feathers in the late first fall and first winter; and in the first summer a complete molt results in adult appearance. Adults likely undergo a complete molt each summer.

Similar Species: When seen close up in flight or perched, Hook-billed Kite is distinctive and unlikely to be confused with other raptors. But when seen at a distance, it can easily be confused with other broad-winged and long-tailed raptors such as Red-shouldered Hawk, Harris's Hawk, and even Cooper's Hawk. Note the Hook-billed Kite's combination of broad wings pinched-in at the base, loose accipiter-like wingbeats, and cupped wings when soaring. The translucent barred primaries create pale wing panels in flight.

Dark-morph Hook-billed Kites are possibly confused with *Common Black-Hawk* in flight, but there are shape and flight style differences of note. Black-Hawk soars on flattish wings (strongly cupped in Hook-billed Kite), has a much shorter tail, and has a more compact overall structure. Perched adult female Hook-billed Kites could be confused with *Red-shouldered* and *Cooper's Hawks*, but note the Kite's broad, rufous collar and very large bill! Kites also have featherless, pale lores, unlike buteos and accipiters.

Status and Distribution: Hook-billed Kites are rare but probably resident in their restricted south Texas range. Populations can quickly appear and disappear based on local conditions, and in times of low snail production, they can be very hard to find in Texas. They are perhaps somewhat nomadic, moving in response to local foraging conditions and may leave the United States altogether during years when habitat and conditions become unfavorable for breeding and foraging. The most reliable sites to find Hook-billed Kite in Texas are Santa Ana NWR, Bentsen SP, and Anzulduas County Park; all best during midmorning when local raptors first begin to soar.

Migration: Presumably resident in south Texas, but local movements probably occur, perhaps mostly postbreeding dispersal. More study is needed.

Vocalizations: Rarely heard, the call is a quick, flicker-like series of *kek* notes, slightly rising and falling in pitch.

Swallow-tailed Kite *(Elanoides forficatus)* STKI page 116

"Ya' think I could get some more of that sunblock?" The sun is beating down on my neck and my eyes are weary from looking into a deep blue sky; it's almost dizzying. Why am I counting hawks into late May… I'm tired of this. It's been three months of the same thing: get up at sunrise, stay out all day, scan the sky for hawks—up, over, down, over, up, over…then a thorough glance overhead. Not only is my neck burnt red, it's sore as heck too. Whoever made up the term "warbler neck" has never done a season-long hawk count! I stare back into the blue sky and wonder *are my binoculars even in focus?* I feel like I can't judge depth or even see straight anymore. What's worse, there's nothing good on the radio…"talkin' 'bout the China Grove"…*uugggghhh.*

There are still a few birds moving, though. Two juvenile Sharpies approach, stocky wings, anxious movements, buoyant flight. I'm used to them by now—*click, click.* But it's a challenge to unravel every ID, and spring watching definitely differs from fall. Birds are faded and tattered, two things that affect their appearance and add to the mystery of identification. Every season is a new experience as well, each with its own dynamics, learning curve, and highlights. But this season has held few surprises— no big flights, no rarities—and I'm ready to put these binoculars down for the summer. I give a one-hand-ed, lazy scan of the horizon and see another raptor approaching. *Whoah!* I steady my binoculars with two hands and can't believe my eyes…a Swallow-tailed Kite! There is no mystery to this bird's ID; just about anybody can identify one. Its profile is sleek, with long, narrow, drooped wings, and even coming

toward me, I can see its magnificent tail *streamers* twisting behind it. But it's the way it flies that makes it so riveting. It is simply effortless, floating on set wings, perfectly graceful. As the bird sails by, it never flaps; it just drifts out of sight to the north and is gone almost as soon as it arrived. I turn back to the south, waiting for the next surprise, but I'm aware that I've just seen the coolest bird on the planet.

Overview: The long, forked tail and striking contrasts in plumage render this large, graceful raptor nearly unmistakable. Swallow-tailed Kites float effortlessly, swooping and diving for dragonflies in spectacular displays of aerial prowess. Although they regularly hunt insects in flight, they also snatch reptiles, birds, and other prey items directly from the treetops. Swallow-tailed Kites are rarely seen perched, except occasionally in early morning before thermals promote efficient soaring.

Swallow-tailed Kites nest in large trees bordering swampy river systems across the Southeast, and they regularly stray north and sometimes west of their mapped range, especially in late spring. Swallow-tailed Kites are generally gregarious, nesting in loose colonies and gathering in large communal roosts, especially just prior to fall migration, when 1000+ may stage together at a single site.

Flight Style: Swallow-tailed Kites are distinct in flight. They appear to float along effortlessly and gracefully, gaining lift when need be with ease. They rarely flap to stay aloft, but when they do so, the wingbeats are slow, elastic, and relaxed, often interspersed with long glides. When soaring, the wings are held slightly bowed, often with the long tail twisting behind them. They glide with wings strongly bowed below the wrists and swept back.

Size and Shape: L 52–62 cm (21–24 in), WS 119–136 cm (47–54 in), WT 325–500 g (11–18 oz) Swallow-tailed Kites are large raptors, similar in size to Ospreys, but much more slender overall. They are unmistakably elegant, with slim proportions and extremely long, pointed wings. The most distinctive trait of Swallow-tailed Kite is the exceptionally long forked tail that looks like 2 streamers trailing behind them.

Plumage: Swallow-tailed Kites are strikingly patterned underneath with a white body, underwing coverts, and head, and black flight and tail feathers. The upperside is dark gray with an iridescent cast, and a black upper back and shoulders. Two ages (adult and first-year) are distinguishable, but they differ only slightly. Sexes appear similar. *Adults* are clean white below, and average longer-tailed than *1st-years* (juveniles). Tail length is not always easy to assess in flight, especially when closed. Be aware that the outer tail feathers occasionally break off, making the tail appear shorter than usual on some adults. Juveniles are washed buffy on the breast when newly fledged, but this quickly fades to white. Swallow-tailed Kites attain adult plumage during the first summer.

Geographic Variation: There are 2 subspecies of Swallow-tailed Kite, but only 1, *E. f. forficatus,* breeds throughout its U.S. range and winters mainly in northern South America. The subspecies are probably not field distinguishable, but northern breeders average larger and have a more purplish sheen above than the greenish-backed southern breeders that reside in Central and South America.

Molt: Juveniles have a very limited molt of body feathers, sometimes lacking, during the first fall/winter, but retain the juvenile flight feathers. A complete molt occurs from late first spring through first summer, after which they become indistinguishable from adults. Adults undergo a complete molt each summer to fall, but may suspend molt of the flight feathers during migration, or may even molt and migrate simultaneously.

Similar Species: If any bird could be considered "unmistakable," this is the one! Swallow-tailed Kites are vaguely similar to *Osprey* in size and plumage, but note Osprey's shorter, squared tail, banded flight feathers, black eyeline, and less pointed wings. When soaring at a distance, Swallow-tailed Kite can be confused with *Magnificent Frigatebird*. Note Frigatebird's blacker overall plumage, especially the underwings, with white limited to the breast and belly in certain ages and sexes.

Status and Distribution: Swallow-tailed Kites are fairly common across most of Florida, but they are local elsewhere in the Southeast along the Gulf Coast. They have withdrawn from their large historic breeding range, which spanned the Mississippi floodplain north to Minnesota. Reasons include logging of bottomland forest, agriculture, and human persecution. But Swallow-tailed Kites are beginning to return to former breeding areas, especially in east Texas and Louisiana. They are rare but regular vagrant north of their mapped range, seen mainly from April through May, but less frequently in September.

Migration: Swallow-tailed Kite is a long-distance migrant, vacating North America for the winter. Trans-Gulf migration takes place mainly from late February through April, and mainly August with a few lingering into September. Large flocks stage in late summer in southern Florida. Migrants leave Florida on favorable winds and cross directly to the Yucatan Peninsula, Mexico, where they stage again before continuing south over land to winter in northern South America. Relatively few move through the coastal bend of Texas. A few are seen along the East Coast as far north as southern Canada almost every spring and fall.

Vocalizations: On the breeding grounds, Swallow-tailed Kite gives a shrill, emphatic whistle *klee klee KLEE!*

Mississippi Kite *(Ictinia mississippiensis)* **MIKI** page 118

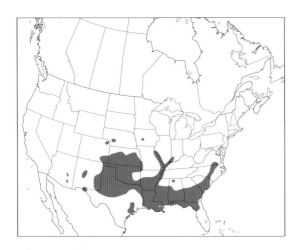

Dawn spreads across the Gulf of Mexico as the sun peeks over the hazy gray horizon. Today the south wind is blowing like a hair dryer, bringing hot, unsettled air across coastal Texas, reminding me of the steamy tropical habitat where I spent the winter in South America. With my grace, agility, and buoyancy I'm already awake and on the wing. Since it's so early, I stay low, moving across the urban sprawl and industrial steam of Corpus Christi, picking up a few associates as I head north. By 10 a.m. our flock has built to several hundred birds, and the strong sun propels us higher into the air. With more dragonflies on the wing now, I pause to snatch one with my agile talons, bringing it forward to be torn apart for a midair snack, as I soar higher over the trees. The river I'm following will lead me north across eastern Texas, and toward my Oklahoma breeding site. By midday I'm making good time, streaking high across the bright white Texas sky; a dark silhouette with pointed wings. I suspect with this tailwind, I'll be able to travel hundreds more miles before dark, taking me that much closer to home. I set my wings and surge northward.

Overview: Mississippi Kites are among the most distinctive North American raptors, not only in their plumage, but also in their shape, flight style, and foraging habits. They occupy a variety of habitats but are closely linked to large deciduous trees for nesting. They nest mainly near water in the Southeast and Southwest, but they also use shelterbelts with adjacent open fields on the southern Great Plains. Mississippi Kites have readily adapted to nesting in sub-

urban landscapes with ample trees. They are solitary or loose colonial nesters but are generally gregarious, and one can find soaring groups of kites at any time of the year, particularly during migration. Mississippi Kites often perch on prominent bare tree limbs early in the morning until sufficient thermal activity promotes aerial hunting. A more versatile hunter than is typically thought, it sometimes perch-hunts, also eating small mammals, frogs, lizards, nestling birds, and other small vertebrates.

Flight Style: Mississippi Kite's direct flight is with deep, easy, fluid wingbeats. They soar frequently, and when doing so, their wings are held flat or bowed, when they may be confused with Peregrine Falcons. They are buoyant on the wing, cutting through the sky with little flapping, twisting their wings and tail in pursuit of aerial insects, which they capture with their talons.

Size and Shape: L 33–37 cm (13–15 in), WS 75–83 cm (29–33 in), WT 240–372 g (8–13 oz)
Mississippi Kites are medium-sized raptors, similar in size and shape to a large falcon. They are slimly built, with a slight body, long, pointed wings, and a long, narrow-based tail that flares at the tip. When perched, they appear small, slim, and small-headed.

Plumage: There are 3 distinct plumages: adult, subadult, and juvenile, with minor plumage differences in the adult sexes. *Adults* are gray overall, with a pale head (slightly whiter on males), whitish secondaries, and rufous highlights in the primaries. *1st-years* (juveniles) are heavily streaked dark below with barred flight feathers and blackish tails with several paler bands throughout the first fall. Some juveniles lack tail bands or show faint bands or spots. By the first spring/summer they acquire a mainly grayish body and upperwing coverts, but retain the barred juvenile flight feathers and tail. At this stage, they are deemed "subadults."

Geographic Variation: No subspecies described. Mississippi Kite is closely related to the Plumbeous Kite (*I. plumbea*) of Central and South America and nearly identical in plumage.

Molt: Juveniles have an extensive molt of body

feathers (but not flight feathers) during the first winter, resulting in grayish-bodied birds with retained juvenile flight feathers by the first spring. A complete molt then takes place from May through August, after which they are adult-like. Adults undergo a complete molt each year from June to September. Most suspend primary molt for migration, resuming on or near the wintering grounds.

Similar Species: Mississippi Kites can be confused with Peregrine Falcon and possibly also with soaring Northern Harrier, but note shape and plumage differences. They are surprisingly like *Peregrine Falcon* when soaring at a distance, but Mississippi Kites are more lightly built with narrow-based wings, and a slimmer tail with flared, square-cut tip (broad-based and round-tipped on Peregrine). The head and body are also slimmer on kites. Peregrine soars on flat wings, but sometimes also with a slight dihedral, whereas Mississippi Kite soars on flat or bowed wings at all times. Unlike Peregrine Falcon, adult Mississippi Kites have pale heads and whitish secondaries above.

Adult female and juvenile *Northern Harrier*, while vaguely similar in plumage to juvenile Mississippi Kite, are longer-tailed, have longer, less pointed wings, and soar with a strong dihedral, rocking back and forth in flight. Harriers also have a bold white rump in all plumages, lacking on Mississippi Kite. Adult male Northern Harrier is grayish on top, similar to Mississippi Kite, but brilliant white below with black-tipped primaries and inner secondaries.

Status and Distribution: Mississippi Kites are fairly common in the Southeast, but they are generally uncommon and local in river systems of the Southwest. Their range is currently expanding north and west, with recent nesting in several states in New England. Mississippi Kites winter in South America, where they are relatively poorly studied, but recent large counts from Bolivia suggest a more southerly winter distribution than was previously thought.

Migration: Mississippi Kites are long-distance migrants, mainly from April through May and August through September. As they are circum-Gulf migrants, large movements occur along the Texas coast, peaking in April and again in August. Mississippi Kites are regular spring overshoots to the Northeast and Great Lakes region, mainly during May and June. From mid- to late May there are usually a few Mississippi Kites, mostly subadults, found along the Northeast and Mid-Atlantic coast, usually in places that are migrant traps, such as Cape May Point, NJ, and Kiptopeke, VA.

Vocalizations: On the breeding grounds, Mississippi Kites make a piercing 2-note whistle, the second note a descending *tee-pheeuww!* Juveniles make an incessant begging *feeeer.*

White-tailed Kite *(Elanus leucurus)* WTKI page 122

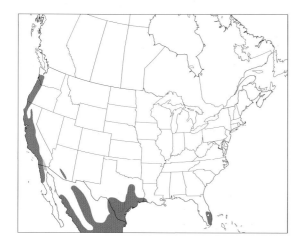

Short, scraggly trees and bushes dot the landscape, providing some relief on the otherwise unbroken coastal prairie. The swaying, tall grasses mixed within the brush bump up against the ocean horizon. Far away, two white birds hover, gleaming like white angels in the crisp evening light. They periodically stoop into the grass, with wings held high in an exaggerated V and legs dangling, only to return quickly to a hovering position 30 feet above the ground. Occasionally, they shift away to another part of the field, flapping with easy, tireless, efficient wingbeats on slim, pointed wings. They are striking in their whiteness, and the only plumage contrast seen at this distance is the boldly marked black shoulders. Rather easily identified, these White-tailed Kites are a distinctive and graceful component of this coastal prairie ecosystem.

Overview: Across their restricted range, White-tailed Kites prefer open country. They hunt grassland, savanna, roadsides, and agricultural areas, and are surprisingly more regular in disturbed areas than most raptors, sometimes even in suburban settings. White-tailed Kites often form large winter roosts (dozens of birds) near optimal foraging areas. Unlike other kites, the White-tailed Kite does not hawk insects in the air; instead it feeds mainly on small mammals. In general behavior, White-tailed Kite recalls a large, white Kestrel, regularly perching on wires, hovering frequently, and pouncing on prey from low to moderate height. White-tailed Kites are generally aggressive toward other raptors, frequently tussling with passing Northern Harriers or Red-tailed Hawks that wander into their breeding territory.

Flight Style: Like Harriers, White-tailed Kites fly with a dihedral, usually strong but smooth when soaring, and modified with flatter hands when gliding. Their direct flight is with languid, Harrier-like wingbeats but faintly stiffer and deeper. White-tailed Kites hover with wings raised above the shoulders and the body angled at 45 degrees, usually with dangling legs. They stoop with wings in a distinctive, strong V-shape, instead of completely folded up like most stooping raptors. Unlike American Kestrel, White-tailed Hawks do not "kite." While hovering for extended periods, they often break off with a few languid flaps, a long glide, and then go straight back to hovering over a new location.

Size and Shape: L 36–41 cm (14–16 in), WS 99–102 cm (39–41 in), WT 305–361 g (10–13 oz)
White-tailed Kites are slim, delicate raptors, with long, pointed wings. Roughly the size of a Northern Harrier, they are generally slimmer and more angular by all comparisons. When perched, they appear small, thin, and somewhat small-headed.

Plumage: White-tailed Kites are distinctly white overall in all plumages, with strongly contrasting black shoulders and dark carpal spots on the underwings that vary slightly in extent. There are 2 distinguishable age classes: adult and first-year (juvenile). *Adults* are clean white below, with plain grayish upperparts and black shoulders; males average paler above than females, with a whiter head, but differences are marginal. *Juveniles* have boldly scaled brownish white upperwing coverts and backs, and a rusty wash on the breast that is gone by winter, earlier in more southerly breeding populations. First-spring birds are similar to adults but have pale-fringed primary coverts. Also note the dusky, thin subterminal tail band on first-year birds. All White-tailed Kites have orange to orange-red eyes.

Geographic Variation: There are 2 subspecies of White-tailed Kite but only 1, *E. l. majusculus,* occurs throughout its North American range. The smaller nominate, *E. l. leucurus,* occurs in South America. These forms are not likely separable in the field.

Molt: Juveniles begin an extensive molt shortly after leaving the nest, replacing the pale-fringed upperwing coverts and rusty breasts over the next several months. Some upperwing coverts and primary coverts are typically retained until the first summer, as well as all the flight feathers. First-summer birds have a complete molt that results in adult-like appearance by fall. Subsequent molts are typically complete, occurring from June to September. Unlike many raptors, White-tailed Kites do not often show obvious gaps in the wings when molting, possibly because of their slim, pointed wing shape.

Similar Species: White-tailed Kites of all ages are generally distinctive, but they can be confused with adult male *Northern Harrier*, which is similar in size and plumage. Compared with Northern Harrier, White-tailed Kite is overall slimmer, especially at the base of the wings, lacks a white rump, and has an all-white tail. In direct flight, both have similarly languid wingbeats, with White-tailed's a bit stiffer and deeper. Also, note White-tailed Kite's slimmer wings, and slightly shorter tail. Harriers hover, but only for a few seconds at a time, usually while hunting just above the ground. White-tailed Kite hovers for extended periods at medium heights.

Status and Distribution: White-tailed Kites are fairly common residents of open country from southern California north through southern Oregon, becoming uncommon to rare coastally north of there. In Texas, they are declining on the coastal prairie, especially in the southern portion of their range. They are likewise uncommon within their restricted range in peninsular Florida. White-tailed Kites apparently underwent historic declines due to habitat loss, but are now thought to be generally stable or increasing, especially to the north on the Pacific Coast. They are exceptional north and east of their mapped

245

range, but have shown up as vagrants on the East Coast (e.g., NJ, CT).

Migration: White-tailed Kite movements are poorly understood and are probably not true migration, but rather extensive postbreeding dispersal events. Wandering birds can be seen away from typical habitat at almost any time of year. Most movement occurs during fall and winter, when nonbreeders gather in large communal roosts, sometimes numbering 50+ birds. Presumed California breeders arrive in Oregon and on the California Channel Islands in fall, and depart over the winter.

Vocalizations: White-tailed Kites are quite vocal on the breeding grounds and during aggressive encounters. The main call is a rising, 2-noted *seee-yrrk*; also a grating, short *grrrrrr* often interspersed with descending, whistled *hew* notes recalling Osprey; also a husky, grating *krr-éerrr*.

American Kestrel *(Falco sparverius)* AMKE page 128

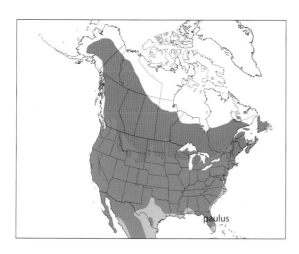

"Ooooh, look at that Kestrel sitting on the fence, bobbing its tail up and down…it's so cute!" Why do they call me "cute"? That really irritates me. I'm not cute, I'm a bad-ass, I'm ferocious…don't they know I'm the most efficient predator in North America? Despite my size, I can catch it all—insects, mice, snakes, birds, whatever I want. How many birds do you know that can hover incessantly, pounce on a mouse, tail-chase a sparrow, or cross the Delaware Bay without breaking a sweat? Sure, I am colorful, but my expression is fierce, not "cute." I can survive the coldest of winters with ease compared to those bigger, *tougher* hawks. You don't see me going hungry. Listen to my call—*kilee-kilee-kilee-kilee*—you call that cute? I don't think those larger hawks think it's cute hearing that as I mob them! *Yeah, that's right, Red-tail, you better get outta here!* I'm sick of being called "cute"… thanks, but no thanks.

Overview: American Kestrels are handsome falcons that inhabit grassland, farms, and open country, regularly visible on conspicuous perches such as roadside wires and fence posts in search of prey. They are lively, active birds that rarely sit still when perched, constantly looking around or bobbing their heads and tails. Kestrels are adaptable to human-altered landscapes, coexisting with man in many places, yet they have declined drastically in some regions in recent years, especially in the Northeast. They are cavity-nesting birds and will accept artificial nest boxes, which are the only available nest sites in some areas. Kestrels feed primarily on small rodents, insects, lizards, and small birds. They often catch dragonflies, butterflies, and other large insects in flight, and consume them on the wing. Kestrels are fantastic mousers, catching an abundance of mice and voles with ease, even when other raptors seem to find it difficult. Prey items are sometimes cached in shrubs, nooks, and clumps of grass for later consumption. Kestrels are often aggressive toward larger raptors, but they are usually wary of becoming prey themselves, given their relatively small size.

Flight Style: In flight, Kestrels appear dainty, elegant, and slim, even at a distance. They often hover for extended periods (the only North American falcon to do so) relatively low to the ground while hunting, but can soar high in the air with ease, especially while on migration. When soaring, Kestrels rise quickly because of their slight weight. Kestrel's direct flight is buoyant and wandering, unique among falcons, and they are more easily buffeted by even moderate winds than are Merlins. Kestrels also flap and glide intermittently more often than other falcons, often causing them to be confused with Sharp-shinned Hawks, especially when seen at eye level. The wingbeats are quick, steady, and flickering, but easy with sweptback hands, generally lacking stiffness and power.

Size and Shape: L 22–27 cm (8–11 in), WS 52–61 cm (20–24 in), WT 97–150 g (3.4–5.3 oz)
At about the size of a jay, American Kestrels are the smallest North American falcon, and indeed among our smallest raptors (only male Sharp-shinned is smaller). Kestrels have long, slim, swept-back wings. In most flight postures, the wingtips are slightly more blunt-tipped, and the tail and body are slimmer than other falcons. At eye level, the wings are hunched at the shoulders, with drooped hands. A Kestrel's wings can look particularly lengthy in a soar, similar to those of Peregrine and Prairie Falcon, but are slimmer at the base. The head appears smaller, and the tail does not taper toward the tip as in these larger species. Females are only fractionally larger than males, but this is not detectable in the field. Perched, Kestrels appear small (even when up close), slim, and fairly long-tailed.

Plumage: American Kestrel sexes are strikingly different, but distinguishing ages is more difficult. *Male American Kestrels* are vibrantly colorful and unlike any other North American raptor. The striking upperside with blue wings and a rufous back, and the black double mustache marks on the face are unique. The primaries are black and the tail is solid orange with a broad black tip (which can be a good field mark for males when seen from below). The outer tail feathers (sometimes the outer few) may have multiple bands, and when folded, the tail can look completely banded underneath. All Kestrels have dark eyes.
Adult males are buffy below with variable black spotting on an orangey breast. *1st-year (juvenile) males* have whitish-buff underbodies with dark streaks throughout (a few juvenile males are fairly heavily streaked), but quickly molt into an adult-like body plumage during the first fall. The upper back of *1st-year males* is usually more heavily barred than on adult males, and the "eye spots" on the nape are often whiter.
Females are distinctive in their overall orangey tone above, but ageing them is very difficult in the field. They have blue on the crown with a variable orange cap. The tail is orange with multiple black bands. *1st-year females* are similar to adults but the

black subterminal tail band is slightly narrower, but this difference is not evident in the field. All females are pale buff below with dark rufous streaks. All Kestrels have whitish spots along the trailing edge of the wings that appear translucent when backlit, but these are typically more prominent in males.

Geographic Variation: There are about 17 subspecies of American Kestrel worldwide, but only 2 definitely occur in North America. The North American forms are only marginally different, and most birds are not safely identified in the field. *F. s. sparverius* breeds across North America, except where it is replaced by the sedentary *F. s. paulus*, which breeds from southern Louisiana to South Carolina and throughout peninsular Florida. Subspecies *paulus* is smaller, more sparsely marked on the underparts and less heavily barred on the back (males). Birds on the Florida peninsula on average are paler overall and more lightly marked, and some can appear similar to the very pale Caribbean breeding subspecies.

Molt: Juveniles molt body feathers during the first fall, resulting in adult-like plumage by late fall to early winter. Typically, a complete molt then takes place from May through September, thereafter putting them on the same annual molt schedule as adults. Adult Kestrels may be finishing flight-feather molt during fall migration, but juveniles do not molt flight feathers in fall. Juvenile males often have a mix of white and rufous feathers on the breast during fall migration. Southern breeders typically molt earlier than northern breeders.

Similar Species: If seen well, Kestrels of both sexes should be straightforward to identify. When seen at a distance or in poor light, which is typical on migration, confusion with other falcons and the similarly sized Sharp-shinned Hawk is possible.
The most likely confusion species is *Merlin*. Kestrel and Merlin are nearly equal in size, with Merlin being only slightly larger; however, Kestrel is rangier overall with slimmer wings and a longer tail compared with the more compact, angular, and solidly built Merlin. The flight of Kestrel is buoyant, unsteady (especially on windy days), and more wandering than that of Merlin (which is steady, fast, and direct), with swept-back, bluntly pointed wings, and wingbeats that appear to lack force (Merlin is very powerful in flight). There are distinct plumage differences as well, with Kestrels typically appearing paler

overall underneath compared with the darker Merlin, which has a heavily streaked body and "checkered" underwing pattern. Be aware that Kestrels can appear dark underneath in overcast light or in shadow, and they are more easily confused with Merlin under these conditions. The topside of Merlin is also darker, with adult males being dark blue and adult females and juveniles being slate-brown, with narrow white tail bands. Adult female and juvenile *Prairie Merlins* are very pale overall and appear most similar to female Kestrels in the field, but Prairie Merlin shows less rufous tone above, being sandier brown overall, and has pronounced chalk-white tail bands.

At long distance, female Kestrels may resemble the much larger *Peregrine* and *Prairie Falcons*, especially the paler Prairie Falcon when seen from below. But note Prairie Falcon's blackish wing linings, steadier flight, slower, more powerful wingbeats, broader tail, and larger head. Be aware, though, that the tail of Prairie Falcon can look reddish when backlit, and thus quite similar to Kestrel.

Sharp-shinned Hawks (especially juveniles) can be confused with Kestrels in flight. There are obvious plumage differences when seen up close (see Sharp-shinned Hawk), but they are nearly equal in size and share a similar flight style. Both are buoyant in flight with quick wingbeats, but Sharp-shinned employs the typical accipiter "flap-flap-glide" mode of flight, whereas Kestrel flaps more consistently, glides less often, and its wingbeats are more fluid, with longer, more swept-back hands. With their wings pulled in (especially flapping into a headwind), Sharp-shinned Hawks can appear more pointed-winged than usual, and so particularly falcon-like, but they still have broad-based wings with shorter "hands" compared with the slim, long wings of Kestrel.

Status and Distribution: Occurring from Alaska across the Americas to the tip of South America, American Kestrel is the most widespread and abundant falcon in the New World. It is common across much of its range but is seriously declining in the Northeast, a result of a combination of factors, including habitat loss, West Nile virus, and possibly depredation by increasing Cooper's Hawk populations. Because of its widespread distribution, it is not yet afforded any special protection or conservation status.

Migration: American Kestrel migration is complex, with northern populations vacating the breeding range from August through November, and overlapping with resident breeders across the Lower 48 during fall and winter. All migration sites in the United States see fair numbers of Kestrels in fall, but especially large numbers migrate along the Atlantic Coast, where the biggest daily counts are tallied at Cape May, NJ, and Kiptopeke, VA. In the West, the Goshute Mountains in Nevada, and Wasatch Mountains in Utah see the highest numbers. Spring migration is more widespread and diffuse, occurring mainly from late March through early May. The largest concentrations in spring occur along the Atlantic Coast and the southern shores of the Great Lakes. The eastern and western foothills of the Rocky Mountains are also good sites for migrating Kestrels.

Vocalizations: Kestrels are quite vocal when breeding and when chasing larger raptors, giving off an excited, high screaming *klee-klee-klee*, at times in prolonged series of 7–10 phrases. Kestrels also give a harsh *chrrrr* when delivering food to the nest.

248

Merlin *(Falco columbarius)* **MERL** page 132

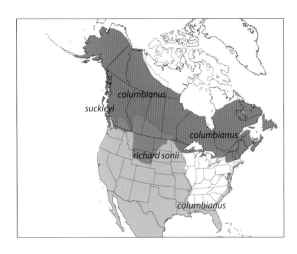

"Over the dunes!" an excited birder yells out from the Cape May Point hawk-watch platform. About 200 yards away, rocketing down the beach with rapid, powerful wingbeats, a small, dark falcon flies. The bird is a Merlin, and it is moving impossibly fast, as if blasted from a cannon. Compact and angular, it streaks over the dunes on its way south. How is it conceivable that a bird only fractionally larger than a Kestrel can fly so differently, with such stability, control, and force? As the bird continues south, most observers on hand can't seem to locate it as others try to convey its whereabouts. Only seconds remain to identify it before it is going, going, gone…across the bay and into the fading orange light, in notorious Merlin fashion.

Overview: Merlins are small birds, only slightly larger than Kestrels, but stockier overall, more angular, and fly with more power, speed, and stability. Merlins can be pugnacious, restless, and easily agitated, often dive-bombing larger raptors on migration, seemingly just for fun; Kestrel rarely does this away from its breeding grounds. Merlins can be quite tame and confiding when perched, seeming to flaunt their apparent fearless nature! They appear small when perched and can be overlooked as Kestrels, but they are slightly bulkier and do not bob their heads or tails as much as Kestrel does.

Flight Style: Like all falcons, Merlins hold their wings flat or slightly drooped when soaring and gliding. They are level, steady, direct fliers with stiff, rapid, forceful wingbeats that propel them to high speeds within seconds. Merlins frequently hunt during migration, and while doing so, males may mimic smaller birds by flipping their wings back in a flashy, rapid, intermittent, undulating fashion before overtaking prey with a quick burst of speed. Female Merlins may attempt to deceive prey with unusually lazy wingbeats before speeding off in pursuit of them. On migration, they frequently soar high up with other raptors.

Size and Shape: L 24–30 cm (9–12 in), WS 53–68 cm (21–27 in), WT 129–236 g (4.5–8.3 oz)
Merlins are small and overall compact. They are more angular in shape overall than other falcons, with broad-based wings, pointed hands, and a short tail, especially compared with the slender, long-tailed, small-headed American Kestrel, to which they are of similar size. The tail of Merlin is typically square-tipped when folded, whereas the tail tip of other falcons is usually rounded. Compared with the larger falcons, Merlins have shorter wings, are slimmer, and have narrow, short tails that do not taper toward the tip. A Merlin's compact proportions carry over to perched birds as well. Merlins are broad-chested and large-headed, with large dark eyes. Their body tapers toward the rear, where the wingtips reach just short of the tail tip.

Plumage: Merlins of all ages, sexes, and subspecies are streaked underneath and uniformly darker on top. Almost all have dark tails with several narrow white bands. Sexes differ in adult plumage but are similar in juvenile plumage. Juveniles are similar to adult females but generally lack the grayish tones above (see below for specifics on ageing each subspecies). Distinguishing juveniles of both sexes from adult female Merlins in the field is difficult, and it is often not possible. There is moderate sexual dimorphism in size, with females larger than males and appearing longer-winged.

There are 3 distinct races of Merlin: Taiga (boreal) (*F. c. columbarius*), Prairie (Great Plains) (*F. c. richardsonii*), and Black (Pacific Northwest) (*F. c. suckleyi*). Plumage among the 3 subspecies ranges from very pale in Prairie Merlin to generally dark in Black Merlin. Typical individuals within a known range are often easily identified to subspecies; however, Taiga Merlin can be nearly as dark as Black Merlin, or almost as pale as Prairie Merlin, and some birds are not safely assignable to subspecies. Some of this overlap is likely due to intergradation between Taiga Merlin and the other 2 subspecies, but more study is needed.

Taiga Merlin is the standard Merlin across much of North America, having well-marked flight feathers and underwings and a neatly banded tail with a white tip. *Adult males* are dark blue above with blackish primaries and distinct pale bluish bands across the tail. They are creamy below with dense, brownish or rufous-brown streaks and a whitish throat. The wrists and leggings of most adult males are yellowish, but noticeable only in good light. *Adult females* are dark grayish brown above, most notably grayish on the rump, with dense brown streaks on a buffy underbody, and paler throat. *Juveniles* are nearly identical to adult females (age and sex with caution) but generally browner above with very clean, pale-fringed upperparts when fresh, and more distinctly streaked below. Juveniles have bluish ceres and orbital rings, but these turn yellow very fast, sometimes before the bird leaves the nest! Some juvenile male Taiga Merlins can have bluish gray tones above, making them easier to age, though they are never as blue as adult males. A few adult female and juvenile Taiga Merlins lack tail bands but have a single, wide dark subterminal band. Adult females and juveniles often appear dark in the field since they are heavily streaked underneath; adult males appear paler since they are rufous or rufous-brown streaked, and they can be similar to Kestrels at times.

Prairie Merlin is paler overall (especially on the upperparts) and shows reduced streaking below compared with the other races, as well as a fainter and narrower malar mark. All Prairie Merlins (especially adult males) have boldly defined tail bands with a prominent broad dark subterminal band. *Adult male* Prairie Merlins are extremely pale below with faint rufous streaking on the body and pale rufous leggings. Some are darker and more heavily streaked below, similar to Taiga birds; these may be intergrades and unidentifiable to subspecies. The topside of adult male Prairie Merlin is sky blue with contrasting blackish primaries. *Adult females and juveniles* are tan above and white below, with pale rufous-brown streaking, and often appear pale-headed. They are very similar to female American Kestrels, but are more boldly streaked underneath, have tan (not rufous) upperparts, and show less contrast between the upperwings and darker primaries. The

overall color on the upperside of adult female and juvenile Prairie Merlin is similar to that of Prairie Falcon. Females and juveniles are more patterned above than Taiga Merlins, with prominent spotting in the flight feathers and upperwing primary coverts.

Black Merlin is the darkest subspecies, often lacking spotting on the flight feathers altogether, and showing reduced tail banding, broken white spotting, or no white at all on the tail. Tail pattern overlaps between Taiga and Black, though the most extreme examples of Black have no tail bands. Black Merlin is dark-headed, lacking the "mustache" markings and whitish throat shown by other races, and heavily marked underneath, looking blackish overall at a distance. *Adult males* are blue-black above with blackish primaries, and dark streaked below. *Adult females and juveniles* are dark slate-brown above and extremely heavily streaked below. Some adult males show a rufous tone to the underbody, and adult females can show a buffy tone, but sexing Black Merlins from the underside is very difficult in the field.

Geographic Variation: Three North American subspecies are differentiated primarily by degree of darkness in plumage, with the Black Merlin of the humid Pacific Northwest being darkest, the Prairie Merlin of the northern Great Plains the palest, and the Taiga Merlin of widespread northern open forest the standard (see Plumage).

Molt: Merlins molt from April to November, typically replacing all their feathers in 1 cycle. Juveniles acquire adult plumage after their first molt. Some fall second-year birds retain juvenile back and upperwing feathers, giving them a "checkerboard" pattern on top, making them identifiable as such. Sometimes second-years may retain the outermost secondary (S1) after their first molt (typically impossible to see in flight). Subsequent molts of adults are typically complete.

Similar Species: In flight, Merlin is most similar to American Kestrel, but can also be confused with the larger Prairie and Peregrine Falcons. Also beware of the superficially similar Sharp-shinned Hawk, which can look falcon-like when flapping or when "tucked in" during strong winds. Merlin is told from the similar-sized *American Kestrel* by its more compact proportions with broader-based wings and shorter, more angular hands, darker overall plumage (beware of Prairie Merlin!), prominent visible white tail bands, and lack of rufous tones above. Note the more direct flight of Merlin, which is steadier and less prone to direction changes and buffeting by strong winds than the buoyant, more wandering flight of American Kestrel.

Prairie Merlin is told from *Prairie Falcon* by its smaller size, more compact proportions, boldly streaked underparts, banded tail, and lack of distinct dark underwing coverts and axillaries. Merlin is told from the larger *Peregrine Falcon* by its more compact structure and shorter wings; also note Peregrine's rolling, fluid, loonlike wingbeat compared with Merlin's short, stiff wingbeats.

Merlin is told in flight from the superficially similar *Sharp-shinned Hawk* by its pointed wings (versus rounded in Sharp-shinned Hawk), more heavily streaked underparts (barred rufous in adult Sharp-shinned Hawks), more compact angular structure with shorter tail, and generally faster, more stable flight. Backyard birders confuse the similarly plumaged juvenile Sharp-shinned Hawk for Merlin when it is perched in trees or near feeders; however, Merlins rarely frequent backyard feeders, instead preferring more open habitats. Merlins have dark eyes compared with the yellowish eyes of young Sharpies, shorter tails with bold banding, darker brownish streaking below, and longer wings.

Status and Distribution: Merlins are widespread breeders across boreal forest habitats, often nesting near clearings around bogs and lakeshores from Alaska east through the Great Lakes, Canadian Maritimes, and south through the U.S.–Canada border region. They are increasing in suburban areas, especially on the Great Plains and into New England. They often nest in ornamental spruce or other conifer stands in suburban areas in abandoned crow and raptor nests, and occasionally on the ground north of the treeline.

The Taiga race occurs throughout most of North America but is the only race seen regularly in the eastern half of the United States. Prairie Merlins occur primarily throughout the western half of the United States across the northern Great Plains and winter from the central Great Plains into Central America. Some winter within the breeding range, especially in cities where House Sparrows and European Starlings are plentiful. They are rare as far west as California, and a vagrant in the East. Black Merlin breeds and winters in the humid Pacific Northwest from southeast Alaska to coastal Washington. Some migrate south in winter along the Pacific Coast to southern California, and inland east to Utah. They are vagrants elsewhere. Populations are currently stable, and likely increasing in certain areas as a result of its ability to use suburban locales for nesting and wintering.

Migration: Merlins are medium- to long-distance migrants; some adults are resident. Northern breeders are migratory mainly from September to November in fall, and March to May in spring. They winter throughout the central and southern United States to northern South America (Peru); Black and Prairie Merlin are partly migratory, but most or some individuals are residents, wintering within the breeding range.

Notable concentrations occur during fall migration (mid-September to late October) at Cape May, NJ, Kiptopeke, VA, and other Atlantic Coast sites. Merlins can also be seen along the western shore of Lake Michigan. The most reliable sites to observe Merlin migration in the West are Wasatch Mountains, UT, and Goshute Mountains, NV. Spring migration is more dispersed than fall and takes place from late April through May. Adults arrive back at their breeding grounds in spring (mainly March–April) before second-year birds. Unlike many raptors, Merlins favor late afternoon for migration. Peak daily flights usually occur from about 3 p.m. to dusk.

Vocalizations: Typically silent away from breeding grounds, but occasionally vocalizes during aggressive encounters with other raptors. Primary call a rapid, loud, high-pitched *kee-kee-kee-kee-kee.*

Peregrine Falcon *(Falco peregrinus)* PEFA page 136

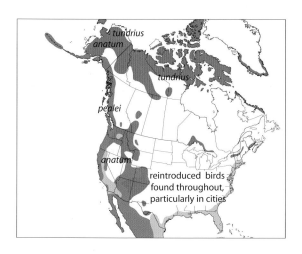

The chase is on! A Peregrine Falcon is closing in on its prey with blinding speed and precision turns. The smaller bird is quick and agile, but no match for the larger, faster, more powerful predator that mirrors its every move. Elegant, graceful, and deadly, the Peregrine Falcon is always one step ahead of its prey, typically outracing and capturing it in midair. Usually, it preys on birds such as waterfowl and pigeons, but this time the target is an American Kestrel! I find myself rooting for the Kestrel to escape: "c'mon, little guy… go!" One raptor killing another seems odd, and almost wrong in a way, but this phenomenon actually happens quite often—survival of the fittest, right? So why, then, does it a bother me to witness such a sight? Are we bothered as much when a Kestrel snares a mouse and flies away with it? This is the way of things in the natural world, and raptors are no different. From time to time a Kestrel's fate is in the hands of another predator, and this bird left itself exposed to predation. As the dashing Peregrine closes the gap, my heart sinks, talons extend, feathers fly…and I almost look away.

Overview: Peregrine Falcon is a large, powerful falcon found in a variety of cliff habitats and open areas across North America. Once nearly extirpated across part of its range, it has rebounded in recent decades, now occupying surprisingly urban areas, where it nests on building ledges, bridges, and manmade structures, especially boxes erected specifically for its reintroduction in certain areas of the United States. It still uses more traditional haunts such as mountain cliffs, but is usually seen only over forested areas during migration.

Peregrine is a bird-hunting specialist—its favored prey include shorebirds, waterfowl, and pigeons (in urban areas). It hunts mainly by way of spectacular stoops, at times reaching speeds of more than 200 miles per hour, earning it the title of "fastest animal on the planet." It is also easily capable of chasing down speedy birds such as Bufflehead and Pintail in direct, point-to-point flight. Peregrines often perch conspicuously on prominent overlooks, including power poles and buildings.

Flight Style: Although known for their speed and long distance endurance, Peregrines are highly capable of soaring, seen high in the sky with other raptors on migration, or when "hiding" from prey before initiating a lethal stoop. Peregrines soar on flat wings or with a very shallow dihedral (sometimes just the wingtips curled upward). Their powerful, fluid, whiplike, rolling wingbeats enable them to accelerate to high speeds in seconds. They are steady in flight at all times!

Size and Shape: L 37–46 cm (14–18 in), WS 94–116 cm (37–46 in), WT 453–952 g (1–2.1 lb)
Peregrines are large, sturdy falcons with elegantly proportioned, long, narrow, pointed wings. The wings are smoothly curved with a slight bend at the wrists, making the overall silhouette resemble a retracted bow and arrow when soaring. Females are distinctly larger than males, the biggest birds confusable with Gyrfalcon. Female Peregrines have broader wings than males, but telling the sexes apart in flight can be difficult without extensive practice. All Peregrines appear stocky when perched, with a flat, blocky head and stout chest and shoulders. The wingtips reach the tail tip on perched birds.

Plumage: Peregrine plumage varies with geography, but 2 age classes are always distinguishable: adult and 1st-year (juvenile).
Adults are whitish below with variable blackish barring on the belly, a white to pinkish chest, and checkered underwings. They are bluish above, with faintly barred upperwing coverts and a blacker head and primaries, sometimes appearing two-toned at a distance. Some darker adults can be blackish blue overall on top, while others have a pale blue rump that contrasts with the darker upperwings and tail.

Males average bluer above than females, but sexes are similar and often not identifiable in the field.

Juveniles are buffy below with darker streaks, checkered underwings, and a pale throat. By spring, the buff color on the underside fades to whitish. From above, juveniles are dark brown to slate-brown with slightly darker primaries, and a dark tail with a white tip. Fresh fall juveniles have a bluish cere and eyering, changing to yellow over the course of the first fall to winter. Often, adults are pale-chested at a distance while juveniles appear pale-throated. First-spring birds can have an adult-like head and upper back, while the remainder of the bird appears juvenile-like.

There are 3 subspecies of the Peregrine Falcon in North America—Tundra (F. p. tundrius), Anatum (F. p. anatum), and Peale's (F. p. pealei). There is plumage variation in all races, and telling the 3 apart can be impossible. In the East, there are Peregrines that resemble Peale's, but many of these birds are of mixed origin as a result of reintroduction programs. Adult Tundra and Anatum typically have unmarked chests and throats, whereas Peale's may have barring throughout the underbody.

Tundra adults tend to be paler overall, especially on the back, and usually have a narrower more defined malar. Juveniles are the palest of all Peregrines in North America, being lightly streaked on the underbody, and most show a pale blonde forehead and crown.

Anatum is typically more heavily marked than tundrius. Adults show a rufous wash to the underside, and often have a dark forehead and broader dark malar. Juveniles average darker than tundrius in all respects, especially in the head characters.

Peale's is extremely heavily marked underneath and dark above. Adults are bluish black above and have heavily marked underparts. Juveniles are heavily streaked dark below with very dark, helmeted heads, similar to a juvenile dark-morph Gyrfalcon. Most juvenile Peregrines have dark malars, or "sideburns," giving a dark helmeted look set off by the white cheeks, but Peale's often lacks white cheeks and sideburns altogether, showing a wholly dark head.

Geographic Variation: Because Peregrine is one of the only truly cosmopolitan raptors, it is perhaps unsurprising that up to 19 subspecies have been described (depending on authority). Subspecies are distinguished primarily by overall darkness of plumage and extent of markings, but overlap between the subspecies occurs, and "introduced" birds of unknown origin complicate identification (some actually brought from Old World populations). Tundra birds of the high Arctic occur across North America and are the most widespread of the races during migration. Anatum birds are seen primarily in the continental West. Peale's (which are slightly larger than the other races) originate from wet areas of the coastal Pacific Northwest and the Aleutian Islands.

Molt: Juveniles undergo a limited (or absent) molt of body, head, and upper back feathers in their first winter. Some juveniles begin to molt in late winter and have an adult-like head, breast, and upper back by March but do not complete their first molt until summer. Some appear to retain all juvenile feathers until the first summer, when they typically initiate a molt cycle and attain adult appearance by the second fall. Second-year birds retain varying numbers of juvenile feathers through the second fall (especially in the montane West), which are brownish and worn, often among the primaries, secondaries, uppertail coverts, and upperwing coverts. Subsequent molts are mostly complete and occur mainly from April to November.

Similar Species: Being widespread and easily visible when present, the Peregrine is a good species with which to become familiar, thereby facilitating comparison with the more range-restricted Prairie Falcon and the overall rare Gyrfalcon. Peregrine is often the default large falcon across much of the East, but in the West it can be confused with Prairie Falcon, and in the far North with Gyrfalcon.

Telling Peregrine from Gyrfalcon can be difficult. Peregrine is smaller and slimmer overall, with a larger head, more distinct head pattern, and narrower wings with longer hands. Also, Gyrfalcon has stiffer, shallower wingbeats lacking the whiplike, "rolling" quality of Peregrine. When perched, Peregrines are shorter-tailed and bigger-headed, with wingtips almost reaching the tail tip.

Peregrine and Prairie Falcon are extremely similar in shape, but Prairie Falcon shows slightly slimmer wings and tail, appearing more Kestrel-like than Peregrine. Peregrine is darker overall in all plumages and lacks the distinct dark wing linings and wing pits of Prairie. Flight style is very similar between the two, but Prairie Falcon has somewhat shallower wingbeats.

Male Peregrines are especially slim and can be

confused with *Merlin*. Peregrine is told from Merlin (and Kestrel) not only by its usually obvious larger size, but also by its longer-handed, broader-based wings, stout chest and head, and long, broad tail that tapers toward the tip when closed. Peregrine soars in wide, slow circles, and the wingbeats are slower and more flexing compared with those of Merlin. Merlins lack the white chest shown by most adult Peregrines, but juveniles of both species have white throats.

Hybrids: Falconers often hybridize Peregrines with various falcon species, including Gyrfalcon and even Merlin. Birds that escape into the wild can be impossible to identify.

Status and Distribution: Generally uncommon, Peregrine is increasing throughout its range. Populations have recovered nicely from extreme lows due to DDT poisoning, and the species has recently been removed from the Endangered Species List. Formerly extirpated from the eastern United States, it now nests with birds of mixed genetic descent through successful reintroduction programs; however, these efforts have introduced European genes into the population that are still visible today, causing subspecific identification headaches for birders, especially in the East. The continental population in the West is more "pure" and typical of the subspecies *anatum*. Tundra Peregrine Falcon breeds across the high Arctic tundra on cliffs. It is generally a long-distance migrant, wintering sparingly in the United States and mainly in Central and South America and the Caribbean. Anatum breeds in the West south of the Arctic tundra to Mexico, and most birds winter within the breeding range. Peale's is resident across the Pacific Northwest coast to the outer Aleutian Islands.

Migration: Tundra Peregrine is the most migratory of the 3 subspecies of Peregrine. Tundra birds migrate south in fall mainly from mid-September through October, and from early April through May in spring. Notable movements occur along the Atlantic and Gulf Coasts, with Cape May Point, NJ, Kiptopeke, VA, and Curry Hammock in the Florida Keys famous for their Peregrine counts. Continental breeders are year-round residents or short-distance migrants, but less is known about their migratory patterns. Peale's is partly migratory, with some individuals wintering as far south as Mexico. Migration of Peale's is poorly understood, but at least some move south of the breeding range and can be seen along the West Coast in fall and winter. Some darker birds resembling Peale's can be seen along the East Coast south to Florida during migration and winter, but it is unknown whether these are truly Peale's, or some mix of genetic descent from reintroduced breeders.

Vocalizations: Peregrines give a loud, harsh, nasal, agitated *kak-kak-kak-kak*, and shrill screams, mainly in alarm or interactions, also drawn-out wailing calls around the nest.

Prairie Falcon *(Falco mexicanus)* PRFA page 140

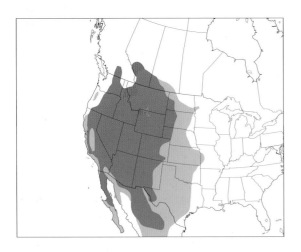

Looking over a vast expanse of blue sky and frost-covered desert, I sit with the sun at my back and face to the wind. Below me, an active colony of ground squirrels bustles about, doing their morning business. Still trying to shake off the previous night's cold, I could use a warm meal…and my stomach is growling. I drop from my perch, and with a few quick flaps, I'm 3 feet off the ground, moving fast toward the colony. I try to stay as low as possible, following the contours of the land. If just one ground squirrel spots my approach, its alarm call will resonate throughout the colony, and all will scatter back into their underground burrows. Nearing the edge of the colony, I pick up speed, streaking across the ground with black wing linings reflecting off the pale ground cover. It's easy to sprint with these long, sturdy, pointed wings, and as I get within 100 yards of my target, my wingbeats become shorter, faster, more intense; just the tips of my wings flickering at high speed. Alarm calls ring out across the colony. I'm spotted, but one squirrel is too far away from its burrow, and with talons extended I pluck it from the ground just before it reaches safety.

Overview: Prairie Falcons are solitary birds of western open country, nesting in cavities on cliffs along rimrock canyons, on buttes, and on rocky outcrops. During winter they can be found more widely across the West, even in surprisingly suburban areas with ample open space. Unlike the similarly sized Peregrine, Prairie Falcon hunts primarily ground squirrels when on the breeding grounds, which are captured through low, surprise-attack flight, as well as by perch-hunting. In certain areas, Prairie Falcons also eat medium-sized open country birds such as Meadowlarks, Horned Larks, and Pipits. Throughout winter, Prairie Falcons catch their own food, but they are also happy to steal voles and mice from Northern Harriers and other raptors. Prairie lacks the respect birders bestow on Peregrines, maybe because it is less defensive on the nest, but in reality it is nearly as impressive in flight.

Flight Style: Prairie Falcons are steady, strong, and fast in flight with Peregrine-like wingbeats, but with a slightly stiffer, shallower quality. Like Peregrines, Prairie Falcons soar and glide mainly on flat or slightly bowed wings. On occasion, they hover or stall in flight while hunting, but only for a few seconds at a time, and never for an extended period like American Kestrel.

Size and Shape: L 37–47 cm (15–19 in), WS 90–114 cm (35–45 in), WT 420–1100 g (0.9–2.1 lb)
Prairie Falcon is a large falcon with long, tapered wings and a medium-length, tapered tail. It is very similar to Peregrine Falcon in size and shape, but with a few subtle differences. Prairie Falcons are slightly slimmer overall than Peregrines, somewhat more Kestrel-like (especially males), but the wings, tail, chest, and head are still broad like those of Peregrine. Distinguishing Prairie from Peregrine at a distance by silhouette alone can be one of the toughest identifications in birding. Female Prairie Falcons are larger than males and have slightly broader wings, but telling sexes at a distance based on structure is difficult without practice. When perched, they appear large and broad-shouldered like Peregrine, but they often bob their head up and down like a Kestrel, a behavior Peregrine does not normally exhibit.

Plumage: Prairie Falcons are overall sandy brown above and whitish below, with contrasting blackish underwing linings that vary slightly in extent, and dark axillaries (wing pits). Even in poor light, the dark wing pits and wing linings of Prairie Falcons are usually obvious. The head shows a whitish supercilium and a pale cheek that offsets a narrow black malar. The tail is brown with faint pale bands throughout. Often, the flight feathers of Prairie Falcons appear pale or translucent against the sky, making the wings look slimmer than normal, and making the tail appear pinkish red.

*Adult*s are lightly spotted below, and the upperwing coverts are faintly barred. Males are more lightly marked below on average, but plumage overlaps between the sexes. Regardless, it is often difficult to age or sex Prairie Falcons in the field without good views. The tail of adults is often paler than the upperwings, showing a slight overall contrast on top.

1st-years (juveniles) are overall plain brownish above with the upperwing coverts fringed paler. They are slightly darker on top than adults, especially in fresh plumage in fall. The underbody is buff or "creamy" with dark streaks when very fresh, but the buff fades to whitish by the first fall. Some juvenile males are lightly marked below. Juveniles have a bluish cere, eyering, and feet/legs, changing to yellow during the first winter or spring.

Geographic Variation: None.

Molt: Juvenile Prairie Falcons may undergo a limited head and body molt during the first winter and early spring, making them look partly adult-like. But adult and juvenile head plumage is very similar and may be difficult to distinguish. Over the first summer, juveniles undergo a complete molt, usually replacing the entire plumage, including all the flight feathers. Rarely juvenile primaries (most often the innermost primary) or secondaries can be retained through the second year, but it is more typical for a few back or upperwing coverts to be retained (this is extremely difficult to see in the field). Adults have a complete molt each year from April to November.

Similar Species: Prairie Falcons have a distinctive plumage: bold head pattern, overall sandy brown coloration above, whitish underparts, and contrasting blackish wing pits and wing linings; the latter being diagnostic for the species. But at a distance or with inadequate views, they can be confused with Peregrine Falcon, juvenile gray-morph Gyrfalcon, "brown" Prairie Merlin, and female American Kestrel.

Prairie is most frequently confused with *Peregrine*, but Prairie Falcon is slimmer overall with a longer-tailed look. The wings are slightly slimmer and more blunt at the tips. Unlike Peregrine, Prairie has pale flight feathers, often appearing translucent in the field, especially the tail when fanned out completely. Prairie appears paler overall in all but the darkest daylight conditions. The flight style of these two large falcons is similar, but Peregrine's wingbeats are more "rolling" or "whiplike"; however, this difference is slight, and judging shape and flight style distinctions between Prairie and Peregrine Falcon takes years of practice!

Female *American Kestrel* and *Prairie Merlin* are distinctly smaller than Prairie Falcon but are generally similar in plumage. "Brown" (adult female and juvenile) Prairie Merlins are the most similar in plumage to Prairie Falcon; both species are pale brown on top and whitish below, but Merlins lack the black wing pits and underwing linings of Prairie. Also, "brown" Prairie Merlins are densely rufous-streaked below, whereas Prairie Falcon is lightly marked with black streaks or spots. Most Prairie Merlins are slightly paler above than Prairie Falcons, including the head, and they always lack the strong head pattern shown by Prairie Falcon. Another major difference is the distinctly banded tail shown by all Prairie Merlins. Even though the tail of Prairie Falcon can look reddish from below when backlit, the black wing pits and underwing linings easily distinguish them from Kestrel. Prairies also lack the buoyant, "fluttery" flight of Kestrel. Both Merlins and Kestrels have slim chests and small heads compared with Prairie Falcon.

Prairie Falcons can be confused with juvenile gray-morph *Gyrfalcons*, but Gyrfalcons lack black wing pits and black wing linings. Rarely, juvenile Gyrfalcons have dark mottling along the underwing linings, but these feathers are never as boldly marked as on Prairie Falcon, and the streaking on the underparts of Gyrfalcon is more prominent. Also, Gyrfalcons are more heavily built than Prairie Falcons, appearing more "chesty" and smaller-headed.

Status and Distribution: Prairie Falcons are relatively uncommon throughout the West and northern Mexico, and rare to exceptional in the East. A few birds make it to the Great Lakes region during fall and winter every few years, but it is generally a rarity anywhere east of the Great Plains.

Migration: Some aspects of Prairie Falcon migration are poorly understood. For the most part, it is a short-distance migrant, leaving the breeding grounds for nearby open terrain abundant with food. Some birds winter throughout the breeding range. Prairie Falcons are solitary on migration, and movements could represent postbreeding dispersal rather than a true north-south migration. Prairie Falcons can be seen migrating along western ridges (especially the Goshute Mountains and the eastern and western foothills of the Rocky Mountains), and across the Great Plains, mainly from March to May and September to November. There are also both easterly and westerly movements, with birds wintering closer to the West Coast and as far to the east as the Mississippi River Delta (rarely).

Vocalizations: Generally quiet away from nesting areas, Prairie Falcons occasionally vocalize during aggressive encounters with other raptors. Their call is very similar to Peregrine Falcon's, but is slightly higher-pitched, a repeated *kak-kak-kak-kak*. Males have a slightly faster and higher-pitched call than females.

Gyrfalcon *(Falco rusticolus)* GYRF page 144

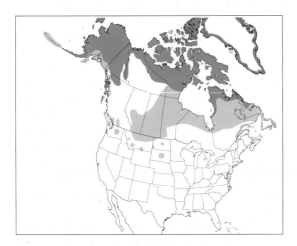

Pheeew!…the smell of manure in the air is putrid! This may be the preferred site of a wintering Gyrfalcon, but it doesn't seem so great to me. The hotline reported a juvenile Gyrfalcon hunting in this agricultural area, and I'm eager to see it. Gyrfalcons are particularly uncommon and difficult to track down in most of the Lower 48, so it would be a "lifer" for me—a dream bird. It's now well past sunrise and I'm no longer alone as a car full of birders pulls up and joins me in the search. The pigeons feeding among the corn stubble are restless and have my attention; they keep flushing from the ground and a nearby grain silo, but every time I scan for the falcon that might have caused the panic, I fail to find one. In the distance, a Pheasant makes a short dash from one stand of the tall grass to another…plenty of food here, but still no falcon.

I've come prepared, having memorized every field guide description of Gyrfalcon available, but I'm nervous that I still might have trouble identifying one, especially a juvenile. *Broad wings, bluntly-pointed wingtips, pale flight feathers, shallow wingbeats, a "flying football"*—all the classic field marks reverberate in my mind. A falcon is spotted

soaring above the cattle. Hands shaking, I have difficulty holding my binoculars steady; it appears massive and mostly dark underneath! The bird stoops but misses an unseen target. Is it a Gyrfalcon? It sure could be. But I'm confused, I just can't tell it from a Peregrine Falcon—*God, they look alike*. The falcon streaks low across the field and out of sight, never to be seen again. For a moment at least, I completely forgot how bad the surrounding odor was. Was that my life Gyrfalcon? I'm still not sure. The birders nearby jump around excitedly; high-fiving ensues. But I'm unsatisfied. I wait it out, sitting patiently all day for the Gyrfalcon to show itself again, but it never does. As sunset comes, I realize that the large falcon I saw may have been the reported *Gyrfalcon*, but my gut tells me it was a Peregrine. I just couldn't see enough to be sure. The truth is revealed the next day when another birder posts photos of the "Gyrfalcon" on the Web. They clearly show a juvenile Peregrine.

Overview: Gyrfalcon is the largest, most heavily built, scarcest, and most sought after of the North American falcons. It is a predator of the Arctic, rarely occurring in winter in the Lower 48 away from a few locations that have Gyrfalcons in most years. Gyrfalcon is usually found in open areas that have ample food and whose habitat roughly mimics the open arctic tundra it prefers (e.g., flat agricultural areas, grassland, dunes, beaches). Many adults remain in the Arctic year-round, but vagrant adults are occasionally also seen in winter; however, juveniles are more typically seen in the Lower 48. Gyrfalcons nest mainly on cliffs above vast treeless expanses where they hunt large birds (e.g., ptarmigan, waterfowl), and sometimes medium-sized mammals (e.g., arctic hare).

Unlike Peregrine Falcon, with which it is often compared, Gyrfalcon hunts primarily using "surprise-and-flush" tactics, cruising low over bumpy or flat terrain hoping to flush avian quarry. When flushed, Gyrfalcon chases down its prey with heavy, forceful wingbeats that enable it to gain speed in a matter of seconds. After a fantastic tail-chase, prey is typically struck in the air, then captured on the ground. Gyrfalcon occasionally stoops from high altitudes as well, when such a tactic is needed. It prominently perches on rock outcrops or hilltops and manmade structures, especially utility poles during winter. Gyrfalcon is sometimes fearless, allowing close approach by humans.

Flight Style: In direct flight, Gyrfalcon's wingbeats are shallower and less "whiplike" or rolling than those of Peregrine, more like Merlin or Prairie Falcon but notably heavier. Gyrfalcon soars on flattish wings, but sometimes also with a slight dihedral in lazy, wide circles.

Size and Shape: L 50–61 cm (19–24 in), WS 110–130 cm (43–51 in), WT 1.0–2.1 kg (2.2–4.6 lb) Gyrfalcon is a real powerhouse, with a hulking chest, back, and shoulders, tapering toward the belly and tail, all combining to impart a small-headed and bulky-bodied appearance. Females can be similar to Red-tailed Hawk in size and bulk, but males are smaller and slimmer-winged and appear equal in size to female Peregrine and Prairie Falcons; thus they are more easily confused with those species. In flight, the wings of Gyrfalcon are slightly broader than those of Peregrine and Prairie (even Peale's Peregrines, which are larger and broader-winged than other races of Peregrine) and the wingtips are more bluntly pointed; this is most apparent on Gyrfalcon when soaring or in a shallow glide. Gyrfalcons have relatively long and broad tails for a large falcon, and the wingtips fall short of the tail tip on perched birds.

Plumage: Gyrfalcons are often described as "large and dark," but they are highly variable in general coloration, ranging from nearly wholly white to completely dark, with a complete continuum in between. For convenience, most birds are lumped into 3 categories: white, gray (intermediate), or dark. Gray morphs are by far the most frequently encountered in North America, while white and dark morphs are rare. Juveniles and adults differ in plumage, but sexes are very similar; females are notably larger.

White-morph adults are beautiful, snow-white below and lightly spotted with dark, with black restricted to the very tips of the wings. The upperparts are white as well, with dark barring on the upperwing coverts. Male averages more lightly marked, but there is overlap between the sexes. *1st-years* (juveniles) are similar to adults but more heavily marked above and below. Juveniles of all plumage variants have a bluish cere, eyering, and feet/legs, changing to yellow during first winter/spring. The tail pattern on all Gyrfalcons is indistinct with faint bands, though some white morphs can be wholly white-tailed (mostly males).

Gray-morph adult Gyrfalcons are similar in appearance to Peregrine Falcon, with which they are often confused. Gyrfalcon is paler overall and evenly spotted underneath, lacking the white-chested look of adult Peregrine. Gyrfalcon is paler gray on top and has a paler head that lacks the distinct black hood of Peregrine Falcon, usually also lacking a bold dark mustache mark. *Juveniles* show dark streaking underneath and a dark brown upperside with pale-fringed coverts. The overall coloration on top is slightly paler than Peregrine. Although Gyrfalcon is said to be "dark" underneath, gray-morph juveniles are often less heavily marked and less buff-colored below than most Peregrines, but often with a more solidly dark head.

Dark-morph adults are slate-gray above with faint barring and a dark head. Adults often have faint pale barring on the underside, but they usually appear solidly dark overall with no distinct field marks. *Juveniles* are either solidly dark or extremely heavily streaked underneath. There is overlap in plumage between these 3 plumage variants, "tweeners" so to speak, and many birds don't fit the classic mold.

Geographic Variation: Previously described subspecies of Gyrfalcon are based largely on poorly understood polymorphism, and they are no longer recognized. Regional frequency of various color morphs requires further study, but gray morphs predominate in North America. Dark-morph birds are thought to be more coastal in distribution, whereas white morphs are thought to be interior breeders.

Molt: Juveniles undergo a limited (if any) molt of body feathers during the first winter, followed by a complete or nearly complete molt mainly from March through October, after which they are usually indistinguishable from adults. *2nd-year* birds sometimes retain a few juvenile back and upperwing coverts, and rarely a few flight feathers. Adults undergo a molt each year mainly from April through

November, but they do not necessarily replace all their feathers each year, sometimes showing multiple generations of flight feathers. Being a high arctic breeder, Gyrfalcons have less time to complete a molt each year compared with more southerly nesting raptor species.

Similar Species: White and dark extremes of Gyrfalcon are usually distinctive and not likely to be confused with other raptors (but beware of albino Red-tailed Hawk, and very pale Ferruginous Hawks). On the other hand, gray-morph Gyrfalcon can appear very much like *Peregrine Falcon.* Many misidentifications are the result of observers being unfamiliar with Gyrfalcon and assuming that one is a Peregrine, but more commonly, overeager observers try to turn Peregrine Falcons into Gyrfalcons. General rule: if you think you're seeing a Gyrfalcon, ask first, "Why isn't this a Peregrine?" Gyrfalcon is sometimes told from Peregrine Falcon by its larger size, but its heavier build, broader wings, longer tail, and smaller head are more reliable structural traits to look for. Also, Gyrfalcon has stiffer, shallower wingbeats lacking the "rolling" quality of Peregrine, but this takes practice to discern.

On adult gray-morph Gyrfalcon, the dark malar and "helmeted" look are less prominent than on adult Peregrine. The upperside is a paler gray, and the underside is evenly marked, whereas Peregrine has a darker belly and paler upper breast. On juvenile gray-morph Gyrfalcon, the upperside is slightly paler brown than Peregrine. The cere, orbital ring, and legs/feet are bluish on Gyrfalcon throughout the first winter and sometimes into the first spring; Peregrine's legs/feet tend to change to yellowish-green by early fall. Almost all juvenile Gyrfalcons show streaks on the undertail coverts compared with barred on Peregrine, and the flight feathers of Gyrfalcon are not as boldly marked, appearing paler at a distance.

Lightly marked juvenile gray-morph Gyrfalcons are superficially similar to *Prairie Falcon* but lack the black wing pits and solid blackish wing linings of Prairie. Rarely, juvenile Gyrfalcon has dark mottling along the wing linings, but these markings are much less bold than on Prairie Falcon, and the streaking on the underparts of Gyrfalcon is more prominent. The topside of Gyrfalcon is noticeably darker than on Prairie Falcon. Also, Gyrfalcon never appears Kestrel-like in flight, as Prairie Falcon sometimes does.

Northern Goshawk is also similar in shape and plumage to adult gray-morph Gyrfalcon. Both are grayish above and pale below, but Goshawk shows a blackish head, white eyebrow, and darker back. Gyrfalcon always shows longer, more tapered wings with black tips to the outer primaries. Gyrfalcon's tail tapers at the tip when closed, unlike Goshawk, which is evenly broad throughout its length. The wingbeats of Gyrfalcon are stiffer, shallower, and more continuous than those of Goshawk.

Adult male Northern Harrier has been confused for white-morph Gyrfalcon, especially when gliding high overhead, when it shows falcon-like, tapered wings. However, Gyrfalcon lacks a black trailing edge to the secondaries, and the extensive black on the primary tips of male Harrier. Harrier is also slimmer-winged and slighter of body compared with the more "chesty" Gyrfalcon.

Hybrids: Hybrid Gyrfalcons are not known to exist or occur in the wild, but hybrids are common in falconry. Peregrine, Saker, Lanner, and Prairie Falcon are most commonly bred with Gyrfalcon. In the United States, Merlin has also been crossed with Gyrfalcon. Hybrids can appear nearly identical to one species or look like a combination of both species, making some impossible to identify with certainty. Occasionally, falconry birds escape into the wild, causing identification headaches for birders. These birds often have jesses (small leather foot straps) or rings on their legs that may be difficult to view in the field. Hybrids or escapees should be considered for any out-of-range Gyrfalcon-like bird.

Status and Distribution: Gyrfalcon is generally scarce and difficult to find, even on the breeding grounds, where large territories are scattered across vast expanses of tundra. A few reach the U.S.–Canada border region each winter, mainly from November to April. One to several usually winter in the coastal Pacific Northwest, especially on the Skagit and Samish Flats, WA. They are also regular winter visitors in and around Sault St. Marie, MI, and on the open expanses of the northern Great Plains. Multiple Gyrfalcons are known to inhabit the open grassland and agricultural areas in and around Pierre, SD, every winter. One or two are usually reported in New England each winter. It is exceptional farther south. Gyrfalcon is also found in northern Eurasia.

Migration: Gyrfalcon migration is poorly understood, but a few birds move south mainly from October to March (mostly juveniles), sometimes staying on the winter grounds into April. Adults may remain on breeding grounds year-round, and recent studies have shown that some Gyrfalcons overwinter on open ice where large sea duck concentrations occur. Migration sites in Alaska are the most likely places to see Gyrfalcon. In the Lower 48, the eastern Rocky Mountain foothills of Montana, the Canadian shorelines of the Great Lakes, and western shore of Lake Superior are the most likely spots to see a Gyrfalcon during migration.

Vocalizations: The call, a harsh, repeated, agitated *kak-kak-kak-kak*, is similar to that of a Peregrine, but usually lower and slower. Drawn-out wailing calls are also given around the nest.

Aplomado Falcon *(Falco femoralis)* **APFA** page 146

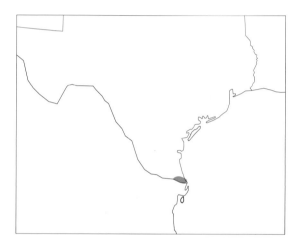

A songbird creeps up to the top of its modest perch, a short shrub amid a sea of grasses and thickets. The Texas sun bakes this open expanse; heat shimmer and haze obscure the distance. As the songird cautiously turns its head, its eyes search for any sign of the sinister shape it has come to fear in recent days. An Aplomado Falcon has taken up residence nearby, though the coast seems clear now. The bird launches into song, head back, delivering its rapid-fire bouncing trill, hoping to attract the attention of a female. Unbeknownst to the singer, a dark slim ghost has broken away from a nearby yucca and dropped just inches above the grass, and is now rushing toward it with flicking, calculating wingbeats. As the Aplomado Falcon draws near, a Botteri's Sparrow's life is soon to be over. As the falcon streaks across the open grass at a speed only a falcon can attain, the sparrow finally sees it, but it has little chance as it takes flight. A few dashing twists and turns later, the sparrow slips away, grappled by long yellow talons and carried off on stealthy, slim wings.

Overview: Aplomado Falcons occupy a very tiny range in the United States, occurring only in south Texas and New Mexico, with all birds currently the products of ongoing reintroduction programs. This elegant, long-winged and long-tailed falcon favors grassy savanna, particularly when dotted with yucca, a habitat that has been all but removed from the southwestern United States where it historically occurred more widely. Aplomado Falcons are sleek and speedy, bursting from a perch to tail-chase their prey, primarily small birds, but also small mammals and insects. Aplomados frequently perch conspicuously on roadside wires, power poles, and bush tops, but they sometimes conceal themselves in the inner branches of a shrub to stay out of view, and especially to find shade during the heat of the day. Distinctive in both structure and plumage, Aplomado Falcon is unlikely to be confused if seen well, but with poor views it can be mistaken for other falcons.

Flight Style: Aplomado's flight is fast and direct with fluid wingbeats, especially when chasing small land birds. Occasionally they soar to high altitudes but typically do not hunt from high elevation. When soaring, they do so steadily and on flattish wings.

Size and Shape: L 35–45 cm (14–18 in), WS 78–102 cm (31–40 in), WT 208–460 g (8.4–16 oz) Aplomado Falcons are medium-sized falcons, only slightly bigger than a Merlin, but completely different in shape and build. Their long wings and exceptionally long tail create a profile that is unique among the North American falcons. When perched, Aplomado Falcons appear particularly lengthy, and the long tail extends well past the wingtips.

Plumage: Aplomado Falcons have 2 age classes:

adult and juvenile (first-year). They attain adult appearance in about 1 year, after their first complete molt. In all plumages note the bold head pattern (black cap and thin sideburn with bold white eyeline and cheek), dark vest, grayish brown topside, and white trailing edge on the secondaries. Adult sexes differ slightly: both have a bright yellow cere and orbital ring, and rufous leggings. *Adult males* are cleanly patterned with unmarked white breasts, bright rufous leggings, and blue-black upperparts. *Adult females* are similar to males, but they have a lightly streaked white breast. The tail of all adults shows 5–6 narrow white bands above. All Aplomado Falcons have dark eyes.

1st-years are tawny below with heavily streaked buffy breasts, tawny leggings, and brownish upperparts. The cere and orbital ring are bluish for the first few months. The tail has 6–7 narrow white bands above. Juvenile sexes are similar.

Geographic Variation: There are 3 weakly differentiated subspecies of Aplomado Falcon, but just 1 occurs in North America: *F. f. septentrionalis*. The North American subspecies differs from the others by being larger overall with longer wings, a more complete, broad black bellyband, and paler blue-black upperparts (adults).

Molt: Information on molt timing is sparse, and date ranges should be considered provisional until further study is conducted. Juveniles undergo a partial molt of body and head feathers in the first winter, but information on extent is lacking. Some may replace most of the juvenile body plumage, but probably no wing or tail feathers. The first complete molt presumably takes place from April to October, after which birds attain adult plumage. Subsequent molts are thought to be complete, mainly from April to November, but as with other medium-large falcons, perhaps not all feathers are molted in 1 cycle.

Similar Species: Distinctive in its restricted U.S. range. Note the especially bold head pattern, which can be seen at great distance and in flight. The slim proportions are unlike any other North American falcon, with long, narrowly pointed wings, an exceptionally long tail (for a falcon) with fine white bands, and relatively long legs. Aplomados are told from the relatively unpatterned *Merlin* and the mainly rufous-colored *American Kestrel* by their bolder head pattern and slimmer, rangier proportions (especially the longer tail). Aplomado Falcons are told from *Peregrine Falcon* by their smaller size, slimmer build, longer, narrower tail, bolder head pattern, and dark "vested" underbody.

Status and Distribution: Aplomado Falcon is rare and local in its U.S. range. Historically, it bred in southeast Arizona, New Mexico, and south Texas but was extirpated in 1952. Wild birds are exceptional in the United States, and the majority of birders' encounters with this species are related to the reintroduced birds in south Texas. The status of wild birds is complicated by ongoing reintroduction efforts, but overall they remain exceedingly rare. A few wild pairs nested in Luna Co., NM, in the early 2000s, but none has done so recently in south Texas or Arizona. Loss of coastal grassland, savanna, and desert grassland to agriculture and development is a continuing conservation problem. Distribution is spotty in Mexico, but Aplomado Falcons are found more broadly south through the tropics and as far south as Tierra del Fuego.

Migration: Mainly resident where reintroduced, but Aplomado Falcons occasionally wander north of their mapped range.

Vocalizations: Usually a high-pitched, whining *ki-ki-ki-ki-ki-ki*…often sustained; female call is lower and huskier.

MYSTERY PHOTO ANSWERS

With mystery photos, generally our first impulse is to look at an image, slap an answer on it, and then look to see if we are correct. Learning in this way will not help you become a better birder. The purpose of these plates is to help you practice identifying birds in a way that can help you become better at it in the field.

As previously mentioned, nothing beats the real thing; however, practicing with these images is the next best thing. To maximize this opportunity, I would recommend a number of things:

1. Take your time! The best are the best because they put the time in. The challenge is to work out each bird's age, sex, and identity—if possible. Quizzes are fun. It is important to recognize that we learn more when we don't know the answers.
2. Study each bird very carefully. Learn the bird—its size, shape, and variations in plumage. A fun thing to try is to look away and draw or write a detailed description of the bird. Doing this well is much harder than it sounds, but it will improve your understanding of a bird's appearance and ultimately its identity.
3. Read the text and compare each bird with other images in the book. This book offers many tools to help you work out the answers. Even after you feel you know the bird in question, compare it with others of the same species. You will probably notice that no two are the same. It is important to note that field guides give only a representative image; here, we are able to show the wide range of variation shown by most species.
4. Birding is a voyage of discovery. It is not about being right or wrong. Try to learn something from images. Appreciate not just the birds, but everything else. It's all great—you just have to see it!

Vultures at the Dinner Table, pages 18–19

1. **Black Vulture.** Black plumage, compact build, with short tails and white outer primaries.
2. **Turkey Vulture.** Note browner plumage of Turkey Vulture and more prominent dihedral.
3. **Black Vultures.** Black plumage, compact build, with short tails and white outer primaries.
4. **Adult Turkey Vulture.** Note red head and pale bill, long wings with silvery flight feathers.
5. **Adult Turkey Vulture.** Red head and pale bill, silvery flight feathers.
6. **Turkey Vulture (center) with Black Vultures.** Note larger size and lankier build of Turkey Vulture, as well as paler silvery flight feathers.
7. **Black Vultures.** Note white outer primaries, short tails.
8. **Adult Turkey Vultures.** Reddish heads with white bills indicate species and age.
9. **Adult Black Vultures.** Black plumage, grayish heads, and short tails.
10. **Black Vulture.** Note black color, flattish wings, and grayish head. Palish-tipped bill and gray wrinkled head indicate it is not a very young bird, but probably an older immature. "Possibly" and "probably" are good words to use unless you are certain.

Vultures from Cape May Point Lighthouse, pages 20–21

1. **Black Vulture.** Black plumage with slight dihedral and gray head. Note paler outer primaries and wing molt.
2. **Turkey Vulture.** Pale brownish with long tail.
3. **Juv./1st-year Turkey Vulture.** Juvenile based on grayish pink head. Note long tail and silvery flight feathers. Large raptors typically retain all their juvenile feathers for much of the first year. Their uniform color and length with smooth trailing edge to the wing is often the best and easiest way to age them.
4. **Black Vulture.** Note the short, broad tail. Short, bowed wings with pale outer primaries.

5. **Turkey Vulture (left) with Black Vulture.** Note larger size of Turkey Vulture and longer tail, as well as uniformly pale flight feathers.
6. **Turkey Vultures.** Silhouette at a distance appears headless with long tail and usually strong dihedral.
7. **Turkey Vulture (top) with Black Vulture.** Note stronger dihedral of Turkey Vulture. Black Vulture sometimes appears flat-winged. The upturned wingtips are typical of Black Vulture.
8. **Turkey Vultures.** Often in large kettles. At this distance, note strong dihedral.
9. **Black Vulture.** Compact build with short tail and white outer primaries.
10. **Black Vulture.** At this angle note short tail and slight dihedral, also blackish plumage.
11. **Adult Turkey Vulture.** Red head with pale bill. Also browner above than Black Vulture.
12. **Turkey Vulture.** Brownish with prominent dihedral.

Eagle Comparisons, pages 34–35

1. **3rd-/4th-year Bald Eagle.** Several adult characters such as white head and tail mixed with immature characters such as dark ear coverts and edges to tail feathers.
2. **3rd-year Bald Eagle.** All the secondaries are replaced but one or two and the belly, head, bill, and underwing coverts are correct for that age.
3. **Juv./1st-year Golden Eagle.** Golden nape and bold white base to the tail. Aged by uniform appearance with smooth trailing edge to the wing.
4. **2nd-year Bald Eagle.** Dark bib, white belly and underwing. Aged by combination of retained juvenile and second-generation flight feathers.
5. **Juv./1st-year Bald Eagle.** Juveniles often appear darker than older immatures. Uniform trailing edge to wing ages it as a juvenile.
6. **4th-year Bald Eagle.** Adult-like with a few retained immature feathers. Some 5th-years can also appear like this.
7. **Adult Bald Eagle.** White head and tail. They often look black and white at a distance.
8. **Adult Bald Eagle.** White head and tail.
9. **2nd-year Bald Eagle.** Note how much further the unmolted flight feathers protrude than the newly molted second-generation ones.
10. **Golden Eagle.** Uniform brown. Compared with Bald Eagle, it looks subtly slimmer with the shorter head projection quite striking. Ageing tough, but 3 years or older.
11. **Immature Golden Eagle.** Even at long range the shape can be diagnostic for the trained eye. Note the dark brown appearance with pale wing panels, indicative of an immature. More specific ageing without better views isn't smart.
12. **Adult Golden Eagle.** Shape, brown color with paler nape. Dark trailing edge to wing contrasting with patterned base to flight feathers and lack of white age it as an adult.
13. **Subadult Golden Eagle.** A somewhat confusing-looking bird. Well-defined terminal band with the dark not extending up the sides of the feathers and pale brown nape and head. Note the different-aged flight feathers. Technically the terms immature and subadult are the same, though subadult implies it is closer to adult plumage than juvenile. There is a tendency when using the term immature to imply the bird is relatively young, but it can include all birds that could be labeled subadult.
14. **Adult Bald Eagle.**
15. **Adult Bald Eagle.** White head and tail. Gliding on flat wings is more typical of Bald Eagle. Golden Eagles usually show at least a shallow dihedral.

Harrier Ageing and Sexing, pages 42–43

1. **Adult female.** Note buffy underparts boldly streaked with dark.
2. **Juv./1st-year.** A difficult one in this pose, but note the rufous-banded tail and unstreaked rufous

underparts contrasting with the darker head.

3. **Unknown.** At a certain distance it is impossible to age and sex harriers, but you can often tell if they are "brown birds" versus adult males. At this angle, though, we must be satisfied to simply leave the identification at Northern Harrier.
4. **Adult female.** Brownish upperparts contrasting with gray-banded flight feathers, including the primary coverts, which are strongly barred. Mottled upperwing coverts, usually strongly tinged rufous in juveniles.
5. **Adult male.** Even at this distance, adult males are distinctive. Note the clean white underparts with bold black wingtips.
6. **Adult male.** Clean white below with black wingtips and dark trailing edge to the secondaries.
7. **Juv./1st-year.** Rufous below with limited fine streaks.
8. **Adult female.** More boldly marked than number 7.
9. **Adult male.** White below and gray above with black wingtips and trailing edge to secondaries.
10. **Adult female.** Buffy underparts with bold dark streaks. Beware first-spring birds that have faded to buffy below, some of which can have faint streaking on the breast, but usually not this dark.

Sharp-shinned Hawk Ageing, pages 46–47

1. **Juv./1st-year.** Brownish above with rufus fringed upperparts and yellow eye.
2. **Adult male.** Pale blue above with dark red eye, short squared tail.
3. **Juv./1st-year.** Brownish above with yellow eye. Short squared tail suggests male.
4. **Adult.** Tough to age from this angle, but note reddish barred underparts, indicating adult.
5. **Juv./1st-year.** Note dense streaking below.
6. **Adult.** Red barring below indicates adult.
7. **Unknown.** Above a certain height or distance, it becomes difficult to age Sharp-shinneds. Juveniles and adults are similar in shape, so plumage details must be seen in order to age them.
8. **Juv./1st-year.** Most have reddish tones to the streaking below, which also tends to be denser than on Cooper's.
9. **Juv./1st-year.** Yellow eyes and brownish upperparts.
10. **Adult molting.** Rarely seen molting during migration, but occasionally in the West. Adult based on reddish barring below.
11. **Juv./1st-year.** Note dense streaking below and upperpart pattern.

Cooper's Hawk Ageing, pages 50–51

1. **Juv./1st-year.** Brownish above with contrasting tawny head and pale yellow-green eye.
2. **Adult male.** Red eye, dense red barring below, and blackish cap.
3. **Adult.** Overall barred reddish below, usually more intense coloration on males.
4. **Juv./1st-year.** Whitish with dark streaks below and brown head.
5. **Juv./1st-year.** High birds can be difficult, but adults do not appear this white below.
6. **Juv./1st-year.** Note contrasting tawny head and whitish underparts at a distance.
7. **Unknown.** Birds headed away at eye level may be difficult to view.
8. **Juv./1st-year.** Brownish above with contrasting tawny head.
9. **Juv./1st-year.** Tawny brown head and brownish streaked underparts, usually paler below than Sharp-shinned.
10. **2nd-year.** Gray above with dark cap. Retained brownish juvenile secondaries and outer primaries.
11. **Juv./1st-year.** At a distance, 1st-years often appear whitish with contrasting tawny heads.

Comparison of Sharp-shinned and Cooper's Hawks, pages 52–53

1. **Adult Sharp-shinned.** Stocky and short-winged with reddish underparts. Also note short, slim tail.
2. **Juv./1st-year Cooper's.** Brownish upperparts indicate 1st-year. Long broad tail and rather lanky build.
3. **Juv./1st-year Sharp-shinned (below) and Juv./1st-year Cooper's (above).** Note larger size and bigger-headed appearance of Cooper's, and especially the longer tail.
4. **Adult Sharp-shinned.** Reddish barring below indicates adult. Note compact, short-winged build, with short, skinny tail. Notched tails are usually indicative of males.
5. **Adult Cooper's.** Bluish upperparts indicate adult. Note long, broad tail with fairly bold white tip. Wings thrown forward mask head projection.
6. **Adult (left) and Juv./1st-year Sharp-shinneds.** Similar in build, but the adult has barred reddish underparts, the 1st-year streaked rufous-brown below.
7. **Juv./1st-year Sharp-shinned.** Compact shape with square-ended tail. Aged by streaked underparts.
8. **Juv./1st-year Sharp-shinned.** Brownish streaked underparts indicate 1st-year. Compact build with small head and rather narrow-based tail.
9. **(2) Unknown Sharp-shinneds, unknown Cooper's (top).** These are tough. The 2 Sharpies are more compact with shorter, squared tails, and the Cooper's is lankier, though its larger size is masked because it is farther away.
10. **Juv./1st-year Sharp-shinned.** Some are more lightly marked below, but note the stocky build with short, slim tail. Notched tip very rare on Cooper's, but common on Sharp-shinned.
11. **Adult Cooper's.** Adult distinguished by reddish barred underparts and orange eye. Note long, broad tail, wings held fairly straight out from the body, and prominent head projection.
12. **Juv./1st-year Cooper's.** Pale underparts with darker tawny head. Note shape, with nearly straight leading edge to the wings and long, broad-based tail noticeably rounded at tip.
13. **Juv./1st-year Cooper's.** Long broad tail with lots of white at the tip, wings held straight out from body on leading edge, and noticeable head projection. Also note fairly light streaking below that is chocolatey instead of reddish in tone.
14. **Adult Sharp-shinned.** A tricky photo. The far wing is just barely visible above the crown, creating a dark-capped appearance like Cooper's. But note relatively compact build and shorter, slim tail. Also the head projection is just past the wrists; it would be more prominent on Cooper's.
15. **Juv./1st-year Sharp-shinned.** Brownish upperparts with compact build, little head projection, and slim tail.
16. **Juv./1st-year Sharp-shinned.** Compact. It's tough for a Cooper's to ever look this compact!
17. **Adult Sharp-shinned.** Stocky build with reddish barred underparts. Note especially the short, slim tail with squared tip.
18. **Unknown.** Many accipiters will give only fleeting views and are best left unidentified.
19. **Juv./1st-year Cooper's.** Brownish upperparts, big head, and long tail.
20. **Juv./1st-year Cooper's.** Rather lanky with good head projection and long tail.
21. **Adult Sharp-shinned.** Blue-gray upperparts indicate adult. Note wings pushed forward at wrist in a glide, creating small-headed appearance. Moderately long, rather narrow tail.

Perched Accipiters, pages 56–57

1. **Juv./1st-year male Sharp-shinned.** Brown upperparts and yellow eye indicate 1st-year. Small head with big-eyed look, and short tail with little white at tip indicate Sharp-shinned. Males usually show square-tipped tails, tiny bills, and white on face.
2. **Juv./1st-year Cooper's.** Streaked brownish underparts and yellowish eye indicate 1st-year. Squared head with small-eyed look, chocolate brown tones to streaking below, and long tail with graduated tip indicate Cooper's. Note bold white tail tip, rarely seen on Sharp-shinned. Cooper's generally have

thicker legs, though this is often hard to judge. Greenish tinge to eyes more common on Cooper's.

3. **Adult Sharp-shinned.** Bluish upperparts and reddish barred underparts indicate adult. Sharpies are slimmer overall, with smaller heads and a bigger-eyed appearance than Cooper's. The legs average skinnier, too.

4. **Juv./1st-year Sharp-shinned.** A tough one. Easy to age based on brownish upperparts and pale eye, though the eye is already turning orange. The bird has also molted a single grayish scapular. The tail is the key. Though shape is hard to judge when tail is spread, Sharpies generally have little to no white at the tip in their 1st-year plumage, and Cooper's have lots of white. The reddish tones in the bit of streaking we can see on the breast also indicate Sharp-shinned.

5. **Adult Cooper's.** Bluish upperparts and reddish barred underparts indicate age. It's a Cooper's based on its long, broad-based tail and dark crown, though the latter is a bit hard to see. Sometimes Cooper's can appear round-headed, and unless their hackles are raised, the head shape can be similar to that of Sharp-shinned. Cooper's usually look smaller-eyed and bigger-headed, though.

6. **2nd-year Cooper's.** The orange eye and faded brownish upperparts mixed with newer gray-blue feathers indicate 2nd-year or 1st-summer. The long, broad tail with moderate white at the tip indicates Cooper's, as do the big head and relatively small eye.

7. **Juv./1st-year Cooper's.** Pale underparts with long, broad tail with much white at the tip. Tough at this angle.

8. **Juv./1st-year Sharp-shinned.** Brownish upperparts indicate 1st-year. Both Sharpies and Coops can have whitish spotting and mottling above, but it's usually not like the more predictable tawny-buff mottling of Goshawk. On this Sharpie, note the small head and short, squarish tail.

9. **Adult Sharp-shinned.** Bluish upperparts indicate adult. Short, squared tail indicates Sharp-shinned.

10. **Adult Sharp-shinned.** A tough one. Easy to age by its bluish upperparts. Species ID is harder, but note extremely short, squared tail, indicating Sharp-shinned.

11. **Adult Cooper's**. Note straight leading edge to wings and long, broad tail. Hard to be certain of species ID, though, at this distance.

12. **Juv./1st-year Cooper's.** Plain brownish upperparts and yellowish eye indicate 1st-year. Contrasting tawny head with squared rear crown and long broad tail indicate Cooper's.

13. **Juv./1st-year Goshawk.** Bulky build with small head and long tail. Note densely streaked underparts, usually chocolate brown. Streaking often continues through undertail coverts.

Accipiters in Flight, pages 58–59

1. **Juv./1st-year Goshawk.** Generally bigger and bulkier than the Cooper's to its right, with more strongly patterned upperparts and a bold buffy eyebrow. Also note longer, broader tail and bulging secondaries.

2. **Juv./1st-year Cooper's.** Plain brown upperparts indicate 1st-year. Note strong head projection and long tail. Goshawk would show a tawny bar along the greater upperwing coverts in this view.

3. **Adult Sharp-shinned.** Reddish barred underparts indicate adult Sharp-shinned or Cooper's. Short wings and short, square-tipped tail indicate Sharp-shinned.

4. **Juv./1st-year Goshawk.** Can hold wings fairly straight along the leading edge at times, inviting confusion with Cooper's. But note this Goshawk's long, broader-based tail and more densely streaked chocolate brown underparts.

5. **Juv./1st-year Cooper's Hawk.** Based on shape and coloration.

6. **Adult Cooper's.** Rich reddish barred underparts indicate adult. Long, rounded tail and big head projection indicate Cooper's, as does the lanky overall structure of this bird.

7. **Juv./1st-year Goshawk.** Tough at this distance. But note the shape rather like Sharp-shinned Hawk, but unmistakably bulkier in all respects, with longer, broader-based tail and more bulging secondaries.

8. **Juv./1st-year Cooper's.** Pale underparts with sparse chocolate streaking most often concentrated on breast. Lanky build with rather long wings and long, rounded tail with much white at the tip.

9. **Juv./1st-year Red-tailed Hawk** (for comparison). Long wings and short, broad tail indicate buteo. Dark patagial bars and speckled dark bellyband indicate Red-tailed Hawk. Lack of distinct dark trailing edge to wings indicates 1st-year.

10. **Juv./1st-year Goshawk.** Rather like Cooper's Hawk in appearance, but note the strongly graduated tail almost appearing pointed, the pushed-forward wrists, and the bulky build of this bird. Can look small-headed at times.

11. **Juv./1st-year Goshawk.** Note big head with prominent white eyebrow, dark chocolatey streaking below that is quite dense, and long tail with pale highlights in the bands.

12. **Juv./1st-year Goshawk.** Broad wings can mask the tail length at this angle, but note the strong white eyebrow and buffy wing bar on the upperwing coverts.

13. **Adult Sharp-shinned.** Bluish upperparts indicate adult. Compact build with short wings and short square-tipped tail indicate Sharp-shinned.

14. **Juv./1st-year Cooper's.** Plain brownish upperparts indicate 1st-year. Straight leading edge to wings, long, broad tail with bold white tip, and contrasting tawny head indicate Cooper's.

15. **Adult Goshawk.** Adult based on bluish upperparts and reddish eye. Note bold white eyebrow and grayish underparts.

Red-tailed Hawks on the Prairies, pages 66–67

1. **Juv./1st-year Western.** Aged as a 1st-year by mainly brown-and-white plumage lacking any rufous tones, and pale eye. Subspecies is likely Western because of barred leggings and darkish throat, but ID to subspecies is not 100% based on this view.

2. **Adult Krider's.** Aged as adult by red tail and lack of prominent paler wing panels. Rufous shoulders and white-based tail indicate Krider's. Unlike Harlan's, Krider's does not show mottling in the whitish tail; instead its tail looks more like a faded and pale version of an Eastern's tail.

3. **Adult unknown.** Aged as adult by well-defined dark trailing edge to wings. Difficult to determine subspecies with this view, but rufous cast would suggest Western.

4. **Juv./1st-year Eastern x Krider's.** Aged as 1st-year by lack of dark trailing edge to wing and pale eye (hard to see). Subspecies difficult to determine, but definitely a paler individual showing Eastern characters likely crossed with Krider's. The very lightly banded flight feathers, pale head, and faint patagial all suggest Krider's, but the tail is more like Eastern, being brownish in ground color with dark bands.

5. **Adult Harlan's.** Blackish upperparts lacking white mottling indicate Harlan's, as does the white tail base with grayish mottling. Aged as an adult by lack of pale primary panels and reddish tail tip.

6. **Juv./1st-year unknown.** Aged as 1st-year by lack of dark trailing edge. Can't see enough to determine subspecies.

7. **Adult rufous Western.** Aged as adult by well-defined dark trailing edge to wings and red tail. Identified as Western by dark plumage with orange breast at a distance.

8. **Adult Western.** Aged as adult by well-defined dark trailing edge to wings and red tail. Identified as Western by overall rufous wash to underparts.

9. **Adult rufous Western.** Aged as adult by solid dark trailing edge to wings and red tail. Rufous morphs with orange breasts, as can be seen on this bird, are fairly typical of darker Western birds.

10. **Adult unknown.** Aged as adult by well-defined dark trailing edge to wings. Tail looks plain reddish from below, but impossible to determine subspecies given this view.

11. **Adult unknown.** Aged as adult by well-defined dark trailing edge to wings and red tail.

12. **Adult Western.** Aged as adult by well-defined dark trailing edge to wings and red tail. Identified as Western by solidly dark upperparts and wholly red tail.

13. **Juv./1st-year dark Harlan's.** Aged as 1st-year by lack of dark trailing edge to wings. Identified

as Harlan's with difficulty at this distance, but close inspection reveals completely banded outer primaries, a field mark that is typical of Harlan's and very rare on similarly plumaged Westerns.

14. **Juv./1st-year Western.** Aged as 1st-year by lack of dark trailing edge to wings and pale wing panel in the outer primaries. Heavily marked underparts indicate western subspecies. This bird will likely become a rufous/intermediate morph as an adult.

15. **Adult dark Harlan's.** Aged as an adult based on solid dark trailing edge to wings. Identified as Harlan's by white tail with smudgy dark tip, but beware: dark Westerns over snow can look white-tailed from below. This bird also lacks the white streaking on the breast typical of dark Harlan's, though many are solid below like this bird.

16. **Adult Western.** Aged as adult by red tail. Entirely brownish upperparts are typical of darker Westerns but generally not seen on eastern birds.

17. **Juv./1st-year Western.** Aged as 1st-year by lack of dark trailing edge to wings and yellow eye. Heavily marked underparts, especially the underwing coverts, and barred leggings indicate western subspecies.

18. **Adult Krider's.** Aged as adult by solid dark trailing edge to wing. Identified as Krider's by mainly white tail and white underparts lacking a bellyband; similar plumages of Harlan's would be darker-backed and usually have a bold, blobby dark bellyband.

19. **Juv./1st-year Western.** Aged as 1st-year by lack of dark trailing edge to wings and yellow eye. Heavily marked underparts indicate Western subspecies.

Red-tailed Hawks on the Southern Great Plains, pages 68–69

1. **Adult unknown.** Aged as adult by red tail. Rufous wash to underparts indicates Western.
2. **Juv./1st-year Eastern.** Aged as 1st-year by long-tailed shape. Identified as Eastern by paler head and lightly marked belly.
3. **Adult Fuertes.** Aged as an adult by dark trailing edge to wings. Creamy unmarked underparts typical of Fuertes and Krider's, but Fuertes generally is dark-headed and has distinctly dark patagial marks.
4. **Adult Fuertes.** Similar to #6, shows a red tail and dark trailing edge to wings, easily ageing it as an adult. The creamy buff underparts with no bellyband and bold dark patagials are typical of *fuertesi*, though more study is needed of this race.
5. **Adult Eastern.** Aged as adult by dark trailing edge to wings and reddish cast to tail. A typical Eastern with spotted bellyband and buffy washed underparts. Some Easterns can have dark throats—generally not a good field mark for distinguishing the races.
6. **Juv./1st-year unknown.** Aged as 1st-year by lack of dark trailing edge to wings. Subspecies not easily determined at this distance.
7. **Adult Eastern.** Aged as adult by dark trailing edge to wings and red tail. Identified as Eastern by blobby dark bellyband and buffy wash to underparts. This bird appears to have a whitish tail base, which could indicate some introgression with Krider's.
8. **Adult Eastern or Fuertes.** Aged as adult by red tail and dark trailing edge to wings. Could be either subspecies, but total lack of bellyband rules out Western.
9. **Adult unknown.** Clear-cut dark trailing edge to wings help age it as an adult, but at this angle determining subspecies is not possible.
10. **Adult unknown.** Aged as adult by solid dark trailing edge to wings and reddish tail. The tail is pale but the underparts are fairly heavily marked. The throat is dark too. Overall a strange mix of characters, but not uncommon for intergrade Eastern x Krider's or Eastern x Western breeding on the northern Great Plains.
11. **Adult Eastern.** Aged as adult by red tail. Easterns usually have a golden cast to the nape and extensive white mottling on the scapulars, as seen on this bird. Easterns breeding in the northern

part of their range and on the northern Great Plains often have banded tails, but the bands average narrower than on a typical Western.

12. **Juv./1st-year Eastern.** A paler example, lacking a dark trailing edge to the wings. Some Easterns can have very faint bellybands and reduced dark patagial bars, and this could be a sign of introgression with Krider's.

13. **Unknown.** At a certain point, it's impossible to age or determine subspecies of Red-taileds, and with a view like this, consider yourself lucky to determine the species! Focus on general shape and wingbeat.

14. **Juv./1st-year Eastern.** Aged as 1st-year by lack of dark trailing edge to wings and pale eye. Pale throat and buffy washed underparts typical of Eastern.

Swainson's Hawk on Migration, pages 74–75

1. **Adult unknown.** Upperparts of all morphs look similar, but this is an adult based on its uniformly dark upperparts. 1st-years usually show pale fringing above.
2. **Adult dark.** Like 4, 7, and 11.
3. **2nd-year light.** 2nd-years look intermediate between adults and 1st-years, with adult-like flight feathers but juvenile-like underparts.
4. **Adult dark.** Like #3, but note solidly brown underparts. Underwing coverts highly variable on all morphs, and even the darkest-bodied birds can have very clean whitish underwing coverts.
5. **Adult intermediate.** Aged as an adult by broad dark trailing edge to wings and broad subterminal band on tail. Also, only adults show solidly dark underparts like this. Told as intermediate by more extensive rufous below than typical "bib" of light morphs, but paler belly than true dark morph.
6. **Adult intermediate.** Rufous underwing coverts and dark breast contrasting with vaguely paler belly. Note broad dark tail tip typical of adults.
7. **Juv./1st-year dark or intermediate.** Aged as 1st-year by lack of broad dark trailing edge to wings and tail. Dark and intermediate birds can be streaked below, and the underwing coverts are highly variable.
8. **Unknown intermediate.** The dark trailing edge and tail tip indicate a nonjuvenile (1st-year), but we can't do too much else with it.
9. **Immature light.** A difficult bird to age. Some 1st-years have a dusky trailing edge to the wings and a marginally distinct subterminal band on the tail. This bird shows those characters, and it really looks clean like a 1st-year. But some really pale 2nd-years are very similar, but they usually show a broader dark subterminal band on the tail and a more strongly defined dark trailing edge to the wings.
10. **First-summer dark.** Aged as 1st-summer by retained juvenile flight and tail feathers combined with newly molted adult-like ones. Dark and rufous/intermediate birds show heavily streaked underparts and in the first summer look very similar to juveniles.
11. **Unknown light.** At a distance light morphs look whitish with dark flight feathers. Can't do much on age with this one.
12. **Juv./1st-year dark/intermediate.** Very similar to #2, and identified using same criteria.
13. **Unknown.** Too high to do much with this one. But, note pale underwing coverts contrasting strongly with darker flight feathers, a typical Swainson's field mark. Also the wings are long and tapered at the tips.
14. **Adult rufous.** Some adults are nearly entirely rufous below, but are usually a bit darker on the breast. Note dark trailing edge and tail tip typical of adults.
15. **Adult dark.** Similar to #4, but a darker example, with nearly uniformly brown body and underwing coverts. Even the darkest adults usually show pale undertail coverts, though they are tough to see on this bird.
16. **Unknown.** When kettling high overhead, Swainson's show a mix of plumages, with some looking

all-dark and others showing the strong contrasts of adult light morphs.

17. **Adult light.** Adult light morphs usually show clean white underwings contrasting with dark flight feathers and a solid brown or rufous bib contrasting with a whitish belly.
18. **Adult dark.** Very similar to #4 and #7 and identified using same criteria.
19. **1st-summer light.** Note molting juvenile inner primaries typical of first-spring birds.
20. **Adult intermediate.** Similar to #3, and identified using same criteria. Note extensively dark subterminal band typical of adults.
21. **1st-summer dark.** Aged as 2nd-year with difficulty at this distance, though only 2nd-year dark morphs can show this white-breasted look. Compare carefully with Harlan's and immature White-tailed Hawks.
22. **Adult dark.** Like #4, 7, 11, and 20, but with a decidedly more rufous cast to the underparts.
23. **First-summer unknown.** Aged as first-summer by uniformly aged juvenile flight feathers with inner primaries molting. The upperparts of all morphs are similar, so you need to see the underparts to determine what morph it is.
24. **Adult dark.** Like #4, 7, 11, and 20.

Ferruginous Hawks over the Canyons, pages 80–81

1. **Adult dark.** Note dark trailing edge to flight feathers visible on the far wing. Dark Ferruginous can be very difficult to age, and a good look is needed to be certain. Adults usually lack tail banding and have a smudgy dark tip to tail. They are also more colorful below, having more distinct rufous tones than 1st-years. Older birds get dark eyes, but this can take many years in Ferruginous.
2. **Adult light.** Note bold rufous shoulders, clean white underparts, and dark rufous leggings.
3. **Adult light.** Like #2, and identified using same criteria. Note tapered "hands" on otherwise broad wings.
4. **Juv./1st-year light.** From above, young light birds are brownish with white-based tails and bold white windows formed by the paler primaries. They generally lack the rufous tones of adults.
5. **Adult light.** White breast with rufous underwings and dark leggings help age this bird, even at this distance.
6. **Adult light.** Note strong rufous cast to upperparts and bold white primary panels. The tail appears whitish with a reddish outer half. Compare with adult Krider's Red-tailed Hawk.
7. **Adult light.** Adults have rufous leggings forming a V and narrow but distinct dark tips to the flight feathers. The grayish head of this bird and generally lightly marked underparts indicate a likely male.
8. **Juv./1st-year light.** Usually lack a bold dark trailing edge to the wings, and have a dusky ill-defined border there at best. Very white below, lacking the rufous tones of adults, especially on the leggings.
9. **Unknown dark.** Note nicely tapered "hands" on fairly broad wings. Dark birds are impossible to age at this distance.
10. **Adult light.** From above, adults show bold rufous shoulders and variable tails, but tails are nearly always a mix of white and red, usually lacking any distinct banding. Also note grayish flight feathers with bold pale window in the outer primaries.

Rough-legged Hawks in the Cold, pages 86–87

1. **Adult male light.** Adult males are quite different from adult females and 1st-years. They often have paler bellies with barred flanks, as we can see here, and some have darker breasts, imparting a bibbed look reminiscent of Swainson's Hawk. Their dark carpal patches are often broken, too. Note the very dark eye typical of older Rough-leggeds.
2. **Juv./1st-year light.** On this bird jumping off a post, note the lack of a dark trailing edge to the wings and the smudgy ill-defined tail band, indicating a 1st-year.

3. **Adult light.** This hovering bird is likely a female, though it's tough to be certain. It has a dark trailing edge to the wings, readily identifying it as an adult, but we'd need a better view to determine the sex.

4. **Juv./1st-year light.** Similar to #1, but with even less dark along the trailing edge of the wings. Adult females and some 2nd-years of both sexes are similar, but they show a bold dark trailing edge to the wings.

5. **Adult dark.** Bold dark trailing edge and broad tail band indicate adult. Sexing is not possible on this bird.

6. **Unknown dark.** Can't really see enough to judge much beyond species on this bird. Some dark 1st-years can have a darker dusky trailing edge to the wings, making them more easily confused with adults.

7. **Adult dark.** Tough to age from this angle, but only dark birds show dark uppertails. Adults can show uniformly dark uppertails with a slightly darker tip, whereas 1st-years usually have faint grayish, broken bands.

8. **Adult dark.** Bold dark trailing edge and broad tail band indicate adult. Sexing is not usually possible on dark adults, though some males show jet-black underparts and a blue-gray cast above.

9. **Unknown light.** Bold dark wrist patches are visible on this bird, making it a light morph, but sexing it is not possible.

10. **Juv./1st-year light.** Quite distinctive, with solid dark wrist patches and dark belly. Underparts are washed with buff. The pale eye and ill-defined dark trailing edge to the wing also help age it as a 1st-year. Sexes are similar among 1st-years.

A Broad-winged Hawk Kettle, pages 94–95

There are 12 Turkey Vultures and 1 Swainson's Hawk (top right)

Widespread Eastern Raptors, pages 96–97

1. **Juv./1st-year Red-tailed.** The classic roadside raptor across much of North America. Note the stocky, chesty build with brown-spotted bellyband and white breast. The yellow eye identifies it as a 1st-year.

2. **Juv./1st-year Broad-winged.** Compact structure with tapered wingtips and plain underwings. The streaking below is mostly limited to the upper breast, but is highly variable on juveniles. Note lack of dark trailing edge to wings and streaked underparts, indicating 1st-year.

3. **Adult Broad-winged.** Compact build with tapered wingtips. Difficult to age given this view, but the boldly banded black-and-white tail is visible, indicating adult. Beware of juveniles that can sometimes show a similar tail pattern when the tail is folded.

4. **Juv./1st-year Red-shouldered.** Note rather square-cut "hands" pushed forward at wrists, and plain, unmarked underwings. Aged as a 1st-year by the lack of black-and-white banding in the flight feathers, and adults are barred reddish below. All Red-shouldereds have pale crescent-shaped translucent windows in the outer primaries, and on 1st-years they are usually buffy.

5. **Juv./1st-year Broad-winged.** Note compact build and relatively pointed wings in a glide. Also note the straight-cut trailing edge to the wing and the long tail. Aged as a 1st-year by the lack of a bold dark trailing edge to the wing.

6. **Adult Red-tailed.** Long, broad wings and a short, broad, red tail. Red tail indicates adult. Also note the dark patagial marks along the leading edge of the wing, a good field mark for Red-taileds of all ages and subspecies.

7. **Juv./1st-year Broad-winged.** Compact structure with tapered wingtips and plain underwings. This is a more lightly marked example, aged as a 1st-year by lack of red barring below and no dark trailing edge to the wings.

8. **Juv./1st-year Red-tailed.** Same as #1, but in flight. The lack of a solid dark trailing edge to the flight feathers indicates 1st-year. Red-taileds are heavy-bodied with long wings and a medium-length tail. Juveniles are notably lankier than adults, with narrower wings and longer tails.
9. **Juv./1st-year Red-shouldered.** Relatively rounded wingtips and plain underwings coupled with a buffy crescent-shaped patch in the outer primaries. Brownish upperparts and lack of bold black-and-white banding in the flight feathers indicate 1st-year.
10. **Adult Red-shouldered.** Striking, with bold rufous shoulders and black-and-white banded flight feathers. Also note white crescent-shaped patch in outer primaries.

Dark Raptors of the Southwest, pages 108–109

1. **Immature Bald Eagle** (p. 108, lower right center). Dark overall with white wing pits, very long broad wings, and large head.
2. **Adult Common Black-Hawk** (p. 108, right of the brown plane that is slightly left of center). Black underneath with white tail band, very short broad wings, and very short tail denote adult.
3. **Subadult Golden Eagle** (p. 108, left of the plane). Dark overall with limited white on wings, very long, broad, tapered wings, and large head.
4. **Hook-billed Kite** (p. 108, above the plane). Hook-billed Kite has rounded, stocky wings that pinch in at body, and short, square-tipped tail.
5. **Adult Mississippi Kite** (p. 108, above the Golden Eagle). Mississippi Kite has falcon-like, long, narrow, pointed wings, small head, slim body, and slim, square-tipped tail.
6. **Adult light Broad-winged Hawk** (p. 109, top right). Light birds can appear dark when shadowed. Note stocky, pointed wings, and narrow, short tail.
7. **Adult Zone-tailed Hawk** (p. 109, 2: center left and center right). Zone-tailed is slimmer than Turkey Vulture, and has buteo-shaped head. White tail band and dark trailing edge to wings denote adult.
8. **Black Vulture** (p. 109, bottom right). Black underneath with whitish outer primaries, and stocky build with short tail.

Mystery Kites in the Southeast, pages 126–127

1. **Juv./1st-year Snail Kite.** Note dark streaked underside, pale eyeline, and lanky, squared-off wings that differ greatly from the narrow, pointed wings of most other kites.
2. **Swallow-tailed Kite.** White body and head, with gray upperwings, black "shoulders," and an extremely long, forked tail.
3. **Snail Kite.** Lanky squared-off wings and dark brown upperside with white tail base.
4. **Mississippi Kites.** Note long, narrow, pointed wings, and short, narrow tail that is square-cut and flared toward the tip.
5. **White-tailed Kite.** White body, head, and tail, and gray upperwings with black "shoulders."
6. **White-tailed Kite.** Pale overall with white body and tail, and long, pointed wings.
7. **Swallow-tailed Kites.** Note long, pointed wings and extremely long, forked tail. Underside is white with highly contrasting dark flight feathers.
8. **Subadult Mississippi Kite.** Note long, pointed wings and small head. Gray overall with whitish head and banded tail denote subadult.

Peregrine or Prairie? pages 142–143

1. **Adult Peregrine Falcon.** Blackish barred underneath (appearing grayish) with a whitish chest and checkered underwings denote adult. Note black head.
2. **Adult Prairie Falcon.** Sandy brown above with pale head (paler than all Peregrines), with a paler

brownish tail, which denotes adult.

3. **Adult Prairie Falcon.** Sandy brown above (paler than all Peregrines), with a paler brownish tail, which denotes adult.
4. **Juv./1st-yr. Peregrine Falcon.** Heavily streaked underneath (denotes juvenile) with overall dark underwings. Also note dark, broad sideburn on head.
5. **Adult Prairie Falcon.** Lightly spotted underneath with dark wing linings.
6. **Juv./1st-yr. Prairie Falcon.** Sandy brown above, and whitish below with lightly marked underbody. Note pale head with dark sideburn. Pale cere and streaked underparts age it as a juvenile.
7. **Juv./1st-yr. Peregrine Falcon.** Dark brown-gray upperside with dark head showing paler crown and cheek denotes juvenile.
8. **Peregrine Falcon.** Pale underneath but buffy, not whitish like Prairie. Also lacks the contrasting blackish wing linings of Prairie Falcon.
9. **Peregrine Falcon.** Dark underneath with checkered underwings, lacking blackish wing pits and wing linings. Note blackish head with broad sideburn.
10. **Peregrine Falcon.** Pale underneath but buffy, not whitish like Prairie. Also lacks the contrasting blackish wing linings of Prairie Falcon.
11. **Prairie Falcon.** Sandy brown above with pale head and narrow sideburn. Pale brownish tail and yellow cere denote adult.
12. **Peregrine Falcon.** Atypical brownish appearance on top due to lighting and variation, but heavily marked underneath with a dark head, broad sideburn, and dark tail.

South Texas Falcons, page 147

1. **Adult Aplomado Falcon.** Note slim build with very long tail and bold face pattern. The plain breast indicates adult.
2. **Female American Kestrel.** Small and mainly rufous with blackish barred upperparts. This is a female based on its rufous upperwings. Habitually bobs head and tail.
3. **Adult Peregrine Falcon.** Big and chunky when perched; note the square head with dark helmeted appearance and wings that nearly reach the tail tip. The black head, gray back, and barred underparts indicate adult.
4. **Merlin.** Tough to be sure at this distance, but overall impression is of a small, compact falcon with a dark back and buffy underparts.
5. **Merlin.** Small and compact with angular, strongly pointed wings and dark-streaked underparts. The throat is usually whitish or buffy, contrasting with the rest of the darkish overall plumage. The dark upperwings and heavily streaked underparts indicate female or immature.
6. **Male American Kestrel.** Any small falcon that hovers for extended periods is likely to be a Kestrel, though Aplomado hovers frequently too. On this bird note the bold head pattern and bluntly pointed wingtips. Kestrels are slim and rangy, with a long tail. Blue upperwings indicate male, as do the boldly blackish spotted underparts.
7. **Adult Aplomado Falcon.** Long wings and long tail, but at this angle note the rufous belly and leggings contrasting with a blackish "vested" look on the lower chest. The plain breast indicates adult.
8. **Adult Peregrine Falcon.** Big-bodied with fairly broad, strongly pointed wings and a relatively short tail for a falcon. The dark helmeted appearance of the head contrasting with the very white breast indicates adult. Peregrines have rolling, loonlike wingbeats that differ from all the other falcons on this plate, but are very similar to those of Prairie Falcon.
9. **Adult Aplomado Falcon.** Slimly built with long wings and a very long tail. Aplomado is dark-winged with a contrasting blackish "vest" on the underparts and rufous leggings and vent. Even at this distance the bold head pattern is visible.

273

Perched Buteos, pages 148–149

1. **Juv./1st-year light Rough-legged Hawk.** Black belly, white chest, and pale head. Pale eye and dusky dark tail tip denote 1st-year.
2. **Adult dark Swainson's Hawk.** Uniformly brownish black overall; wingtips reach tail tip.
3. **Juv./1st-year light Red-tailed Hawk.** Brown overall with pale mottling on upperwings, and pale eye. Wings fall short of tail tip.
4. **Adult light Swainson's Hawk.** Pale belly with dark chest "bib," dark head with white throat; dark upperwings lack mottling, and wingtips reach tail tip.
5. **Adult male light Rough-legged Hawk.** Grayish head with black eyeline and white throat, grayish upperwings with pale mottling throughout; tail is banded.
6. **Adult Swainson's Hawk.** Brownish black upperside that lacks mottling, dark indistinct tail, and dark head with white throat and grayish cheek.
7. **Adult rufous Red-tailed Hawk.** Orangey underbody with dark bellyband, and reddish tail.
8. **Juv./1st-year light Ferruginous Hawk.** Warm brown upperwings, whitish underside, large, pale brown head with faint eyeline.
9. **Juv./1st-year light Red-tailed Hawk.** Pale underneath with brown head and distinct bellyband.
10. **Adult light Ferruginous Hawk.** Brownish upperside with vibrant rufous upperwing coverts and tail. Head is pale with a grayish cheek and cap.
11. **Juv./1st-year light Red-tailed Hawk.** Pale belly with dark streaks, and light leading edge to the wings (shown on several buteos but not all). Brown upperside lacking golden nape, and pale eye denote 1st-year.

Buteos on the Midwest Prairie, pages 150–151

1. **Adult light Ferruginous Hawk.** Snow-white underneath with rufous leg feathers, underwing mottling, and upperwing coverts.
2. **Adult light Red-tailed Hawk.** Pale underneath with dark patagial bars and belly streaks. Note that rufous tint to underside, dark trailing edge to wings, and reddish tint to tail denote adult.
3. **1st-summer light Red-tailed Hawk.** Brown overall on top. Broad wings with new, darker inner primaries, outer primaries showing 1st-year paleness or "window." Brownish, faintly banded tail with new, reddish adult feathers.
4. **Juv./1st-year light Red-tailed Hawk.** Pale underneath with dark patagial bars and bellyband. Lacks the buffy or rufous tint to underbody, dark trailing edge to the wings, and reddish tail of adult. Shows translucent primaries.
5. **Juv./1st-year dark Western Red-tailed Hawk.** Broad, somewhat long wings in a full soar. Note that uniformly brownish body and underwing coverts is uncommon plumage. Lack of defined trailing edge to wings and reddish tail denote 1st-year.
6. **Juv./1st-year light Western Red-tailed Hawk.** Pale underneath with dark patagial bars and belly streaks. Note that translucent primaries and plain buffy coloration denote 1st-year.
7. **Adult intermediate Swainson's Hawk.** Long, pointed wings in a shallow glide. Note dark flight feathers and chest "bib" contrasting with a paler body and underwings. Many intermediate adults are mottled on the belly.
8. **Adult light Red-tailed Hawk.** Pale underneath with dark patagial bars and belly streaks, and reddish tail. Somewhat long but broad wings.
9. **Adult dark Ferruginous Hawk.** Dark underneath with whitish, plain flight feathers, and minimal dark on wingtips. Wings are long and tapered. Dark trailing edge to the wings, rufous overall body plumage with whitish throat, and lack of dark on the tail tip denote adult.
10. **Adult light Rough-legged Hawk.** Pale underneath with blackish belly and wrists. Dark trailing edge to the wings and defined dark tail tip denote adult; single dark tail band, complete bellyband,

and wrist patches denote female.

11. **Adult Krider's Red-tailed Hawk.** Pale and nearly unmarked underneath with minimal dark on patagials, reddish and whitish tail, and dark trailing edge to wings. Broad wings slightly tapered in shallow glide is classic Red-tail shape.

12. **3rd-year light Swainson's Hawk.** Pale underside with dark bib and flight feathers with darker trailing edge to wings and tail. Bib is near complete, and paler outer primaries help denote age.

13. **Juv./1st-year light Rough-legged Hawk.** Pale underneath with solid blackish belly and wrists, and buffy, unmottled underwing coverts. Dark trailing edge to the wings is ill defined, but appears to have a dark tail tip. Translucent primary panels somewhat visible. 1st-years and adult females can be difficult to tell apart at times.

14. **Adult light Ferruginous Hawk.** Snow-white underneath with rufous leg feathers, underwing mottling, and minimal dark on wingtips. Wings are long and lack bulge along secondaries, body is robust.

15. **Adult female light Rough-legged Hawk.** Pale underneath with blackish belly and wrists. Dark trailing edge to the wings and defined dark tail tip denote adult, single dark tail band, rufous underwings, complete bellyband, and wrist patches denote female.

The Widespread Common Raptors, pages 152–153

1. **Adult male Northern Harrier.** Distinct grayish topside with black border on flight feathers, back is often browner. All Harriers have a white "rump," a classic field mark!

2. **Adult female Northern Harrier.** Pale underneath with slightly darker flight feathers, and narrow streaks on chest. Note long, narrow wings and tail (showing bands when spread). Head is small with owl-like facial disk.

3. **Juv./1st-year light Broad-winged Hawk.** Stocky pointed wings, large head, and short, narrow tail. Pale underside with dark streaking on sides of breast, and indistinct tail pattern with darker tip denote 1st-year. Some (like this bird) have streaks on belly similar to Red-tailed.

4. **Juv./1st-year Eastern Red-shouldered Hawk.** Somewhat stocky squared-off wings with translucent "commas" along the primaries. Pale underside with buffy underwing coverts, and dark, evenly spaced streaking on body denote 1st-year.

5. **Juv./1st-year Cooper's Hawk.** Pale underneath with dark streaks throughout underbody, and brown head denote 1st-year. Note long wings for an accipiter, large head, and long tail with white tip.

6. **Juv./1st-year Cooper's Hawk.** Note brown upperside with tawny head that projects well past wings, and long tail with white tip.

7. **Turkey Vulture.** Blackish overall; reddish head can be difficult to see at a distance but white bill usually glows. Note long, broad, squared-off wings, broad tail, and modified dihedral when gliding.

8. **Juv./1st-year Sharp-shinned Hawks.** Note short, stocky wings and body, long, slim tail that is short for an accipiter, and small head. Plumage is difficult to see on distant birds but 1st-years lack a rufous tone underneath.

9. **Juv./1st-year Red-shouldered Hawk.** Note somewhat stocky squared-off wings with translucent "commas" along the primaries. Pale underside with buffy underwing coverts, and dark, evenly spaced streaking on body denote 1st-year.

10. **Juv./1st-year Broad-winged Hawk.** Pale underside with dark streaking densest on sides of breast, translucent primary "windows," and indistinct tail pattern with darker tip denote 1st-year. Note stout body, large head, stocky, pointed wings, and narrow tail.

11. **Adult male Northern Harrier.** Very distinct brilliant white underside with a black border on flight feathers. Note long, slim wings and tail, and small head.

12. **Immature Bald Eagles.** 1st-years are dark overall with white wing pits, 4th-years are similarly dark overall but show a whitish head and minimal white on the wing pits. Note somewhat broad,

straight, very long wings that lack a sharp taper and are held drooped in a glide, large head, and broad tail.

13. **Juv./1st-year Peregrine Falcon.** Classic silhouetted long, narrow, pointed wings that are angled at the wrists, and long tail that resembles a cocked bow and arrow. 1st-years are dark-streaked underneath, lacking the paler chest and black head of adults.

14. **Juv./1st-year Peregrine Falcon.** Pale underneath with heavily streaked body, heavily "checkered" underwings, and dark head. Note very long, pointed wings, heavy body, and broad tail and head. Wingtips are less sharply pointed in a full soar.

15. **Adult light Red-tailed Hawk.** Quintessential broad-winged, short-tailed buteo shape. Plumage is pale underneath with dark patagial bars and bellyband. Note: dark trailing edge to the wings and reddish tail denote adult.

16. **Juv./1st-year light Red-tailed Hawk.** Pale overall underneath with dark patagial bars and bellyband. Lacks a dark trailing edge to the wings and reddish tail, and shows translucent primaries, identifying it as 1st-year.

17. **Adult Eastern Red-tailed Hawk.** Pale underneath with buffy wash, dark patagial bars and belly streaks, dark trailing edge to the wings, and reddish tail. Note pale throat and lightly marked underwing coverts.

18. **Second-year Red-tailed Hawk.** Pale underneath with dark patagial bars and bellyband. Dark trailing edge to the wings and reddish tail denote adult, but shorter retained juvenile secondaries denote 2nd-year bird.

19. **Adult Western Red-tailed Hawk.** Note dark upperside with only minimal pale scapulars and rufous uppertail coverts, but tail lacks bands. Reddish tail, golden head, dark edge to back of wings denote adult.

20. **Merlin.** Juvenile and adult female are pale below with heavy, dark streaking, heavily "checkered" underwings, and distinct tail bands. Merlin has stockier, more sharply pointed wings, broader, shorter tail, and is "chesty" compared with Kestrel. Likely an adult female based on buffy underside, thick streaks, slaty head, and yellowish leg feathers.

21. **Male American Kestrel.** Note pale underside with orangey chest, black spots on belly, 2 black "sideburns" on head, and blue upperwing coverts, orange tail with black tip.

22. **Merlin.** Juvenile and adult female are pale below with heavy, dark streaking, heavily "checkered" underwings, and distinct tail bands. Merlin has shorter wings and shorter, slimmer tail and body compared with Peregrine. Likely an adult female based on buffy underside, thick streaks, slaty head, and yellowish leg feathers.

Hovering Birds, pages 154–155

1. **Female American Kestrel.** Plumage entails rufous upperwing coverts, black primaries, rufous color to mottling on underwing coverts and streaks on chest. Note long, slim, pointed wings.

2. **Juv./1st-year light Red-tailed Hawk.** Buffy underneath with dark patagials and bellyband, brown head, and completely banded tail that lacks reddish color. Note that dark trailing edge to the wings is less prominent than on adults.

3. **Male American Kestrel.** Note long, pointed wings, and short body. Pale underbody with contrasting darker, silvery underwings identify this as a male.

4. **3rd-year White-tailed Hawk.** Note buteo-shaped, broad wings and short tail. The white tail with darker flight feathers help identify this as White-tailed Hawk, but subadult underwing plumage denotes 3rd-year.

5. **Light Red-tailed Hawk.** Buffy underneath with dark patagials and bellyband, but difficult to age at this distance or pose.

6. **Dark adult Rough-legged Hawk.** Note the uniformly dark underbody with paler flight feathers that show a dark trailing edge, and pale underside to the tail with a well-defined dark tip. The broad,

dark tail tip and lack of multiple tail bands make this a likely female.

7. **Male American Kestrel.** Note 2 facial sideburns, blue upperwing coverts, and orange tail with black tip. No other North American raptor shows this coloration.
8. **Dark adult Swainson's Hawk.** Note the uniformly dark rufous-brown underbody with darker flight feathers, and tapered wingtips.
9. **Osprey.** Ospreys are large, distinct birds. Note pure white underside with darker flight feathers and black wrists, and white head with black eyeline and nape. An adult based on pure white chest, and lack of dark streaking on crown.
10. **White-tailed Kite.** White underside with grayish flight feathers and black wrists; head and tail are pure white. Note long, slim, pointed wings.
11. **Juv./1st-year male American Kestrel.** Note pale underbody with black spots on belly and chest, 2 sideburns on face, and reddish tail. Checkered flight feathers appear silvery on males. Some new rufous chest feathers denote 1st-year in fall; by winter the chest is fully rufous and lacks spots.

Hazel-Bazemore Hawk Watch, pages 156–157

1. **Juv./1st-year Cooper's Hawk.** The pale underside with dark streaks, rufous-brown head, and yellow-green eye denote 1st-year. Note the long, rounded tail with obvious white tip, and streaking on body is heaviest on the chest.
2. **Juv./1st-year Northern Harrier.** Rufous underneath with darker flight feathers and brown head. 1st-years lack prominent streaking on the underbody. Note long tail and white "rump."
3. **Immature Crested Caracara.** Very distinctive raptor. Very long tail, long, squared-off wings, long-necked appearance. Blackish with white primaries, dark belly with streaked chest, white undertail coverts, and blackish head with pink face
4. **Adult Zone-tailed Hawk.** Very similar to Turkey Vulture but smaller. Large, dark bird with silvery flight feathers, and always flies with a dihedral or modified dihedral. The head appears buteo-like, and the tail is slimmer than Turkey Vulture's.
5. **Juv./1st-year White-tailed Kite.** Note the white body, head, and tail, and grayish topside with hint of black shoulder, and pointed wings. The faint orange patch on the chest denotes 1st-year.
6. **Juv./1st-year White-tailed Hawk.** Dark body with pale mottling on chest and pale ear coverts identify this as 1st-year White-tailed. Note broad but long tapered wings that are slightly dark, and long tail. Wing shape similar to Swainson's Hawk but slightly less tapered.
7. **Adult Aplomado Falcon.** Distinctly plumaged white body, black bellyband and wing pits, yellowish lower belly, dark checkered underwings, and very long tail with narrow white bands. Note "sideburn" like that of most other falcons, and long, pointed wings.
8. **Adult White-tailed Hawk.** Very dark upperside with chestnut shoulders, and pure white tail with black tip. Note broad wings, but pointed at the tips.
9. **Broad-winged Hawks.** Small buteo with stocky, pointed wings, and large head. Tail is slim when closed, but appears short when fanned. Note dark tail tip and buffy underside, and translucent primaries of 1st-year birds. Soars on flat wings or very slight dihedral.
10. **Mississippi Kites.** Very Peregrine-like in shape, but the wings and body are slimmer, and the tail is shorter with a square tip that flares out instead of tapers. Note overall grayish underside with whitish head of adult plumage, but combined with mottled underwing coverts denotes subadult.
11. **Adult light Red-tailed Hawk.** Buffy underneath with dark patagials and bellyband, brown head, and dark trailing edge to the wings. Red-taileds with dark throats can be several races, but the lack of markings to the underwing coverts and well-defined belly streaks make this more likely an Eastern.
12. **Adult Fuertes Red-tailed Hawk.** Very pale with a faint rufous wash underneath, unmarked belly, but dark patagials, wrist commas, and a dark trailing edge to the wings. Note reddish tail and golden-brown head.

13. **Osprey.** White body with darker flight feathers, white head with dark eyeline and cap, and extremely long, narrow wings, that taper but are not pointed at the tips.

14. **Osprey.** White body with darker flight feathers, white head with dark cap, and extremely long, narrow wings, that taper but are not pointed at the tips

15. **Female American Kestrel.** Plumage is pale underneath with rufous streaks on body and underwing coverts, checkered flight feathers, and 2 sideburns on side of head. Note long, slim, pointed wings that are blunt at the tips.

16. **Turkey Vultures.** Large, dark birds with silvery flight feathers, and flies with a dihedral or modified dihedral at all times. The head appears small in flight, but shows long, broad wings, and a somewhat long, broad tail.

Topsides, pages 158–159

1. **Juv./1st-year Swainson's Hawk.** Dark brown on top with blackish flight feathers and tail, pale uppertail coverts, and obvious buffy fringes to upperwing coverts. Note long, tapered wings.

2. **Juv./1st-year Swainson's Hawk.** Dark brown on top with blackish flight feathers and tail, pale uppertail coverts, and obvious buffy fringes to upperwing coverts. Note long, tapered wings.

3. **First-spring Golden Eagle.** Dark brown on top with a golden wash on head, and white-based tail. Note that 1st-years in spring have a broad fade to the upperwing coverts that resemble the narrow, pale mottled upperwing bar of older birds. Also note shorter inner primary still growing in.

4. **Adult Bald Eagle.** Unmistakable, uniformly dark with a white head and tail, and large yellow bill!

5. **Adult Golden Eagle.** Overall brown above with paler mottling along the upperwings, golden head, and grayish bands on tail. Note, in bright sunlight, grayish areas can look white.

6. **Juv./1st-year Red-shouldered Hawk.** Brownish on top overall with translucent primary "commas." Note squared-off wings and somewhat long tail with indistinct banding.

7. **Juv./1st-year Northern Goshawk.** Pale underneath with heavy dark streaking throughout. Note somewhat short wings that are very broad but taper at the hands, a broad chest, and long tail.

8. **Osprey.** Blackish on top with a white head and black eyeline. Note white underbody and long, narrow wings. An adult based on pure white chest, and lack of dark streaking on crown.

9. **Juv./1st-year Sharp-shinned Hawk.** Dark brown on top with faintly banded tail. Note long, narrow tail, short, broad wings, and small head.

10. **Immature Bald Eagle.** Dark brown overall with blackish flight feathers. Note significant whitish mottling in tail and uneven secondaries denotes subadult. Also, note browner back with darker upperwing coverts. 1st-year is even-toned throughout back and upperwings.

11. **Adult Red-shouldered Hawk.** Plumage is a beautiful rusty underneath with a brown head, and blackish on top with clean, narrow white bands throughout the flight and tail feathers, and whitish comma-shaped primary windows.

12. **Adult Red-shouldered Hawk.** Rusty underneath with a brown head, and blackish on top with clean, narrow white bands throughout the flight and tail feathers, and whitish comma-shaped primary windows. Note reddish "shoulders" of adult.

13. **Juv./1st-year Broad-winged Hawk.** Brown on top with slightly paler primaries, faint pale mottling on upperwings, and indistinctly banded tail with darker band at tip. Note stocky, pointed wings and large head. Tail appears somewhat long on 1st-years.

14. **Adult Red-tailed Hawk.** Dark brown on top with a bright rufous tail, and golden wash to head. Rufous uppertail coverts rather than whitish much more common on Western race than Eastern.

15. **Juv./1st-year Red-tailed Hawk.** Indistinct plumage. Brown on top with pale uppertail coverts, and pale mottling on upperwings. Note long but broad, bulging wings that taper slightly at the tips.

16. **Juv./1st-year Cooper's Hawk.** Dark brown on top with faintly banded tail similar to Goshawk but lacks the pale mottling along the upperwings, and pale eyeline. Note long tail with obvious white tip, short, broad wings, and noticeable head projection. Wings and tail are slightly longer in relation

to other accipiters.

17. **Osprey.** Note blackish topside with white crown, and very long, narrow wings. Aged as adult based on lack of pale fringes on upperwing coverts.

18. **Juv./1st-year Northern Goshawk.** Brown on top with tawny-streaked nape, pale mottling on upperwing coverts, whitish eyeline, and long banded tail. Note broad wings compared to other accipiters.

19. **Juv./1st-year Broad-winged Hawk.** Brown overall on top with slightly paler primaries, and indistinctly banded tail with darker band on tip. Note stocky tapered wings and big-headed look.

Southeastern Raptors, pages 160–161

1. **Adult Florida Red-shouldered Hawk.** Note pale rufous wash to underside, pale head, reddish shoulders, and black-and-white banded flight feathers.

2. **Adult Florida Red-shouldered Hawk.** Note the strikingly black-and-white banded flight feathers and tail, and reddish shoulders of all adult Red-shoulders. Florida adults are the palest of the races, with very pale heads and pale brown backs.

3. **Adult dark Short-tailed Hawk.** Uniformly dark underbody, paler flight feathers with dark trailing edge, and pale tail with dark tip. Note stocky wings similar to Broad-winged Hawk, but slightly broader and less pointed at tips.

4. **Swallow-tailed Kite.** Brilliant white underneath with highly contrasting blackish flight feathers, and extremely long, black forked tail. Note the long, pointed wings.

5. **White-tailed Kite.** White underside with white head, grayish secondaries, darker primaries, black wrist spots, and white tail. Note gray upperside, long, slim, pointed wings, and slim, square-tipped tail.

6. **Black Vulture.** Nearly all black with pale outer primaries. Note stocky proportions, especially the short tail.

7. **Swallow-tailed Kite.** Note extremely long, narrow, pointed wings that are dark on top, and contrasting whitish head. Even in a head-on view, the tail seems to trail well beyond the body.

8. **Light Short-tailed Hawk.** White underneath with dark flight feathers, and a short tail. Similar in plumage to Swainson's Hawk but lacks the dark bib. Note stocky, pointed wings.

9. **Juv./1st-year light Broad-winged Hawk.** 1st-year is pale underneath with unmarked to lightly marked underwing coverts, and dark streaks on the body. The tail is faintly banded with a dark tip. 1st-year lacks a prominent dark trailing edge to the wings, and shows pale primary windows. Note stocky wings and large head.

10. **Adult Peregrine Falcon.** Adult has pale body with faintly (such as this) to heavily barred belly, checkered underwings, and a black head with pale cheek. Note long, pointed wings and stout body.

11. **Subadult Mississippi Kite.** Overall grayish underside with whitish head of adult, but mottled underwing coverts and banded tail denote subadult. Very Peregrine-like in shape, but the wings and body are slimmer, and the tail is shorter with a square tip that flares out instead of tapers.

12. **Female American Kestrel.** Plumage is pale underneath with rufous streaks on body and underwing coverts, checkered flight feathers, and 2 sideburns on side of head. Note long, slim, pointed wings that are blunt at the tips.

13. **Juv./1st-year Red-shouldered Hawk.** Note somewhat stocky, squared-off wings with translucent "commas" along the primaries, and fairly long tail for a buteo. 1st-years such as this one are pale underneath with buffy underwing coverts, and dark, evenly spaced streaking on the body.

14. **Merlin.** Juvenile and adult female are pale below with heavy, dark streaking, heavily "checkered" underwings, and distinct tail bands. Merlin has shorter wings and shorter, slimmer tail and body compared with Peregrine, but is slightly stockier overall than Kestrel.

15. **Osprey.** Brilliant white body with darker flight feathers, black wrist patches, and white head with dark eyeline. Note extremely long, narrow wings that taper at the hands and create an M shape in a glide.

16. **Turkey Vultures.** Dark overall at a distance with small head and somewhat long, broad tail, and flying with a dihedral. Silvery flight feathers are noticeable in good light.
17. **Juv./1st-year light Eastern Red-tailed Hawk.** Pale underneath with dark patagial bars and streaked bellyband. Note translucent primaries, plain whitish coloration overall, and lack of reddish on the tail, denoting 1st-year. Note long but broad, bulging wings. Eastern birds tend to have a pale throat and lack significant marking on the underwing linings.
18. **Northern Harrier.** Note brown upperside with bold white rump, banding on tail, and long wings. Slight grayish cast to upperside of wings denotes likely adult female instead of 1st-year.
19. **Adult female Snail Kite.** Charcoal upperside with blackish flight feathers and white-based tail. Note lanky, squared-off wings.
20. **Subadult Bald Eagle.** Note dark overall with white wing pits, and whitish head with dark streaking. Overall plumage combined with even trailing edge of wings denotes 3rd- or 4th-year. Also note large head with yellow bill, and long wings.
21. **Osprey.** Note very long, narrow, bowed wings that taper slightly but are not pointed, and white body with darker flight feathers.
22. **Black Vulture.** Nearly all black with pale outer primaries. Note unfeathered blackish head, grayish bill, and stocky proportions, especially the short tail.
23. **Immature Snail Kite.** Dark underbody and head with pale eyeline. Note lanky, squared-off wings.
24. **Adult Red-tailed Hawks.** These are both of the local race *umbrinus*. At their darkest, they have noticeably darker heads and necks than other Eastern Red-tailed Hawks. Most birds are paler-headed. Their tails are typically barred.
25. **Adult Crested Caracara.** Very distinctive in plumage with blackish upperside, white outer primaries, white tail with broad, black tip, dark belly with pale chest, and blackish head with orange facial skin. Note very long wings and tail, and long-necked appearance.

Dark Raptors in the South, pages 162–163

1. **Adult Turkey Vulture.** Dark overall with a reddish, unfeathered head, whitish bill, and pale legs. Eats carrion exclusively, especially roadkill.
2. **Adult Black Vulture.** Black with pale outer primaries. Note stocky proportions, especially the short tail. Dark, unfeathered head with pale bill denotes adult.
3. **Adult Crested Caracara.** Very distinctive appearance with blackish underside, white outer primaries, white tail with broad, black tip, white undertail coverts, pale chest, and blackish head with pinkish orange facial skin. Note long wings and tail, and long-necked appearance.
4. **Adult dark Ferruginous Hawk.** Dark rufous-brown underneath with whitish, plain flight feathers, and minimal dark on wingtips. Wings are long and tapered. Dark trailing edge to the wings, rufous body with grayer bib, and lack of dark on the tail tip denote adult.
5. **Adult Zone-tailed Hawk.** Blackish underbody with silvery flight feathers similar to Turkey Vulture, but with dark trailing edge to wings, buteo-shaped, feathered head, and slimmer wings, body, and tail.
6. **Adult Common Black-Hawk.** Black overall with very short tail, and broad wings. 1st-year is mottled underneath and has longer wings and much longer tail.
7. **Dark Short-tailed Hawk.** Uniformly blackish underbody, paler flight feathers with dark trailing edge, and pale tail with dark tip. Note stocky wings similar to Broad-winged Hawk, but slightly broader and less pointed.
8. **Adult dark Rough-legged Hawk.** Dark underbody and wrists with slightly paler underwing coverts, and pale tail with well-defined, dark tip. Also note dark trailing edge to adult wings. Male and female adult plumages overlap, but this is most likely a female based on quite brownish underside.
9. **Juv./1st-year Bald Eagle.** Dark overall with white wing pits. Note long, broad wings that taper in a

glide but not sharply pointed, long tail, and large head.

10. **Turkey Vultures.** Dark overall with paler flight feathers. Note long, broad wings held in a dihedral, small head, and long, broad tail. Often fly in groups or "kettles."

11. **Adult dark Rough-legged Hawk.** Dark underbody and wrists with slightly paler underwing coverts, and pale tail with well-defined, dark tip. Also note dark trailing edge to wings. Wings are long and broad, but fairly straight across and less stocky than those of Red-tailed.

12. **Adult Turkey Vulture.** Blackish on top with a reddish, unfeathered head, and whitish bill. Note long, broad wings, and small head.

13. **Juv./1st-year Turkey Vulture.** Dark overall with paler flight feathers, and a dark unfeathered head, and dark bill. Note long wings held in a dihedral.

14. **Adult Zone-tailed Hawk.** Blackish underbody with silvery flight feathers similar to TV, but with dark trailing edge to wings, buteo-shaped, feathered head, and slimmer wings, body, and tail.

15. **Juv./1st-year Turkey Vulture.** Dark overall with paler flight feathers, and a dark unfeathered head, and dark bill. Note long wings held in a dihedral.

16. **Adult Turkey Vulture.** Dark overall with paler flight feathers, a reddish, unfeathered head, and whitish bill. Note long, broad wings held in a dihedral.

17. **Adult dark Short-tailed Hawk.** Uniformly blackish underbody, paler flight feathers with dark trailing edge, and pale tail with dark tip. Note stocky wings similar to Broad-winged Hawk, but slightly broader and less pointed at tips.

18. **Adult Turkey Vulture.** Dark overall with paler flight feathers, a reddish, unfeathered head, and whitish bill. Note long, broad wings held in a dihedral.

Going Away! pages 164–165

1. **Juv./1st-year light Ferruginous Hawk.** Warm brown upperwings with bold, whitish primary panels and a white tail base. Wings are long and tapered, tail is long, head is large.

2. **Adult Red-tailed Hawk.** Dark brown on top with slightly paler golden head, and rust-reddish tail with black subterminal band.

3. **First-spring intermediate Red-tailed Hawk.** Pale underneath with dark-streaked bellyband, dark patagials, and mottled chest and underwing coverts. Beginning its first molt (flanks and legs) but still has almost all 1st-year feathers including flight and tail.

4. **Adult Red-tailed Hawk.** Pale underneath with dark patagial bars and bellyband, and reddish tail.

5. **Juv./1st-year Golden Eagle.** Dark brown on top with white base to tail. 1st-year is only age that lacks any molt or pale mottling on upperwing coverts. Note long wings held in a dihedral.

6. **Adult female Northern Harrier.** Long, narrow wings and tail, and slim body. Pale underside with sparse, dark streaking on body denotes adult female. This is a lightly marked individual. Also note brownish upperwings.

7. **Adult Bald Eagle.** Note long wings held flat, heavy body, and dark overall plumage with gleaming white head. Tail is white but less obvious when shadowed, still sharply contrasts with dark body.

8. **Male American Kestrel.** Note long, pointed wings, long, narrow tail. Orangey tail, and checkered underwings that appear silvery and contrast with the paler underbody denote male. Underside is pale with black spots compared with rufous-brown underside streaking of female.

9. **Turkey Vultures.** Dark overall with paler, silvery flight feathers, Note long, broad wings held in a dihedral, small head, and broad tail. Often fly in groups or "kettles."

10. **Osprey.** Note white underside with darker flight feathers, black wrists, and broad, black eyeline on head. Very long, narrow wings. Has slight rufous wash to underwing coverts, clean, even trailing edge to wings, dark bib, and no signs of molt, but age is uncertain because of plumage overlap.

11. **Adult Red-tailed Hawk.** Pale underneath with dark patagial bars and streaks on belly, and reddish tail.

12. **Adult male Northern Harrier.** Snow-white underneath with black primary and secondary tips.

Wings are long, narrow, and tapered, and tail is long and narrow. Head is grayish.

13. **Male American Kestrel.** Distinct plumage, bluish upperwing coverts, orangey back and tail, and blackish primaries. Underside is pale with black spots, and checkered underwings.

Black and White! pages 166–167

1. **Juv./1st-year light Red-tailed Hawk.** Pale underneath with dark-streaked bellyband. Pale eyes and banded tail denote 1st-year.
2. **Adult Prairie Falcon.** Pale underneath with dark spots on body (instead of streaks as on 1st-year) and dark wing pits and underwing linings. Note falcon shape and dark sideburn on head.
3. **Northern Harrier.** Long, narrow wings that taper but are not sharply pointed, long, narrow tail, slim body, and small head. Uniformly dark underneath, lacking the bold, black border to the wings (and white underside, which is not always obvious on shadowed birds) of adult males. At a distance, dark streaking on body of adult female, or lack of, may be difficult to see.
4. **Adult female Northern Harrier.** Long, narrow wings and tail with obvious white rump. Adult female, such as this, is pale underneath with dark streaking on body.
5. **Juv./1st-year male American Kestrel.** All Kestrels have long, pointed wings, long, narrow tail, and 2 sideburns on head. Dark spots on body of male are less dense than dark rufous streaks of females. Lacks the pale, clean chest of adult male.
6. **Merlin.** Stout, relatively short-winged falcon with sharp angles, and sharply pointed wings. Appears dark on top, but narrow; white tail bands are visible. Note tail is narrow and does not taper toward tip like those of larger falcons.
7. **Juv./1st-year light Red-tailed Hawk.** Pale underneath with dark-streaked bellyband and dark patagials. Dusky trailing edge to the wings denotes 1st-year. Note long, broad wings held in slight dihedral, stout body, and broad tail.
8. **Adult Peregrine Falcon.** Adults are dark (bluish in good light) on top with blackish primaries (appearing slightly two-toned) and black head with broad sideburn. Note slightly paler rump on many adults, and classic falcon-shaped wings.
9. **Prairie Falcon.** Pale underneath with markings on body and dark wing pits and underwing linings. Almost identical in shape to Peregrine but slightly narrower wings.
10. **Unknown (left) and adult male Northern Harrier.** Both have long, narrow wings that taper but are not sharply pointed, long, narrow tail, slim body, and small head. Compare white underside with black border on wings of adult male Harrier (right) to darker underside overall of Harrier on left. Dark streaking on body of adult female, or lack of streaking on 1st-year, is often not visible on distant birds.
11. **Juv./1st-year light Red-tailed Hawk.** Pale underneath with dark-streaked bellyband, and dark patagials. Dusky trailing edge to the wings and obvious translucent primaries when backlit denote 1st-year. Note broad wings, and stout body.
12. **Juv./1st-year light Red-tailed Hawk.** Pale underneath with dark-streaked bellyband, and dark patagials. Dusky trailing edge to the wings and banded tail denote 1st-year. Note broad wings, stout body, and broad tail.
13. **Adult dark Rough-legged Hawk.** Dark underneath with paler flight feathers, and narrow, pale tail with well-defined, broad, dark tip. Also note dark trailing edge to wings. Wings are long and broad, but less stocky than Red-tailed and more sharply pointed in a glide.
14. **Golden Eagle.** Dark underneath with a large head showing a pale nape. Note long, broad wings, and long, broad tail. Most likely an adult based on lack of white on wings or tail, but impossible to know for sure since tail is folded and bird is shadowed.
15. **Adult Bald Eagle.** Note long, planklike wings in a soar, and gleaming white head. Tail is white but less obvious when shadowed, still sharply contrasts with dark underside.
16. **Turkey Vulture.** Blackish underneath with paler (silvery) flight feathers, and a small, unfeathered

head. Note long, broad wings held in a dihedral, stout body, and long, broad tail.

17. **Adult light Rough-legged Hawk.** Note dark belly and wrist patches. Dark trailing edge to wings, and well-defined dark tail tip on all adults, but heavily mottled underwings and mottled belly and chest denote male, compared with typically solid belly and paler underwings of adult female.

18. **Adult Bald Eagle.** Blackish overall with pure white, large head and yellow bill. Tail is pure white, but sometimes look dark when shadowed. Note long, straight wings.

19. **2nd-year Bald Eagle.** Dark overall with white wing pits, white mottling on underwing coverts, belly, and crown. Note long, broad wings with jagged edge to secondaries as a result of first molt. Also note large head, and large, dark bill.

20. **Adult light Ferruginous Hawk.** White underneath with dark leg feathers (or leggings), and dark mottling on underwing coverts. Note long, pointed wings, large head and body, and fairly long tail.

21. **Adult light Swainson's Hawk.** Two-toned underneath with pale underbody strongly contrasting with dark bib (adult trait) and dark flight feathers. Note long wings that are especially pointed when flapping, and square-tipped tail.

22. **Adult light Swainson's Hawk.** Distinctly two-toned underneath with pale underbody strongly contrasting with dark bib (adult trait) and dark flight feathers. Note long, pointed wings and fairly short, square-tipped tail.

Sunrise on the East Coast, pages 168–169

1. **Juv./1st-year Cooper's Hawk.** Note short, stocky wings and very long tail. Head projects well past the wings, and is paler than upperwings.

2. **Juv./1st-year Sharp-shinned Hawk.** Note stocky wings, long, narrow tail, small head that barely projects past wrists, and thick, dense streaking on underbody.

3. **Juv./1st-year Northern Harrier.** Note long tail, small head with pale eyeline, and white rump. Underside is pale and lacks visible streaking, denoting 1st-year.

4. **Juv./1st-year Northern Harrier.** Note long tail and long, narrow, tapered wings. Harriers often look "hooded," even at a distance. Underside is pale and lacks visible streaking, denoting 1st-year.

5. **Osprey.** White underside with darker flight feathers, black wrists, and broad, black eyeline. Very long, narrow wings that form an M shape in a glide.

6. **Juv./1st-year Cooper's Hawk.** Note long wings compared with other accipiters that are held slightly drooped, and tail that appears short head-on, but still broader than Sharp-shinned.

7. **Sharp-shinned Hawk.** Note stocky wings and body, small head, and long, square-tipped tail that is narrow and short for an accipiter.

8. **Juv./1st-year Red-tailed Hawk.** Pale underneath with dark-streaked bellyband, and dark patagials. Dusky trailing edge to the wings denotes 1st-year. Note stout body.

9. **Sharp-shinned Hawk.** Note stocky wings and body, long, square-tipped tail that is narrow (and short for an accipiter), and small head.

10. **Juv./1st-year Peregrine Falcon.** Pale underbody but heavily streaked, appearing dark in flight. Note broad sideburn, dark cap, very long, pointed wings, and long, broad tail.

11. **Turkey Vultures.** Appear dark overall in poor light, but show long, broad wings, small head, and broad tail. Wings are almost always held in a dihedral. Top bird is virtually unidentifiable from this perspective without noting two-toned underwings.

12. **Adult Red-tailed Hawk.** Pale underneath with dark patagial bars and belly streaks. Dark trailing edge to wings denotes adult. Note somewhat long but broad wings, broad tail, and stout body.

13. **Osprey.** White underside with darker flight feathers, black wrists, and broad, black eyeline. Very long, narrow wings that taper slightly but are not pointed.

14. **Sharp-shinned Hawks.** Note stocky wings and body, relatively short, square-tipped tails, and small heads compared with other accipiters.

15. **Male American Kestrel.** Kestrels have long, pointed wings, long, narrow tail, and 2 sideburns on

head. Dark spots on body of male are less dense than dark rufous streaks of females.

16. **Adult Red-shouldered Hawk.** Note pale underside with faint dark streaks on chest, unmarked underwing coverts, banded flight feathers with a dark trailing edge, and stocky wings that are pointed only in a steep glide or when flapping such as this.
17. **Juv./1st-year Cooper's Hawk.** Note short, stocky wings and very long tail. Head projects well past the wings and is paler than upperwings.
18. **Black Vultures.** Appear uniformly black in poor light with small head, stocky wings, and short tail.
19. **American Kestrel.** Kestrels have long, slim, smoothly curved wings, long, narrow tail, and 2 sideburns on head.
20. **Merlin.** Note heavily dark-streaked underside, single, narrow sideburn, and checkered underwings. Wings and tail are slightly broader, and chest is bulkier compared with Kestrel.
21. **Juv./1st-year Cooper's Hawk.** Note short wings, and very long tail that is broader than Sharp-shinned and has more prominent white tip (rounded when closed). Streaking on underside is less dense than on other accipiters and head is large in comparison with Sharp-shinned.

Into the Sun! pages 170–171

1. **Adult Peregrine Falcon.** Bluish upperside appears dark in poor light, but note long, pointed wings, long tapered tail, large, blackish head, and stout, whitish chest.
2. **American Kestrel.** Kestrels have long, pointed wings that are often blunt at the tips, and long, narrow tails. Chest is not stout as on Merlin.
3. **Adult Red-tailed Hawk.** Pale underneath with dark patagial bars and bellyband, and reddish tail. Somewhat long but broad wings, and short tail.
4. **Adult Eastern Red-tailed Hawk.** Pale underneath with dark patagial bars and bellyband, and reddish tail. Underwing coverts are unmarked, typical of eastern bird. Note somewhat long but broad wings.
5. **Adult Bald Eagle.** Dark brownish black overall with highly contrasting white head and tail, and yellow bill and feet!
6. **Juv./1st-year Red-shouldered Hawk.** Note the stocky wings that are squared off at the tips in a full soar, and the translucent primary "commas." 1st-years are pale underneath (not rufous) with dark streaking on the body, and an indistinctly banded tail with a dark tip. They also lack the clear banding on the flight feathers of adults.
7. **Juv./1st-year Broad-winged Hawk.** Note stocky, pointed wings and narrow-based tail. 1st-years are pale underneath, typically with moderate streaking on the underbody, and the tail has a defined dark tip. Also note translucent primaries.
8. **Adult Cooper's Hawk.** Very long, straight wings (for an accipiter), large head, and long tail with rounded tip. Orangey chest can be seen in direct sunlight.
9. **Adult Krider's Red-tailed Hawk.** Pale underneath with very faint, dark patagial bars, and lack of bellyband. Tail is reddish and head is dark, suggesting Krider's x Eastern intergrade. Also note dark trailing edge to wings.
10. **Female American Kestrel.** Note narrow, pointed, smoothly curved wings, and visible reddish tail with multiple bands.
11. **Juv./1st-year Cooper's Hawk.** Very long, straight wings (for an accipiter), large head, and long tail with rounded tip. Pale underside with dark streaks is visible when backlit.
12. **Peregrine Falcon.** Note long, pointed wings (especially at the hands), long tapered tail, and stout chest. Broad sideburn is visible.
13. **Juv./1st-year Cooper's Hawk.** Large head, very long tail, and short wings that lack the bulge of Goshawk. Also note slim body.
14. **Merlin.** Note long, pointed wings that are shorter than Peregrine, and stout chest.

GLOSSARY

adult plumage – Definitive plumage type for a bird

axillaries – Wing pits (see Anatomy)

bib – A dark patch of feathers on the breast (see Swainson's Hawk)

buffy – A pale tan color

carpal – Underwing area at the "wrist" (see Anatomy)

crown – Top of the head

dihedral – Wings held above the body in a V

flight feathers – Includes primaries, secondaries, and tail feathers, but most often referred to as the "wing feathers"

glide – To fly forward with wings pulled in

hand – Consists of the primaries, the outermost part of the wing (see Anatomy)

head-on – An eye-level front profile

hover – To remain stationary in flight while flapping

hybrid – An offspring of two species breeding with each other

immature – Includes all ages other than adult

intergrade – A bird showing traits of two different races or forms

juvenile – A bird in its first plumage

kettle – A group of birds soaring together

leggings – Feathers that cover the legs and sometimes feet (see Anatomy)

leucism – Presence of some or all-white feathers on a normally darker-plumaged bird. Also referred to as albinism. Leucistic birds usually have normal colored eyes; albinos have red eyes.

melanism – Presence of dark feathers on a normally lighter-plumaged bird

modified dihedral – Position of wings raised at the shoulder and level at the wrists

molt – Replacement of old feathers with new feathers, usually occurs from April through August in raptors

montane – The biogeographic zone comprising high elevation, mountainous habitat

morph – Color form

nape – Back of the neck (see Anatomy)

patagium – Area between the wrist and body along the leading edge of the wings (see Anatomy)

primaries – Ten outer wing feathers (see Anatomy)

rectrices – Tail feathers

rufous – An orange-rust color

rump – Feathers that cover the base of the uppertail coverts (see Anatomy)

scapulars – Feathers along the sides of the back (see Anatomy)

secondaries – Flight feathers from the wrist to the body making up the base of the wing (see Anatomy)

sexual dimorphism – Difference in plumage or size between male and female of the same species

soaring – Rising in a circular motion on outstretched wings

stoop – To dive with wings folded, usually when hunting

subadult – A bird in plumage between juvenile and adult

subterminal band – The next to last band on the tip of the tail

superciliary line – Pale feathers over the eye that form an "eyeline" (see Anatomy)

tawny – Dark ocher-brown color

terminal band – A band at the tip of the tail or wings

undertail coverts – Feathers that cover the underside of the base of the tail (see Anatomy)

underwing coverts – Feathers covering the underwings (see Anatomy)

uppertail coverts – Feathers that cover the topside of the base of the tail (see Anatomy)

upperwing coverts – Feathers that cover the upperwings (see Anatomy)

wing-on – An eye-level, side profile.

wing panel – A pale or partially translucent "window" in the primaries (see Anatomy)

wrist – Joint at the leading edge of the wing where the secondaries and primaries meet (see Anatomy)

ACKNOWLEDGMENTS

In a major project such as this, there are always many people involved who should be thanked. Our immediate families contribute in so many ways and have much to endure. Special thanks to Debra, Sophie and Samantha Crossley, Sherry Liguori, and Sophie De Beukelaer. My right-hand man Ciprian Patulea makes just about everything possible. The staff at Princeton University Press—led by Robert Kirk—always provide indispensable help.

Thanks to everyone who helped to make this book better. I apologize to anyone I unintentionally omitted from the following list (RC). Some of the helpers include

Vic Berardi, Jeff Bouton, Jessi Brown, Tommy DeBardeleben, Bill Clark, Brian Gibbons, Pete Gustas, Larry Hancock, Julian Hough, Steve N.G. Howell, Paul Lehman, Tony Leukering, Ian Lewington, Larry Manfreddi, Marshall Iliff, Michael O'Brien, Peter Pyle, Mike Shaw, Dave Tetlow, Lucy Treadwell, Brian Wheeler, and Chris Wood.

PHOTOGRAPHY CREDITS

Nearly all the images in this book were taken by the authors. Thanks to the following photographers for filling in the gaps and making this book better.

Jeff Bouton – RTHA p.161
Bill Clark – HBKI p.115
Michael Engelmeyer – Cover portrait
Mary Gustafson – HBKI p.114, p.115
Tony Leukering – MIKI p.118
Bruce Mactavish – GYRF p.145
Jeff Poklen – GYRF p. 145
Jonathon Wood – GYRF p.144

INDEX

Numbers in bold refer to color plate pages.

Regular breeding range—birds are typically faithful to breeding sites from year to year.

Regular year-round range—few birds stay year-round in one place; they often make local movements and are replaced seasonally by others.

Regular winter range—tends to change from year to year and day to day due to factors such as food supply and weather. Assume that species showing no winter range winter to the south of our region, in the Caribbean, Central, or South America.